DeS

W9-DCV-591

Dear Reader:

The book you are about to read is the latest bestseller from the St. Martin's True Crime Library, the imprint *The New York Times* calls "the leader in true crime!" The True Crime Library offers you fascinating accounts of the latest, most sensational crimes that have captured the national attention. St. Martin's is the publisher of John Glatt's riveting and horrifying SECRETS IN THE CELLAR, which shines a light on the man who shocked the world when it was revealed that he had kept his daughter locked in his hidden basement for 24 years. In the Edgar-nominated WRITTEN IN BLOOD, Diane Fanning looks at Michael Petersen, a Marine-turned-novelist found guilty of beating his wife to death and pushing her down the stairs of their home—only to reveal another similar death from his past. In the book you now hold, PICTURE PERFECT, award-winning author Shanna Hogan documents the high-profile case of Jodi Arias.

St. Martin's True Crime Library gives you the stories behind the headlines. Our authors take you right to the scene of the crime and into the minds of the most notorious murderers to show you what really makes them tick. St. Martin's True Crime Library paperbacks are better than the most terrifying thriller, because it's all true! The next time you want a crackling good read, make sure it's got the St. Martin's True Crime Library logo on the spine—you'll be up all night!

Charles E. Spicer, Jr.
Executive Editor, St. Martin's True Crime Library

ALSO BY SHANNA HOGAN

Dancing with Death

PICTURE PERFECT

THE JODI ARIAS STORY

A Beautiful Photographer, Her Mormon Lover,

and a Brutal Murder

Shanna Hogan

St. Martin's Paperbacks

NOTE: If you purchased this book without a cover you should be aware that this book is stolen property. It was reported as "unsold and destroyed" to the publisher, and neither the author nor the publisher has received any payment for this "stripped book."

PICTURE PERFECT: THE JODI ARIAS STORY

Copyright © 2013 by Shanna Hogan.
Update copyright © 2014 by Shanna Hogan.

All rights reserved.

For information address St. Martin's Press, 175 Fifth Avenue, New York, NY 10010.

ISBN: 978-1-250-00353-9

Printed in the United States of America

St. Martin's Press edition / September 2013
St. Martin's Paperbacks edition / November 2014

St. Martin's Paperbacks are published by St. Martin's Press, 175 Fifth Avenue, New York, NY 10010.

10 9 8 7 6 5 4 3 2

To my Mimi, Carol Hogan
&
To the memory of Travis's Mum Mum,
Norma Sarvey

AUTHOR'S NOTE

All of the people, places, dates, and facts in this book are true and no names have been changed. Some of the quotes used to compile the narrative were taken from police reports, trial testimony, and television and newspaper articles conducted with sources connected to the case.

Although a jury of her peers has convicted Jodi Arias of first-degree murder, in the American legal system she has the right to appeal her verdict. Such an appeal would have to await her final sentencing in this case.

CHAPTER 1

June 9, 2008

Slivers of light pierced the white wood blinds, illuminating a single window on the second floor. It was the only trace of light in the house—the rest lay shrouded by the night sky.

From where he was parked on the street, Dallin Forrest studied the property. It was an expansive, beige stucco house with a brown tile roof. A stream of river rocks snaked across the gravel, dividing a lawn of sparse trees and desert plants.

Dallin glanced at the clock on his car radio. The numbers glowed 10:05 P.M. In the passenger seat, his girlfriend, Michelle Lowery, stared at her lap and toyed with her cell phone. Her long, dark hair hung loose around her face, masking a fearful expression.

At the end of the street a set of headlights came into view. A car pulled alongside Dallin's and parked on the opposite side of the road. A petite brunette emerged from the vehicle—Michelle's friend Mimi Hall. Dried tear tracks stained her cheeks, and her normally olive complexion had gone starkly white.

Dallin and Michelle stepped out of their car into the warm summer night. Mimi met them at the driveway, smiling weakly.

Without uttering a word, Dallin walked to the porch and

rang the doorbell. Inside he heard the muted sounds of a dog barking. He hunched his lanky frame and peered through the decorative glass cutouts in the front door. In the dark, he saw the silhouette of the dog yapping in the foyer, pawing excitedly at the door.

A moment passed, but no one answered.

Michelle broke the silence. "The light's on. Someone must be in the house."

Clutching her cell phone, she made a call. "We're here," she said to the voice on the other end. "No one is answering."

Dallin rang the doorbell again, five times in quick succession. *Ding. Ding. Ding. Ding. Ding.*

Approaching the garage, Michelle repeated four numbers—0187—into her phone as she typed the digits into the keyless entry pad. With a rumble, the door began to rise.

Parked inside the garage was a 2004 black Toyota Prius. There was no license plate, but a temporary registration card was affixed to the back window. Dallin immediately recognized the vehicle as belonging to the homeowner—Travis Alexander.

Dallin had only met Travis a few times and knew little about the thirty-year-old motivational speaker and entrepreneur. His girlfriend was close friends with Travis, whom she had met through the local Mormon church.

Just a half hour earlier, Michelle had been at the house that twenty-year-old Dallin shared with his parents. They had gone to a nearby Walmart to run errands and had barely pulled back into his driveway when her cell phone rang. It was Mimi.

"Hey, have you heard from Travis recently?" she asked, her voice hollow.

"No, I guess I haven't heard from him for at least a week," Michelle said. "Why?"

"We are going to Cancún tomorrow and I haven't heard from him." Mimi swallowed involuntarily. "We're supposed to leave in the morning."

Michelle knew about the trip. Travis and Mimi had been dating and a few weeks prior, he'd invited her to join him

on a business trip to Cancún. As the date grew closer, however, Mimi had had second thoughts. She'd called him and
confessed she no longer wanted to pursue a romantic relationship.

"I would totally understand if you wanted to take someone else to Mexico," she'd added.

But it was too late to change the vacation plans. Because
the tickets had already been purchased and arrangements had
been made, they had agreed to go as friends. Their flight was
scheduled for 9:25 the following morning, yet Mimi hadn't
heard from Travis for more than a week.

"I just went by his place, but no one answered the door,"
Mimi told Michelle. "I've tried calling him and his voice mail
is full. I've called his house and cell phone. I'm really worried. Have you heard anything at all?"

"No," Michelle said. "I don't have any idea. Let me call
Taylor and I'll call you back in a bit."

Taylor Searle was Travis's close friend and business partner. If anyone had heard from Travis, it would be Taylor,
Michelle reasoned.

"Other people have been asking me if I've heard from
Travis too," Taylor told Michelle on the phone. "I thought he
was out of town."

Michelle explained that she had just spoken to Mimi and
that their flight was departing in the morning.

"I'm concerned," Michelle said. "Do you think we should
go over there?"

Michelle covered the receiver with her palm and whispered
to Dallin. "Do you mind if we drive over there and see what's
going on?"

Moments later, they were headed toward Travis's house on
the outskirts of Mesa's suburbs. Michelle phoned Mimi, and
she agreed to meet them outside the residence. On the drive,
Michelle told her boyfriend how Travis had seemed upset over
his recent breakup.

"But he seemed like he was getting better," she said. "He
was getting over it." Travis was organized and responsible.

There's no way he wouldn't respond to numerous e-mails, text messages, and phone calls. "This isn't like Travis." She shook her head.

Turning onto East Queensborough Avenue, Dallin eased down on the brake, canvassing the block in the dim light of the street lamps. He parked along the curb painted with the house number, 11428.

Travis's two-story, five-bedroom house blended into the neighborhood. Ubiquitous stucco homes lined the blocks for miles in all directions. During the recent housing boom, new homes had cropped up rapidly across the desert, expanding the population to nearly 500,000. Despite being the third-largest city in Arizona, behind Phoenix and Tucson, Mesa was still a quiet community. Quaint boutiques, family-owned restaurants, and elaborate Mormon churches peppered the city.

Mesa was a hub for the Latter-day Saints residing in the Phoenix metro area. Travis himself had moved to the city in part to build a life in a strong Mormon community.

Through the church, Travis had cultivated a large network of loyal friends. Now, three of those friends were at his house trying to determine his whereabouts.

With growing apprehension, Dallin, Michelle, and Mimi entered the garage. Taylor Searle had given Michelle the code to the garage door.

"All right . . . well, his car's here," Michelle informed Taylor over the phone. "Could someone have taken him to the airport? Maybe something happened, and he had to go out of town all of a sudden?"

Dallin approached a door leading into the house, tried the handle, and found it unlocked. Groping the inside wall, he flicked on the light. The door opened into a narrow space with a washer and dryer. He stepped into the laundry room, which led to the main area of the house. To the left were the formal living and family rooms. On the right, a wide hallway opened up into the kitchen, TV room, and the stairway.

The walls were painted taupe, the floors a mottled brown tile. Dallin didn't know the layout but quickly became familiar.

As he stepped into the house, Dallin noticed a foul odor hanging in the air.

"What is that smell?" he muttered to himself.

Once inside, a black pug scurried toward them, wagging its tail. Michelle bent down and ran her fingers through its fur. In the kitchen she noticed the dog's bowl, full of food.

"Well, someone's taking care of his dog," she said.

In the living room, on top of the couch, two tall bar stools rested on their sides. Dallin noticed a tile-cleaner machine sitting upright in the middle of the floor, as if someone was preparing to clean.

Dallin, followed closely by Michelle and Mimi, checked each downstairs room, flicking on lights. Left of the TV room was a short hallway leading to a bathroom with a shower and tub. Across from the bathroom, on the opposite side of the hallway, was a den.

Mimi stepped in the bathroom and pulled back the shower curtain. It was empty. Turning back toward the hallway, she noticed the door to the home office was closed.

"Let's check his office," Mimi said. "That's where he spends most of his time."

A large mahogany desk took up most of the width of Travis's office. Atop the desk sat a silver Dell laptop, leather wallet, set of keys, and cell phone. Dallin picked up the phone and saw it was turned off. Inside the wallet, he discovered cash, credit cards, and the picture ID of an attractive man with cropped brown hair and vivid green eyes—Travis Alexander.

Dallin shuddered.

Where would he go, leaving his car, cell phone, and wallet? Dallin wondered. *Where is he?*

Dallin left the den and headed back toward the stairwell; Michelle and Mimi trailed behind. Digging his nails into the wooden banister, he began to climb the steps, leading the way.

At the top of the stairs to his left were tall, white double doors, firmly shut. To his right was a spacious open loft, furnished with a leather sofa and three oversize beanbag chairs. A movie projector sat in the corner of the room next to a small table displaying a chess set.

As Dallin stepped onto the second-floor landing, he heard the faint sounds of music coming from the direction of the loft. The sounds became louder as he approached the hallway, blocked off by a dog gate. Dallin stepped over the gate, while the girls stayed behind in the hallway. Dallin pounded on the bedroom door where the sounds were coming from.

"Hold on," someone inside the room hollered. "Just a sec."

Half a minute passed and a tall young man with tousled dark-blond hair appeared at the entrance. Dallin didn't recognize him but would later learn it was Zachary Billings, one of Travis's roommates.

Immediately, Dallin spoke.

"Have you seen Travis?" he asked urgently.

"He's in Mexico," Zachary said.

Mimi piped up behind them in the hallway. "He's not in Cancún. I was going with him. We're supposed to leave in the morning."

"Have you checked his room?" Zachary asked.

"No. I heard the music so . . ." Dallin let the thought trail off.

Zachary stepped over the gate and headed across the loft to the double doors on the other side of the staircase.

"Travis?" Zachary shouted as he pounded on the door. No response. He shook the handle, but it was locked.

"Wait here a second," Zachary said. He left the three friends standing by the double doors.

As they waited, Michelle updated Taylor over the phone.

"His roommate is here," she said. "He's getting a key."

A moment later Zachary reappeared with a key he'd retrieved from a rack downstairs. He inserted it into the door, which unlocked with a rickety click.

As the doors swung open, Dallin grimaced. Inside the bedroom, the putrid stench permeating the air was more pungent.

From the doorway Dallin could see Travis's king-size bed—the sheets had been removed and a duvet was piled in a ball in the middle of the bed. Next to the bed were two pillows, minus pillow cases, tossed on the floor.

Zachary slipped inside the room. Dallin followed.

A long, tiled hallway led into the master bathroom. A light gleamed from the direction of the bathroom—the same light Dallin had noticed from the street. Paralleling the hallway was a walk-in closet, which had a second entrance to the bathroom on the opposite end.

As Dallin moved deeper into the room, a rust-brown mass on the floor caught his eye. A chunky, dark-red pool had congealed on the carpet.

"Oh my God," Zachary muttered.

Dallin's heart began to race; his breath hastened. The two men exchanged a terrified look.

What is that? Is that blood? Dallin thought. *This is bad. Nobody does that to the carpet and leaves.*

Dallin stepped outside the double doors. "Don't come in," he told the girls. "Stay out here."

By the time he turned back, Zachary had disappeared into the closet and toward the other entrance to the bathroom.

Dallin paused, unsure whether he wanted to continue. *If there is blood here, what more is there?*

He followed the crimson stains on the carpet toward the edge of the long bathroom hallway, where the muddy red puddles trailed over the tile like a path of footprints.

"Oh my God," Zachary gasped. He rushed out of the room, past Dallin.

Dallin turned the corner and entered the bathroom. It took a moment to grasp the nightmarish sight.

"No," he whispered.

The glass shower door was open, exposing a corpse in a crumpled heap on the shower floor. Bloody punctures branded Travis's body, a deep gash severed his throat. He was naked, his skin a ghastly mosaic of blue and purple. Travis's once handsome face was unrecognizable.

"I saw him curled up in the shower on the ground and I turned, I turned right back around," Dallin later recalled.

Backpedaling out of the master bedroom, he closed the doors, instinctively barricading himself from the horror.

"He's not alive," he said, his voice trembling. "Call 911."

* * *

Red and blue rotating lights reflected off the dazed faces of the witnesses standing by the curb. The house on East Queens-borough Avenue was surrounded by ambulances and police cruisers. Yellow police tape cordoned off the perimeter of the property. A uniformed officer stood guard by the front door.

At 11 P.M. Mesa Homicide Detective Esteban Flores arrived on the scene. By then, Travis's friends and roommates were already being questioned by officers.

Flores, a seasoned investigator with more than fourteen years on the force, was assigned as lead detective on the case. In his forties, with a husky build, thick black hair, and a dark complexion, Flores came across as stoic, with a staunch demeanor.

He approached one of the first responding officers on the scene and was briefed on the situation: the homeowner had been found in the master bathroom, deceased. He had been there at least a day or two and had wounds on his neck and chest.

"Who found him?" Flores asked.

Consulting his notes, the officer identified two of the people standing by the curb—Dallin Forrest and Zachary Billings.

"No one had heard from the guy for about a week," the officer told Flores. He reiterated what the witnesses had told him about Travis's planned trip to Mexico and how they had gained entry into the house.

Later, Flores would take official witness statements, as well as request DNA and fingerprint samples. First, however, he needed a closer and more careful look at the victim.

From what the witnesses had reported, the deceased had suffered a laceration wound to the neck. Flores had heard of cases where individuals had committed suicide in such a manner, although it was uncommon. Before launching an investigation he needed to assess the situation and determine if a crime had been committed.

Donning protective footwear and gloves, Flores entered the house through the front door, along with two fellow detectives and a commander. As Flores stepped inside, he winced. The odor was repulsive—rank and sweet, the smell of decay.

The detectives inspected the downstairs, making note of the stand-up floor cleaner in the living room, and the chairs on the couch. Discovering nothing else out of the ordinary, the detectives approached the stairwell.

Slowly, they climbed the steps and entered the loft. As Flores glanced around, he jotted down notes about the layout of the upstairs. Near an oversize beanbag chair he noticed an open black camera bag. The camera was missing, he wrote in his notepad.

Flores focused his attention back toward the master bedroom. Flanking the king-size bed in the center of the room sat two nightstands. In the corner of the bedroom, adjacent to a chair with an ottoman, a treadmill was hidden behind a wooden room divider.

As Flores entered the room he immediately noticed the reddish brown stains on the carpet. Instantly he knew it was dried blood. Instead of traipsing over it, the detectives walked through the narrow walk-in closet, which was neatly organized with color-coordinated men's clothing, shoes, ties, and belts. Flores stepped into the bathroom through the door on the opposite end of the closet.

He paused for a moment to take note of the carnage. Dried blood covered the walls, mirror, and sink and had pooled in thick puddles on the floor. The body coiled in the shower was well into the stages of decomposition. The corpse was grotesquely bloated, the skin marbled with discoloration.

Approaching the body, Flores noted the deep laceration across Travis's neck—his throat had been slit open in a gruesome gaping grin. Dried blood caked his nose and mouth. A thick dark fluid oozed from a puncture wound in the center of his chest.

"This guy didn't go quietly," Flores said softly.

The crime scene told the story of a victim who fought back. Such a profuse amount of blood spatter was an obvious sign of a violent assault.

"The large amount of blood throughout the bathroom and

bedroom areas indicated to me there was either a struggle or the victim was attempting to flee his attacker," Flores later recalled. "He had numerous injuries and trauma to his body, which indicated he had attempted to defend himself."

Travis Alexander had suffered an agonizing, cruel death. Right away Flores knew he was searching for a cold-blooded killer, someone who likely knew the victim and wanted him to suffer.

The medical examiner would later determine Travis had been shot in the face, stabbed twenty-seven times, and his throat had been slit from ear to ear. The cause of death: rapid blood loss.

There was no question—it was homicide. And this was now a crime scene.

"Let's get out of here and come back with a warrant," Flores told the detectives.

A search warrant would ensure the integrity of the investigation and any ensuing criminal charges. They left the corpse where he lay, curled in the shower.

Retreating out of the master bedroom, the detectives descended the staircase and passed through the kitchen and living room, heading toward the garage door in the laundry room. As they were exiting the house, a curious stain caught Flores's attention. On the washing machine was a small reddish-brown smear. It appeared to be blood—unusual since nearly all the other evidence had been confined to the upstairs.

Flores made a note of the stain. He would wait to sift through the contents of the machine until he obtained the warrant.

As Detective Flores left the crime scene that evening, he had no way of knowing that lurking inside was a peculiar piece of evidence that would come to play a crucial role in untangling the twisted murder mystery—a camera.

appeared like that of any large brood. In one photo, a young Travis, doe-eyed with pouting lips, grinned mischievously, crowded on a small leather couch with his three brothers and one of his sisters. In another, he stared fretfully at the ground as his older brothers cradled him in their arms. In yet another, Travis was wide-eyed, his palms splayed around his face in a moment of elation.

These photos showed some of the happier times, the picture-perfect moments suitable for framing. The camera's lens wasn't there to capture the abuse.

In the slums of Riverside, in a shabby house on Allwood Drive, Travis's childhood was consumed with violence, poverty, and neglect. At the time of his birth, Travis's parents were already poverty stricken and both addicted to crystal meth. When the children were still very young Gary and Pamela divorced. Gary was largely absent and for the most part the children were left in the care of their drug-addicted mother.

In the months before his murder, Travis had started writing a book about his life, which he intended to call *Raising You*. In it, he recounted his own tragic upbringing.

"My childhood, unfortunately, was very much like any child's that had drug addict parents," he wrote. "My father was never around which left my siblings and I to the fate given by my mother—a good woman, with the intent at an early age to be a loving mom. A few poor decisions changed that."

As Travis's mother progressively became more involved in drugs, she became less capable of raising children. Pamela was often prone to violent outbursts, staying awake high on crystal meth for up to a week at a time. When she ran out of meth, she would sleep for days. If one of the children woke her up from her drug-induced state, they were beaten.

"Most commonly was a beating for waking her up. It hurt but we got used to it," Travis wrote. "I learned how to turn so that when she hit me she would strike my back and arms, the pain was less there. If it was just that I think it would have been relatively manageable. It was not just there, however."

While their mom was high on meth, the children were neglected. They consumed almost everything edible within

CHAPTER 2

It would take months for Travis's friends to fully comprehend the staggering loss. It was an unspeakable tragedy. Travis was only thirty years old and so full of life—so driven, so accomplished.

Tall and broad-shouldered with bright green eyes, Travis was a handsome young entrepreneur who appeared to have the world at his feet—a lifetime away from his impoverished beginnings.

Travis Victor Alexander was born on July 28, 1977, in Riverside, a large city in Southern California. He was one of eight children born to Gary and Pamela Alexander. He had two older brothers: Gary Jr. and Greg, and was followed by sisters Tanisha, Samantha, Hillary, Allie, and a younger brother, Steven.

With a population of more than 300,000, Riverside was a diverse community with pockets of upscale suburban homes checkered by sections of concentrated poverty. The hilly landscapes and palm tree–lined streets were interspersed with luxury condos and sprawling estates. The poor areas were bursting with crumbling properties and illegal trailer parks, where residents lived in squalor.

In the pages of his family album, Travis's childhood

reach, and after several days whatever remained had begun to rot, attracting cockroaches that infested the home. Many times Travis would wake to bugs crawling on his body. He developed an intense phobia of roaches that would stay with him his entire adult life.

"I don't remember much of this, I can only think of one instance where I found a moldy piece of bread on the side of the fridge that represented the last thing we could eat. I remember being teased by canned food. Knowing full well what was in the can but not knowing how to use a can opener," he wrote. "I remember the filth, admittedly caused by us kids, which compounded on itself for weeks and months at a time. With that came thousands and thousands of roaches."

For years, the Alexander family lived in a tiny, deteriorated house. When Travis was a toddler, his family was evicted and forced to move into a camper, parked in their aunt's garage alongside a washer and dryer. The conditions in the camper were squalid. The washer wasn't hooked up to the plumbing and the dirty water would drain into the backyard and stagnate. The camper was just four feet tall, five feet wide, and six feet long. For more than a year Travis, his seven siblings, and his mother lived in the cramped quarters.

Without being able to bathe, the children tended to stink. As a boy, Travis didn't mind being dirty. He was actually scared of bathing, because if he got the bathroom floor wet, his mother accused him of urinating on the ground and threw him against the wall. Not just physically violent, his mother was cruelly mentally abusive as well.

"I have never heard in any movie, on any street corner, or amongst the vilest of men any string of words so offensive and hateful, said with such disgust as was the words that my mother said to my sisters and me," he wrote.

On the occasions when his father was around, his parents' fights would turn violent. Once, during an argument, Pamela emptied a revolver into Gary's car. Subsequently, Gary took an ax and destroyed her belongings. That night he burst into the home while Travis was on the other side of the front door. The police were called, as they so often were.

While Travis didn't mind being dirty when he was young, he and his siblings were mocked for their filthy clothes. After school Travis and his sisters found small comforts in watching *Sesame Street*. It helped them escape into a world of fantasy where children were happy and learning.

Among the few fond memories Travis cherished from his childhood were occasional visits with his great grandfather Vic. His mother didn't have much family but about twice a year she would fix herself up enough for a visit with her grandfather, who lived an hour away from their home in Southern California.

All the children adored Great Grandpa Vic. Visits with him were one of the few times in Travis's young life when he got to be a child. Grandpa Vic would play checkers, take the children out for pizza, and entertain them with a trunk full of toys he kept for their visits. He taught the children to read and write the alphabet.

Despite Pamela's attempts at concealing their horrid living conditions, their great grandfather knew what the children endured. At the end of each visit Grandpa Vic would grab Travis by the shoulder and shake him, his tone suddenly becoming serious. "Travis, you need to know that you are special, that there is not anything that you can't do. There is something great inside you," his great grandfather said. "You're special, Travis, don't you ever forget it."

That was quickly followed by a rigid hug. For Travis, those words would alter every aspect of his life.

"The words my grandfather said were spoken with such conviction that I believed him," Travis wrote. "You see what I wasn't aware of then, that I have since figured out was my grandfather was savvy to the way mother was raising her children. She would often make remarks while coming down from drugs about how miserable we all were, that we ruined her life, that we were worthless. Although those words hurt very deeply, as you could imagine, every time she would scream those words I would hear his words instead, every time I would feel her fist sink into my back, I could feel my grandfather's hands on my shoulders, and I knew she couldn't reach what was great inside of me."

When Travis was six, he came to the conclusion that there was a God. In anguish he screamed all day, begging the Lord for his grandmother Norma to hear his cries and take him away for the weekend.

"I screamed so long and loud that I actually woke up my comatose mother long enough to beat me for waking her up. When she went back to bed I went back to screaming to God," he wrote. "Sure enough that evening my Grandma came and picked me up while my mother slept."

Grandma Norma would become one of the most influential people in his life. Travis's abuse at the hands of his mother continued until he was eight, when he ran away and never looked back. He went straight to his grandmother Norma's house.

"I'm going to live with you now," he told her.

Travis and his younger siblings were taken in by their father's parents, Jim and Norma Sarvey. Shortly after, Pamela died of a drug overdose. Living with their grandparents, the children experienced having a loving, functional family for the first time in their lives. Grandma Norma became like a second mom and the children affectionately called her Mum Mum.

A devout Mormon, Norma introduced them to her faith. It was a turning point in Travis's life.

Also known as the Church of Jesus Christ of Latter-day Saints, Mormonism is the fourth largest religious body in the United States, with more than fourteen million members across the world. Adhering to the gospel in *The Book of Mormon,* church members believe, first and foremost, that Jesus Christ is the Savior of the world and the Son of God.

Among the main tenants of Mormonism is the belief that a person's existence doesn't begin with birth on this earth. Rather, Mormons consider that all people lived as spirits before being born and receiving a physical body.

The purpose of an earthly life is to learn, grow, and progress in knowledge and worthiness. The temporary trials of life represent a mere blink of an eye on an eternal scale for Mormons. Once a person passes, their spirit spends eternity in one of three heavenly kingdoms.

Given his cruel upbringing, Travis felt a strong connection to the Mormon faith. His past wasn't a punishment, it was a lesson—one that strengthened his spirit and character. It was now up to him to decide his fate. If he wanted a different destiny, a better life than his mother and father had provided, it was in his power to make it happen.

By accepting Jesus Christ, fully and completely, living the gospel and receiving the proper ordinances—including baptism, confirmation, sacrament, endowment, and celestial marriage—Travis's life, and afterlife, would be blessed.

At ten years old, Travis was baptized. When he was sixteen, he became fully active in the Church of Jesus Christ of Latter-day Saints. His faith guided his life.

Attending Rubidoux High School in Riverside, at first Travis was uncharacteristically shy, at times eating lunch in the library alone. As he became active in the church, however, Travis flourished. He became social and outgoing—personality traits that would stay with him throughout his life.

As he reached adolescence, Travis grew tall and brawny, his chin strong and defined. He used his newfound physical strength as a member of the high school wrestling team.

While the Alexander children were living with their grandparents, their father came back into their lives, having since recovered from his drug addiction. With Gary, Travis and his older brothers would engage in push-up, sit-up, and arm wrestling matches.

As he invested in his faith, Travis became inspired to better himself, and began working part time after school. In 1995, he graduated from high school. The following year he used his savings to serve a two-year mission to spread the Mormon message.

Mormons believe it is essential to disseminate the word of God and the church maintains a large missionary program that proselytizes and conducts humanitarian services world-wide. To serve as a missionary is considered a rite of passage for young Latter-day Saints, both men and women, although the majority are young, unmarried men.

Travis was called to serve his mission in Denver, Colorado, a Rocky Mountain city with a population of more than five million. Dressed according to the required code—conservative dark trousers, white dress shirts, and ties for men—Travis traveled across Denver with another young male missionary, his companion, switching companions every few months as part of the Mormon custom.

As a missionary, Travis was known as Elder Alexander. Each morning he and his companion woke at dawn, ate breakfast, exercised, and spent two hours studying the scriptures. The remainder of the day was spent knocking on doors, attempting to convert non-Mormons to their faith.

Travis considered this time among the best two years of his life, said his sister Hillary Wilcox, a blonde with big green eyes who closely resembles her brother.

"Travis loved his mission. He loved the people there in Colorado. He actually wanted to move there one day," Hillary recalled. "He truly loved to serve the Lord."

On July 28, 1997, while still on his mission, Travis turned twenty. That same day his father died in a car accident. Travis flew back to Riverside to be with his family for the funeral. When he returned to Denver just one week after his father's death, Travis showed tremendous strength and resolve, according to his companion at the time.

"We had talked a lot about death, and what our purposes were here on earth in the weeks to come, but never did he let his father's passing or grief stop him in his pursuit to help others," recalled Hyrum Dean Nichols. "I really do not think there was a day that went by that Travis did not seek out someone to help, whether with service, work, or spiritual help."

Travis refused to let his life's tragedies haunt him. He viewed the early trauma he had endured as transformative, rather than destructive, and eventually came to believe that there had to be a reason for everything that happened in life.

"I would change nothing. I have thanked and continue to thank the Lord for these experiences," Travis later wrote. "I see them strictly as blessings and count myself fortunate for them."

In spite of his humble beginnings, Travis was determined to do great things. Success, however, would not come easily.

CHAPTER 3

Travis Alexander had ambitious goals for his life. He wanted to be independently wealthy, travel the world, and get involved in politics. Near the end of his life, his main aspiration was to get married and have a family.

Tragically, Travis wouldn't live long enough to kiss his bride at his wedding or cradle his firstborn child in his arms. His murderer cut short his life, robbing him of the chance to fulfill many of his dreams.

Still, Travis squeezed an extraordinary amount of life into his thirty short years on earth. He approached each day as an opportunity for discovery, soaking up as many experiences as possible. Determined and goal oriented, Travis continuously strove to improve himself—to do better, be better.

"Travis thrived on thinking big and achieving his goals," recalled his friend Aaron Mortensen. "He wanted to see the world, challenge his fears, and help others on a grander scale than most permit themselves to aspire."

Throughout his adult life Travis devoured personal development books, over time building an impressive library. His favorite titles included *Think and Grow Rich, How to Win Friends and Influence People, The Slight Edge, The Richest Man in Babylon, You Were Born Rich, The Greatest Salesman in the World,* and *Atlas Shrugged.*

But Travis not only wanted to be inspired, he wanted to inspire others.

"He was so hungry to change the world," said Taylor Searle, a close friend and business partner. "He was all about, 'How can I create change?' 'How will I become my best self?' 'How do I influence people around me?'"

For years, after returning from his mission, Travis began each day by writing the ending—creating a list of tasks he hoped to accomplish. On a three-by-five index card, he would write down six things he found essential to achieve, along with other things he needed to do.

In his writing, Travis often referenced his aspirations and methods to staying focused.

"Some of my days I create the day with ultimate productivity in mind. Others I am looking for a lesson to be learned or to have a life experience," Travis wrote. "Sometimes the goal is to do some service or philanthropy, but always when all is said and done, you tend to get what you focus on. It is as simple as that. Write down what you want life to bring you today, and chances are life will bring it to you on a silver platter."

As time passed Travis made a habit of accomplishing his six achievements each day, after which he would add a seventh and then an eighth, and so on. Eventually, he had dozens of daily goals on his list.

"Once I fill out my three-by-five card, I take a moment and look at it. I ask myself, 'If this was all to get done would it be an amazing day?'" he wrote. "Sometimes the answer is 'yes,' sometimes 'no.' However, I never start the day until I can say that this is going to be a day for the ages. Once that is done, I am jacked out of my mind and I get to work. I have increased my productivity more than five times what it used to be and I have mastered certain aspects of my life that I would have never done if I didn't keep myself conscious to do it."

An example of Travis's daily list would include activities like praying, reading scriptures, listening to thirty minutes of motivational recordings, working out, writing in his journal, affirmation, and visualization.

"Now that is a full day, with getting things done in mind," he wrote. "Granted it's not creating oceans and countless animals but based on the same principles that our Father in heaven followed, I am able to create my own amazing days. May you live all the days of your life, we have a limited supply of them and the clock is ticking."

Despite his enormous drive to succeed, in his early twenties Travis struggled as he began carving out his professional path in life.

In 1998, after returning from his mission, he moved to Provo, Utah, and enrolled in college. He quickly learned, however, that while he loved learning, college was not for him. After a few classes he dropped out and moved back to Riverside, where he rented an apartment with three single male roommates, and purchased an older-model Honda Civic.

For the next couple of years he worked a variety of menial jobs, including telemarketing, retail sales, and a stint as a "substance abuse professional," testing urine for drug and alcohol use. For a few years he also worked as an insurance agent for Allstate, an auto insurance agency.

During this period Travis often faced financial hardships, but he never lost his unshakable belief in himself, said his best friend, Deanna Reid.

"Since I first met Travis I always saw something special in him—at a time even when not many people might have," recalled Deanna. "At the time others might have just seen him as a young punk kid, living in a house with a bunch of other guys in Riverside, California, driving around in his beat-up Honda Civic, telling everyone that he was going to be rich and he was going to change the world."

Deanna, a fellow Mormon, lived with three other female roommates in an apartment complex across the street from Travis. Eventually the four men and four women became close friends. A curvaceous brunette with wide brown eyes and wavy brown hair, Deanna dated Travis on and off for the next five years. When they stopped dating, they remained the best of friends.

Upbeat and outgoing, Travis made dozens of close friends through the Mormon church in Riverside. There, he was a member of the Riverside Singles Ward, a congregation dedicated solely to young single Mormons from the ages of eighteen to thirty.

Singles wards are established in areas with high populations of unmarried Mormons, providing young people a chance to serve in offices in church. The wards also facilitate opportunities for LDS members to meet other singles.

"He loved to be social and date and made special efforts to be friends with everyone," Deanna recalled. "He also continued as a missionary and strived to find those who were searching for something more so that he could share his knowledge of the gospel with them."

Early in their friendship, Deanna discovered Travis's passion for his faith. One evening Travis was speaking with one of Deanna's roommates, who played on the women's volleyball team for California State University. The roommate was the only Mormon on the volleyball team, a detail that piqued Travis's interest.

"He busted out a piece of paper and a pencil and he said, 'Now let's write down the names of all those friends and let's set a date for when you're going to share the gospel with them,'" Deanna recalled. "The rest of my roommates and I just looked at each other and we thought it was cute because he was a newly returned missionary and that's what newly returned missionaries do. But Travis never changed. He was always like that."

By the age of twenty-three, Travis held three jobs, working eighty hours a week. His best job was in retail sales at the local mall, which paid just $9 an hour. Travis's commute was up to three hours a day, as he drove from job to job in his Honda, which frequently broke down.

With little income, and growing expenses, Travis was also deeply in debt. By 2000, he owed about $20,000 to various credit cards, and was at his credit limit, unable to secure ad-

ditional credit cards. At one point, after being unable to afford rent, he found himself sleeping on a friend's couch. It
was the lowest point in his adult life. Years later he commented
on that period in a 2005 motivational speech.

"I didn't know what I was going to do," Travis said. "I was
not very excited about where I was going. I didn't know what
I was going to do to get out of that mess."

As he searched for his career path, Travis spent a lot of
time at church and in the temple. In the LDS faith Mormon
churches are considered public places where members and
visitors meet for weekly worship services to pray and study
scripture. The temples are reserved for special forms of worship and are dedicated to be the House of the Lord. Considered by Latter-day Saints to be the most sacred structures on
earth, only members who are living by the standards of the
church are permitted to enter.

The primary purpose of the temple is to conduct the sacred ordinances LDS members need for an eternal life. Additionally, the temple is thought to be a place to commune
with God and receive personal revelations.

The nearest temple to Riverside was about an hour's drive
away in Los Angeles. The Los Angeles California Temple,
on Santa Monica Boulevard in the Westward District, was
then the second largest LDS temple in the country.

Each week Travis and Deanna, who was preparing to serve
her own mission in Costa Rica, made the trek from Riverside to Los Angeles.

During this time, Travis often reflected on his purpose in
life. He felt it wasn't God's plan to work as many hours as
possible to simply survive. He truly believed he was capable
of doing something more meaningful.

"He worked many different jobs in search for a career,"
Deanna recalled. "None of them seemed to be working out
so he prayed that he would find something."

Soon, Travis's prayers were answered. At a church func-
tion in the fall of 2001, he met a man named Chris Hughes,
who would play a prominent role in transforming his life.

With a kind, round face and light blue eyes, Chris was a successful executive and personal development lecturer, and a Sunday school teacher.

One day in 2001, Chris was teaching a class Travis was attending. As part of his lecture on parenting and family values, he read an essay entitled "Father Forgets," by Dr. W. Livingston Larned.

The story began with a father standing by his son's bed as he sleeps, feeling remorse for scolding his son.

"What has habit been doing to me? The habit of finding fault, of reprimanding—this was my reward to you for being a boy. It was not that I did not love you; it was that I expected too much of youth. I was measuring you by the yardstick of my own years.

"Nothing else matters tonight, son. I have come to your bedside in the darkness, and I have knelt there, ashamed. It is a feeble atonement; I know you would not understand these things if I told them to you during your waking hours. But tomorrow I will be a real daddy."

Immediately, Travis recognized the essay. It had been republished in one of his favorite personal development books, the bestseller *How to Win Friends and Influence People,* by famed motivational writer Dale Carnegie.

After class Travis approached Chris. At the time they were merely acquaintances and had never really spoken. As they discussed the book, both men discovered their shared interest in personal development and self-improvement.

Little did Travis know at the time that while he had been praying for a career path, Chris too had asked God to bring him a leader to help grow his business. Both men would come to believe that God had destined them to meet.

The conversation turned to Chris's career. Travis knew Chris was financially successful, but was unsure how he made his money. For some reason, that day Travis felt compelled to ask.

"Have you heard of Chippendales?" Chris said with a smirk.

They both laughed. Chris then explained he was one of

the top executives with a company that sold legal insurance. Prepaid Legal Services, Chris told him, had been in business for more than three decades and provided legal services to more than 1.5 million across the United States and Canada.

The legal insurance plans were sold through independent contractors, utilizing multilevel marketing, also known as network marketing. Part of the Prepaid Legal business model involved recruiting new salespeople. The associates earned a commission off each sale, as well as a percentage of the contracts each person they recruited sold.

In 2001, Prepaid Legal was a growing company with promising earning potential. New recruits could make a few hundred dollars or hundreds of thousands of dollars, depending on how much they sold and how many associates they recruited to their organization.

Chris extended an invitation to Travis to attend a Prepaid Legal seminar to learn more about the company. Soon after, Travis attended the business briefing, at which several executives gave inspirational presentations about how the company had made them rich.

For a motivated individual like Travis, the presentation was life-changing. In September 2001, he scrimped together the $249 application fee and was soon working as a Prepaid Legal associate under Chris Hughes.

His first day, Travis started making phone calls and immediately closed three deals. Soon after, Travis was making more money than he had ever made in his entire life. Simply by selling Prepaid Legal plans he was earning about eight times what he made working eighty hours a week at three jobs.

Within weeks Travis quit two of those jobs, but for a while he maintained his position working part-time at the mall. One day before his shift in late 2001, Travis spent the morning making sales calls for Prepaid Legal. That day he was on a streak, going three for three—making three calls and closing each deal. His commission that morning: about $400 for thirty minutes of work.

Later, as he walked through the mall toward his job, Travis felt empowered. He was on a precipice—his dream of independent wealth was nearer than ever.

By the time he made it to work, Travis's outlook had shifted. Strolling casually into the store, he didn't even realize he was late. His employer, however, did notice.

"You're three minutes late," his boss told him.

"Yeah, well guess what? I'm going to be ten minutes late tomorrow!" Travis shot back. "You need to get used to this."

Travis was fired on the spot for insubordination. But he didn't care. He had developed a new attitude.

CHAPTER 4

At the age of twenty-four, Travis was ready to reinvent himself. He had always been extraordinarily driven and goal-oriented. With Prepaid Legal, he now believed he had the vehicle to succeed.

Training with Chris Hughes, Travis developed his sales skills. Very early on, Chris saw something in Travis. He could tell the young man had the personality and positive perspective necessary to flourish in network marketing. The two men shared a mutual respect that developed into a great friendship.

"Travis was so disciplined, such a great guy, just larger than life. He was charming, hilarious, and super-outgoing. He had a huge heart and he loved helping people," Chris said. "There never was and there never will be another quite like him. He is the most unique person I have ever known."

Through Chris, Travis discovered how to utilize the Prepaid Legal business model in a way that would maximize his earning potential. The company provided compensation on an escalating scale. The more an associate sold, the more they made per sale. In early 2000, Prepaid Legal plans cost $300 to $500 a year. For each plan sold, the sales associate received $103. After three sales, that commission was raised to $138.

While a salesperson with Prepaid Legal could earn money

simply by selling legal plans, only a small percentage made
a substantial living. Those who recruited and managed a team
of associates rose through the ranks of the company and
earned significantly more money.

For the next few years Travis sold legal plans and worked
to develop a team of associates. Each week he spent about
twenty hours making calls, selling an average of five plans a
week. He sold legal insurance to friends, family, neighbors,
local business owners, and even strangers.

At one point he sold a legal plan to Barney the Purple
Dinosaur—or at least the actor inside the costume.

"I didn't believe it at first, but he verified it. He showed
me pictures of him getting in and out of the costume and him
on the set," Travis said in a 2005 speech. "He autographed a
picture and I gave it to my nephew."

When selling Prepaid Legal Travis would often use that
story to say, "Now if a purple dinosaur needs legal insurance,
do you think you might need it?"

As he worked to build a team of associates, however,
Travis faced some obstacles. The Southern California area
was relatively oversaturated with Prepaid Legal sales representatives. To climb to the next level in his business, he felt
he needed an untapped market—a place where the Prepaid
Legal concept would seem new and exciting. Travis decided
to relocate.

In choosing a new city, it was important to him to find an
area with a large Mormon community. Eventually he settled
on Mesa, a suburb east of Phoenix, Arizona.

Mesa was founded in the 1870s when Brigham Young, the
leader of the LDS church at the time, sent a group of Mormons to Arizona to colonize the region. More settlements followed, homes were erected, schools were built, and canals
were widened to subsidize the farming community.

In addition to a growing Mormon population, Mesa was
home to one of the country's oldest and largest LDS Temples,
the Mesa Arizona Temple.

In 2004, Travis packed his belongings and headed toward

Mesa to establish his new life. Soon after relocating, Travis became active in the local LDS community, joining the Desert Ridge Young Single Adult Ward.

Each week the ward hosted several social functions, in which Travis quickly became a regular. In addition to Sunday school classes, the ward organized weekly church get-togethers designed for members to socialize and study scripture.

On Mondays the ward held an activity night called Family Home Evenings. For families, FHE is one night a week designated for study, prayer, or any other fun, wholesome activity. In the church singles ward, FHE was held as a group get-together at a member's house or venue. In addition to FHE, ward members also regularly gathered for camping trips or picnics, to play sports, or engage in any number of social activities.

His first few years in Mesa, Travis met a lot of new people through the church, many of whom would become loyal, lifetime friends.

Michelle Lowery first met Travis through the single ward's campout. He approached her and before saying hello, or even his name, he blurted out, "You look like you're thirteen."

Michelle laughed. Indeed she was small in stature and had a youthful face framed with long, chocolate brown hair. However, she was actually eighteen at the time. Despite their eleven-year age difference, Travis and Michelle became close friends. Travis became like an older brother to Michelle; she, in turn became his close confidant.

In the singles ward, Travis was quite popular. Earnest and upbeat, he made a strong first impression. He had a way of greeting people so that they felt they were the most important person in the world, as if he had been waiting all day to speak with them, Michelle recalled.

"Travis had many great qualities. One in particular was that he was never shy," Michelle recalled. "He was in his element standing in front of hundreds of people. If he had something to say—a joke, his testimony, a compliment to someone, he would share it. If he was feeling any emotion—love, excitement, passion, tenderness, he couldn't help but show it."

Travis was also extraordinarily giving of himself and his time. Whenever a volunteer was needed at church, Travis would raise his hand. Every Sunday, without exception, he would collect the trash from the bins throughout the church building and take them outside to the Dumpster.

"Travis was a beautiful example of service. He was always serving others and thinking of others," Michelle recalled. "If you needed someone to talk to, he would sit with you for hours. If you were sick, he was over in a second, and he was never empty-handed."

As his social network grew, so did Travis's business. Networking through the church, he recruited many fellow LDS members to take part in the company. Some simply purchased a legal plan; others came to work as Prepaid Legal associates under Travis. Although some of his associates only sold one or two plans, a handful sold up to seventy-five a month. With a large and growing sales team, Travis quickly rose through the ranks of the company. By 2004, Travis had mastered his sales pitch and the contracts came easily. As a salesman, he was ranked second out of a team of five thousand.

Travis enjoyed training fellow associates on leadership skills, commitment, and personal development. One of his favorite mantras was: "The greatest leader is the greatest servant." By mentoring many of these new salespeople, Travis discovered his gift for motivation.

"As a mentor he was able to reach people and create growth and progress and personal development," said Aaron Mortensen. "He wanted to help people to grow and teach people to be their best selves, in a very open and honest way about his own weaknesses."

Hosting regular team meetings, Travis preached many of the philosophies he had learned from self-improvement books. He taught visualization, successful habits, and the power of positive thinking. Many of the associates he mentored also became close friends.

"Travis was a positive individual who was not simply a motivational speaker to me. He was a motivational friend," said
Aaron. "He found the good in people and situations. Spending time with him helped me want to be a better person."

By 2004, Travis had money in the bank, which afforded him
the luxury of designing his own life. With his newfound financial wealth, he bought new clothes, ate at nice restaurants,
and traveled.

Travis always dressed the part of success, wearing flam-
boyant designer suits in bright colors. At Prepaid Legal conferences, he stood out in the crowd. Donning royal blue and
pinstripe suits, he appeared bold, successful, and confident.
Travis became known as the guy in the flashy suits.

After moving to Mesa, Travis also sold his broken-down
Honda Civic and bought himself a blue BMW 3 Series. His
"beemer," as he called it, was his prized possession. While
he spent lavishly on himself, Travis was also extremely gen-
erous with his money—he gave selflessly without asking for
anything in return.

Throughout their friendship, Aaron Mortensen, a dentist
with narrow brown eyes and a broad, flawless smile, spoke
with Travis several times a week about girls, the future, or
insignificant things like movie quotes. They regularly went
on road trips, double dates, and out for dinners.

On one occasion Aaron invited Travis to meet up with him
and a group of friends for a late-night meal at an Applebee's
restaurant. They all ordered food and milkshakes, and at the
end of the night Travis excused himself to go to the bathroom.
Aaron watched as Travis, instead of heading in the direction
of the restroom, snuck around the bar and found the waiter.

"I knew that he was picking up the table's tab. Eventually,
the server came over and told us to have a good night. Everyone was surprised and assumed the restaurant had just comped
us or something," Aaron said. "I didn't say a word. No one
else saw him do it besides me. I didn't expose his kind act to
everyone else."

Later Aaron sent a text to Travis to express his gratitude.

At first Travis was disappointed that he had been caught—he truly wanted to keep it a secret. Then Travis, who always called Aaron "brother," simply told him, "Pay it forward, Brother."

"The natural man would say you can pay me back another day. Not him. Pay it forward means do something good for someone else. It speaks to Travis's character that he used moments like this to teach those around him," Aaron recalled. "He lifted people up and shared the lessons he'd learned."

In his mid-twenties, Travis had a near-death experience.

One late night he was at a Mimi's Cafe restaurant in San Bernardino, California, with a few friends when a man dressed all in black walked in brandishing a gun.

"Get the fuck on the ground," the robber screamed, waving the pistol.

Many of the patrons dropped to their knees, cowering underneath the tabletops. Travis and one of his friends tried to duck under the table, but there was no room. They both bolted toward the other side of a partition. His friend made it to the other side of the room and sought cover.

But the gunman stopped Travis, forcing him to the ground. Nudging the butt of his gun into Travis's temple, the robber demanded his wallet. Travis, however, didn't have a wallet. He was carrying some cash, which he handed over, along with his cell phone.

When Travis didn't hand over the wallet, the thief became enraged. "You have five seconds to distribute the wad," the man screamed.

Travis's thoughts raced.

This is how I'm going to die, he thought. *He's going to kill me. All he has to do is squeeze the trigger.*

"I'm seeing myself, facedown in a puddle of blood," Travis said in a 2006 recorded conversation. "I'm like, 'This is death. This is death.'"

In his peripheral vision, he could see a woman under another table crying uncontrollably. Travis closed his eyes, considering his last moments on earth.

"They say that your life flashes before your eyes—well, I can't say that—but it's amazing how many thoughts go through your mind," he said. "I thought hundreds and hundreds of different things in just a few seconds."

Eventually, someone took out a wallet and slid it across the floor. The gunman followed the wallet, picked it up, and moved on to the next table. A few minutes later, the robber was gone.

Travis's adrenaline was still pumping through his veins. That night he cheated death. The next time someone put a gun to his head, he would not be so lucky.

In 2004, the country was in the midst of a dramatic housing boom, which would ultimately change the landscape of Arizona. The Phoenix metro area led the charge with new home construction, transforming the vacant desert parcels and undeveloped farmland into instant master-planned communities. Uniformly designed tract homes cropped up seemingly overnight—the suburban sprawl stretching to the edge of the city limits.

For Travis, the housing boom came at the ideal time in his life. He was twenty-seven and ready to purchase his first home. On July 27, 2004, a few months after moving to Arizona, he put up a $10,000 down payment to build a new house in an east Mesa development known as Mountain Ranch. Half an hour's drive away from downtown Mesa, the far-flung community sat along a vacant swath of desert.

Travis selected for his design a spacious two-story house at 11428 East Queensborough Avenue. The five-bedroom, three-bathroom home was built with a formal living room, dining room, recessed lighting, a loft, three-car garage, and a covered patio. The price: $259,834.

As Travis settled into his first home, he discovered he had a passion for decorating. His home became a symbol of his success.

"He had a specific goal on how he wanted to decorate the house and he truly made it happen, from colors he was going to paint the walls, to the theater room he wanted," Deanna

Reid recalled. "He was proud of his closet and took special measures to have it organized. It was important for him to be in style and looking good."

Travis designed the home in dark shades—brown marbled tile floors, beige carpet, oak cabinets, and tan walls. It was decorated with a masculine touch, furnished with leather couches, dark wood tables, and stainless steel appliances.

He even purchased Martha Stewart and feng shui books to help him achieve his vision. As he was improving his property, he would often call his older brothers for advice on how to fix things, such as wiring in the ceiling fan.

The heart of his home was the loft. Strewn around the floor were oversize beanbag chairs known as LoveSacs. Black-and-white framed posters of celebrities from the 1950s covered the walls. In the center of the room was a theater-style projection TV, which he purchased to host regular Ultimate Fighting Championship (UFC) parties.

Travis didn't like to spend much of his time watching television, joking it was "for the weak." As a sports fan, however, he often invited his buddies over to watch basketball or football on the hundred-inch projection screen. Perhaps because of his wrestling background, Travis's favorite sport was Mixed Martial Arts, which at the time was the fastest growing sport in America. Travis became famous for his UFC parties. Each week, cars would line the block as friends came by to watch the UFC matches on cable or pay-per-view.

With his friends, Travis hosted regular gatherings to watch movies or play board games. For his business, Travis hosted training seminars and recruitment sessions for prospective salespeople. Throughout the time he lived in the house, he also rented out his spare bedrooms and had several different roommates.

Travis enjoyed owning a place where everyone could congregate. Friends so frequently came and went that Travis rarely even locked his doors.

"His house was always open. It didn't matter if he had known you for years or if he had just met you," Michelle Lowery recalled. "If you needed a place to sleep for the night, his door was open."

For Travis's friends, the house on East Queensborough Avenue would be the setting for many happy memories. It would also represent the site of a tragedy.

The house was where Travis lived. It was also where he would die.

CHAPTER 5

auntering across the stage, Travis Alexander gazed out into the crowd of hundreds. He was dressed in a loud three-piece suit, a small microphone attached to his colorful tie. Displayed on a large screen behind him was the phrase THE SYSTEM WORKS, alongside a picture of a blindfolded woman holding balanced scales—the symbol for justice.

"With this company, I went from three jobs to no jobs," Travis said, his voice oozing confidence. "I went from a three-hour commute to a three-foot commute. I went from a broken-down Honda Civic to a BMW. I went from bumming a couch off a buddy to owning a four-thousand-square-foot home."

Travis paused.

"It sounds like I'm bragging." He smirked. "There's a reason for that—I'm bragging."

The crowd erupted into laughter.

"Not bragging to impress," Travis said quickly, "but impress upon you that you can do it as well."

The audience cheered, bursting into a chorus of applause. The smirk on Travis's face spread into a wide, unabashed grin.

It was 2008, and Travis was speaking at a Prepaid Legal seminar. By the age of twenty-seven, he was a true success

story. He had about thirteen hundred people in his organization, earning him the title of Gold Executive Director.

Along the way his gift for public speaking had become
recognized by the executives, and Travis became a regular
motivational speaker at Prepaid Legal seminars around the
country.

On stage, at the center of attention, Travis was completely
at ease, completely in his element. Using his own background
as a motivational tool, he preached "limitless thinking" and
encouraged others to strive to achieve their ultimate potential. He spoke of God's plan and finding one's purpose in life.

In his speeches, Travis was earnest and self-deprecating,
his enthusiasm infectious.

"He was an excellent speaker," Chris Hughes recalled. "He
brought a spiritual flair to his speaking. He would talk about
his relationship with God. People just really connected with
him."

As a public speaker, Travis had a gift for inspiring. He
never used his background as an excuse or to gain pity. Instead, he encouraged others not to allow setbacks to stymie
their dreams.

Dave Hall was an executive with Prepaid Legal who first
met Travis shortly after he joined the company. Husky with
round cheeks and short thinning hair, Dave believed Travis's
troubled childhood was one of the things that made him such
a dynamic speaker.

"He took the audience on an emotional roller coaster,"
Dave said. "When he would speak, he could literally take
people from laughing their heads off with sarcasm and in-
nuendos to crying, in the matter of minutes."

On stage, in moments of bleak honesty, Travis spoke about
working three jobs and being tens of thousands of dollars in
debt.

"Before I got started I wasn't doing so well, to be honest
with you," Travis said in a 2005 speech. "I just wasn't going
what I thought was the right direction."

It wasn't God's plan for anyone to toil away their life, barely making a living wage, Travis would say. No one should confine themselves to that lot in life. Using stories from the Bible, Travis compared today's nine-to-five workforce to the children of Israel, the Hebrew-speaking slaves of the Pharaoh of Egypt, who were led by Moses to the promised land.

"The children of Israel worked all day. They were told when they could use the restroom, when they could go home. And when they got to go home, the next day they had to come back and do the same thing again," Travis said. "Does that sound like anyone you know?"

Many in the audience chuckled, nodding in agreement.

Travis also sold the concept of legal insurance by sharing his personal experiences.

After being fired from his job at the mall, Travis's former boss refused to provide his final paycheck. After three months of battling over the phone, Travis called an attorney that specialized in labor law in the Prepaid Legal plan.

"Two days later I got the check," he said. "Attached to it was a one-word note that said, 'Sorry.'"

On another occasion, Travis discovered he was being fined $515 for a conviction for robbery, contempt of court, and assault and battery that he had not committed. When he called the department of corrections to learn the origin of these charges, he learned that a man using his identity had just served time in jail. Travis's identity had been stolen.

Later, Travis would learn the perpetrator was his own brother Greg, who was on drugs when he committed the offense and chose to use his brother's identity. Travis called his Prepaid Legal attorney and his record was eventually expunged.

"This is a viable product everyone needs and no one has," Travis said in his speeches. "There's not a lot of selling to do. It sells itself. That's why we make so much darn money. That's why this business is easy. You'll never, ever, ever find an opportunity where someone with no money can make a lot of money so easily."

Not everyone involved with Prepaid Legal—which was later renamed to LegalShield—made a fortune. But in 2005,

Travis honestly believed in what he was selling. He was truly passionate about the product and felt he was helping people by protecting them from a legal disaster.

"We're changing society for the better," Travis told audiences. "We're not only making a living, we're making a difference. It's one thing to make a living; it's another to be able to sleep at night."

Working as a motivational speaker for Prepaid Legal, Travis spoke at conferences in California and New York, as well as exotic locations such as Hawaii and the Bahamas.

Chris Hughes and his wife, Sky, also attended many of these trips. Sky was pretty and petite, with bright blue eyes and long brown hair. The couple had married in 2005, and later had three children: two boys and a girl.

Both Chris and Sky took Travis under their wing and the three became great friends. Sky was like a big sister and throughout their friendship would often play a supporting role in Travis's search for love—talking up his good traits as he courted potential partners.

When Travis wasn't traveling, he conducted the majority of his business in his downstairs den. He spent most weekdays in the office making sales calls.

At night he typically went to church gatherings and social events. When he returned home, he regularly worked until the early-morning hours—sending e-mails and creating business proposals. Whenever he became excited about a new project or endeavor, Travis was unable to sleep. His friends became accustomed to waking up each morning with late-night e-mails from Travis in their inboxes.

By early 2006, Travis's business was practically running itself. The first week of the month, he trained and motivated his team. For the rest of the month, he made sales calls a few hours a week and raked in the commissions from the sales his associates closed.

In an e-mail to a friend he explained how his business had evolved, freeing up much of his spare time. Travis realized he could work to grow his Prepaid Legal business, but by this time he was more interested in expanding his horizons.

"PPL is very automatic these days," he wrote. "Now I could work harder if I want to, but I have a problem with doing the same thing every day all day. I don't want to get burned out on something I love so much."

After five years of selling, he was ready to explore other entrepreneurial endeavors. He didn't want Prepaid Legal to be his legacy. He told several friends that when he died he feared his gravestone would read, "Travis Alexander, Prepaid Legal."

"Something else to spin my wheels on will be good for my business I think," he wrote. "I need to do about two hours of Prepaid a day. Then I have my personal development to take care of. And the rest of the time I have free to do what I want."

Throughout the years Travis had recruited several of his peers and friends into his business. One of these men was Taylor Searle, whom Travis met in the fall of 2004 through Prepaid Legal.

Although he was six years younger than Travis, Taylor possessed a similar entrepreneurial spirit. Tall and lean with light brown hair, Taylor was attending Arizona State University to study accounting while working part-time for Prepaid Legal.

One day in 2006, as they were discussing business, Taylor shared an idea he had first developed in high school. Back then belly shirts and skimpy skirts were fashionable among his female classmates. As a Mormon, Taylor was instilled with a sense that women should dress conservatively and he wanted to create a clothing line to promote modesty among women, to be called CAFGSS, an altered acronym for the Coalition Against the Flagrant Flaunting of Flesh.

"Our mission is simple: We want people to start wearing clothes again," Taylor had posted on the company's Facebook page. "Many of us are fed up with this blatant showing of skin. Now it's time we band together."

The motto for the clothing line: "More than a shirt, it's a quest!"

Immediately, Travis took to the cheeky idea. He was also excited about the prospect of building a business with his close friend. Out of all of his associates, he felt Taylor was as much a visionary as he was.

Travis decided he wanted to partner with Taylor to create the clothing line. At 2:30 one morning in 2006, Travis sent an enthusiastic e-mail to Taylor.

"I am just gonna give it to you straight. We have been talking about getting rich for a long time together," he wrote. "I think CAFGSS is a million dollar idea, truly I do—a fun one at that. It's one of those unique ones that doesn't come around every day. I think about it all the time."

Soon the pair began building the business—creating logos and developing a Web site. Because Taylor was busy with school, Travis volunteered to lead many of their projects. With his undemanding schedule with Prepaid Legal, Travis had a lot of time to devote to CAFGSS. At their peak, the company sold about five hundred shirts a month on the Internet.

"This is what I am good at," Travis told Taylor. "I feel like a caged lion, just ready for the gate to open so I can go tear something to shreds."

CHAPTER 6

T he 1980s rock tune "Pour Some Sugar on Me," by Def Leppard, reverberated in the background as Eddie Snell burst into the conference room. He was barefoot—dressed in cutoff jean shorts, a black sleeveless T-shirt, and oversize black sunglasses. His curly, dark mullet was swept into a ponytail.

"Woo," he grunted. "I friggin' love that song!"

Eddie kicked his leg high and flexed his biceps, showing off his muscles to the crowd of professionally dressed Prepaid Legal representatives.

"It's a plum, pleasing pleasure to be with you again," he said in a Southern accent.

Eddie glanced around the podium, searching for his notes.

"All right, where's my crap," he exclaimed.

"Eddie Snell from Alabama" was Travis's alter ego—a lazy, crude, inappropriate salesperson he created as a humorous way to show associates how not to behave. Eddie insulted customers, dressed inappropriately, and made bad jokes. Travis's redneck persona made appearances at Prepaid Legal seminars, giving presentations like "Ten Poor Commitments," a play on the "Ten Core Commitments" for Prepaid Legal associates that were fundamentals of success.

Eddie Snell was a hit at conferences. When Travis leaped

out on stage in his mullet wig, shaking his pelvis, the audience was in hysterics.

For many who knew Travis professionally, his alter ego was an entirely unexpected side to his personality. Yet for close friends, this was simply Travis being Travis.

Travis, who jokingly called himself the T-Dogg, had a saucy sense of humor. Whether he was singing, making jokes, or dressing up as Eddie Snell, he loved making people laugh.

"Travis was hilarious," his sister Hillary Wilcox said. "There's not one person he couldn't bring a smile to your face."

Often his jokes were sarcastically cocky, as he made quips about his own physique. Fit and trim with large, muscular biceps, Travis was proud of his build. If he had an opportunity to show off his muscles, he took it. Rolling up his sleeves, he would say things like, "This is my ridiculously large arm, also known as a shameless ploy."

"He loved his biceps," Hillary said. "He was always flexing them, especially if you were a girl."

On one occasion, Travis and Taylor Searle were going out to dinner at a Mexican restaurant with their dates. Walking up to the hostess Travis asked, "How long is the wait?"

"About forty-five minutes," the hostess said.

Travis smirked and pulled up his sleeve. "How about now," he said, flexing his biceps. "You can touch it."

The hostess giggled. Travis turned his behind toward her and pointed to his butt. "You can touch that, too."

"I think the hostess maybe touched his butt for a second," Taylor recalled with a smile. "We still had to wait at least thirty minutes."

On another night the two men were hanging out when Travis challenged his friend to a dare. He wanted to select two random girls in each other's phones and send a text message, "I want to get you pregnant."

Taylor laughed. "There's no way I'm doing that."

Travis took the challenge upon himself, selecting two phone numbers in his own phone and sending the raunchy message. One of the women replied: "Funny, funny."

"He had a sick sense of humor," Taylor recalled. "He was just that way with the irreverent wit."

But despite his irreverence, Travis's flirty personality was playful, not lecherous. He found it hilarious to act the part of a lothario, but only in a teasing manner, said Sky Hughes.

"He was super flirtatious, but it was just his way of being funny," she said. "He wasn't Mr. Smooth, he was Mr. Hilarious."

Part of Travis's zany charm was his affinity for singing. Friends called him a "walking musical" because he so often spontaneously sang. The soundtrack to his life was upbeat with a catchy hook.

"He would always bust out in song. I'd sometimes catch him looking in the mirror singing a song or talking to himself," Hillary recalled. "But I think he did it on purpose because he knew someone was going to walk by and he wanted to make us laugh."

Travis's musical taste was diverse—he enjoyed adult contemporary classics by Neil Diamond as well as the punk rock tunes by the Ramones. He listened to obscure rock, hip-hop, punk, and ska bands from the 1990s. When Travis heard something that reminded him of a song he knew, he couldn't help but sing the lyrics.

"Every time I saw him, he would flash his big smile and sing his salutation," recalled Michelle Lowery. "The best thing was checking my voice mail after he had called. Because without fail there would be a two- to three–minute-long message of him singing. He would go on and on and on, loud and as dramatically as possible—with a little vibrato and a few crescendos for effect."

Another aspect of Travis's silly side was the sayings he often used that became known among his friends as "Travisisms."

"We knew that he said some weird things, but he was known for them," recalled a former girlfriend Lisa Andrews.

If he did something goofy that caused someone to roll their eyes, he'd say, "If you died, you'd miss it."

His biggest Travis-ism came every time he was asked,

"How are you doing?" Travis would always respond with, "If I was any better I'd be twins."

"He'd always have the biggest, goofiest smile on when he said it, and we'd laugh," recalled his friend Chad Perkins. "Then, after hearing this same dang response for years, it finally dawned on me that I have no freaking clue what that means."

So one day Chad asked.

Travis started laughing. "I don't know either!" he said.

"He heard it once from someone and he thought it sounded funny and positive, so it stuck and Travis made it his own," Chad recalled. "Travis's influence is still with me, encouraging me to be fuller of life like he was."

"I'm a simple man, really. Smart, successful, smashing good looks, a real suitor," Travis wrote on his MySpace page. "I love nature, helping the homeless, and cooking with my grandmother just to create memories."

In 2006, Travis signed up for MySpace, a social networking site where users posted photos, blog entries, and videos to keep in contact with their friends. At that time social networking had become an integral part of the Internet mainstream and MySpace was the most visited social networking site in the world. In June 2006, it surpassed Google as the most visited Web site in the United States.

On his MySpace page, Travis posted funny photos and videos of himself dressed as Eddie Snell. But it was his description of himself in the "About Me" section that lent the true glimpse into his unique brand of humor.

"Do I work out you ask? Well I'd like to be modest, but can you say, 'tri-athlete.' And if you can't say that well simply say, '16½ inch biceps,'" he wrote. "If I look familiar you are probably an avid reader of *GQ* or *Men's Health*."

Travis listed his interests as attending church, teaching English to foreign children, and gourmet cooking. He bragged about a list of fictitious accomplishments.

"You might say to yourself, 'Yes but what are Travis's talents?' Well, if I must answer: poetry, playing the Spanish

Guitar (or what I like to call the strings of love) and understanding more than just people's voices, but understanding people's hearts," he wrote. "At least that's what Maya Angelou said at the awards ceremony when I was nominated for my first Nobel Peace prize."

On his profile, Travis had ninety friends who kept in contact with him through short messages. Each year his friends posted birthday wishes and regular comments, noting that they were thinking about him.

"Just want to say, 'Hi,' since I haven't talked to you forever," one friend wrote.

"I have to tell you, every time I see a Prepaid Legal sticker I think of you," wrote another.

In June 2006, housing prices had ballooned to their peak. Nationwide, home costs were overvalued by about 10 percent compared to income. The real estate bubble had been inflated to its bursting point.

In two short years Travis's house value had climbed by more than 30 percent. In August, he refinanced his home for $336,000, pulling out more than $75,000 in equity. He used the money to finish furnishing his house, make some investments, travel, and fund his lifestyle.

With his extra money and his newfound spare time, Travis was able to pursue many of his goals and interests.

One of those interests was politics. A staunch Republican, Travis often sported a PROUD TO BE A REPUBLICAN baseball cap and planned on one day running for office.

In the fall of 2006, Arizona was holding a state election. That year Travis campaigned for many political issues, including one he felt strongly about—Proposition 204, which would mandate humane treatment of animals before slaughter. The proposal created misdemeanor fines and penalties for confining a pregnant pig or calf for the majority of the day.

A popular slogan against the proposition was "Prop. 204—It's Hogwash." Travis was in support of the proposition, explaining to friends how he felt about the character of the people fighting against it.

"If I get the opportunity to speak with them, I'll explain what hogwash really is," Travis said.

"Travis was always out to protect those that couldn't protect themselves, even if they were 'just animals,'" recalled former girlfriend Lisa Andrews. "This is just one of the things I learned early on that Travis was so passionate about."

Travis later adopted a little black pug he named Napoleon, which he often shortened to Naps or Napster. Travis took his dog everywhere and was often seen walking him around the neighborhood.

"Travis loved this dog like he would a child," said Deanna Reid. "He would teach him all kinds of tricks and take him along on road trips."

Another hobby Travis enjoyed was genealogy, tracing his family lineage. Charting his ancestry, he was excited to find a new family member and discover more about his own heritage.

Perhaps due to their dysfunctional upbringing, several of Travis's siblings struggled as adults. At least two of his brothers and sisters got involved in drugs; another had trouble with the law. After he moved to Mesa, Travis drifted some from his siblings, who always considered their brother the shining star of the family. But Travis always valued his family—especially Grandma Norma.

"Travis was the type of person who wanted to be close to everyone," Hillary Wilcox recalled. "He would find those similarities in anyone he came in contact with and feel really close to him. That's how he was."

The majority of Travis's spare time was devoted to fitness. As motivated as he was about his spiritual development, he was equally passionate about his physical health.

Wearing a pedometer, he monitored how many calories he burned each day. He exercised regularly, ate healthy, and did not smoke, drink alcohol, or consume caffeine. Friends remember his dedication to self-improvement was rivaled only by his devotion to fitness.

"Because he was self-employed, I would go to his house and he'd be on the treadmill listening to some author's book on tape, working out listening to personal development," said Taylor Searle.

Much of his exercise routine was done at home, where he kept gym equipment, including a treadmill, weight set, and punching bag. Almost daily Travis ran on a treadmill he stored in the corner of his bedroom. He lifted weights, did yoga, and hiked the vast desert trails on Arizona's mountain ranges. When he was near the beach he loved wakeboarding.

Among his favorite activities was cycling. When riding his bike, even just around the neighborhood, he dressed as if he were racing in the Tour de France. He donned a bicycle helmet and wrap-around sunglasses, knee-length black biker shorts, and a checkered yellow cycling jersey emblazed with a logo for Dad's Root Beer.

"Travis enjoyed biking. He had this really decked-out outfit that he would wear," Hillary recalled. "It was really funny. I don't know about cute, but really funny. He liked to strut his stuff in it."

By 2006, Travis had built the ideal life for himself. He had everything he ever wanted—a spacious house, a nice car, a dream job, and an amazing group of friends.

Travis savored each day to a degree beyond that of a typical optimist. His zest for life was fervent and contagious.

"I love my life. Why I have been so blessed, is hard for me to understand," Travis wrote on a blog he would later launch in 2008. "I have fantastic visionary friends, a supportive family, and most importantly the Gospel of Jesus Christ. I can honestly say that I awake every single day happy. I feel as if it is the way to live—to have purpose, to have righteous desire to make this world a better place because you are in it."

CHAPTER 7

Travis relished his single status. Throughout his twenties, he lived a bachelor lifestyle, dating a score of attractive young women.

Handsome, charismatic, successful, and funny—Travis knew he was appealing to the opposite sex. When he approached a woman, he'd often flex his biceps or make a playfully cocky quip about his "dangerous good looks."

Travis loved it when, at speaking engagements, the host would state, "By the way, ladies, Travis is single," an announcement that was usually followed by cat calls from the crowd.

"He really tried to be a ladies' man," Taylor Searle recalled. "He loved to charm the ladies, loved to flirt."

Travis was popular among women in general, and Mormon women in particular. Many of the women he dated were single Mormons he met at church.

Among the functions of an LDS singles ward is to facilitate opportunities for church members to meet their future spouses. Latter-day Saints place an unusually strong emphasis on marriage, believing it is ordained by God. Every LDS member who is able to is expected to marry.

Because of this belief, Latter-day Saints take dating and

courtship more seriously than those for whom marriage has less religious significance.

Unlike many of his peers, however, Travis was not interested in finding a spouse, at least not throughout his twenties. He enjoyed dating and had no plans to settle down.

Dating in Mormon culture comes with boundaries. Celibacy before marriage is one of the basic tenets of the Mormon faith and sex of any kind prior to marriage is considered sinful.

As part of the Law of Chastity, the church teaches its members not only to abstain from adultery and fornication, but also to refrain from masturbation and sexually inappropriate thoughts. In addition, members of the LDS church are encouraged to avoid pornography and adult-themed movies and shows.

Before going on his mission, Travis swore a covenant to God not to have sexual relations with anyone but his lawful wife during the Endowment Ceremony, a sacred Mormon ritual that involves secret gestures and passwords as well as scripted Biblical reenactments. As a constant reminder of his promise of celibacy, Travis was provided with special temple garments, consisting of a top and bottom piece, which he was expected to wear every day for the rest of his life, only removing them to shower and change, or acceptable times like swimming or intense sports.

As a further reminder of his faith, Travis wore a silver ring engraved with the initials "CTR," as a prompting to "Choose the Right," a motto of his religion and a saying among members of the LDS church, which is taken from a hymn of the same title.

Everyone who met Travis knew he was devout. He was rarely absent from church, prayed daily, and did not use alcohol or drugs, which are forbidden by the church. He had read *The Book of Mormon* more than twenty times and could recite hundreds of passages by heart. He preached the gospel and spoke with passion about his covenants with God— including the importance of celibacy.

As far as his friends and family knew, Travis's faith extended to his covenant not to engage in sexual relations prior to marriage. His older brothers bragged about Travis's dedication, proudly referring to him, up until the end of his life, as a "thirty-year-old virgin."

But unbeknown to his friends and family, Travis had failed to keep his vow of chastity.

It is impossible to know exactly the extent of his sexual activity or how many partners he had throughout his life. But at least two women he had dated would later come forward, admitting to prosecutors that they had had a sexual relationship with Travis.

One of those women was Travis's longtime friend and ex-girlfriend Deanna Reid. The couple had dated exclusively from 2002 to 2005, when Deanna broke up with Travis because she was ready to marry and he was not. Over a period of about a year they had sex several times, although they both kept it a closely guarded secret.

Several of Travis's friends were aware he had engaged in sexual activity, but were under the impression that it didn't reach the extent of actual intercourse. With most people, however, Travis didn't discuss his sex life. He tried to be an example and would have likely been ashamed of his indiscretions.

The extent of his sex life was a secret Travis would take to the grave. It was only after his murder that it would be exposed.

When the truth came out, there were those who would call Travis a hypocrite for breaking his vow of chastity. The reality, however, may be much less seedy.

Breaking sacred covenants is a most serious matter in the Mormon church. Unfortunately, it is something that happens among members of every congregation around the world. When this occurs, LDS members have a chance to repent and seek forgiveness.

While sex before marriage is forbidden in the Mormon religion, that standard is not always maintained in modern society. There are a small minority who ignore the covenants. Other, less devout Mormons may justify their behavior by loosely interpreting the Law of Chastity, engaging in sexual activity but excluding intercourse prior to marriage.

There are also some who incorrectly interpret the Law of Chastity as not to have sex with the woman they plan to marry in the temple prior to the wedding night. In other words, they may engage in intercourse prior to marriage with partners they are dating casually, but with their future husband or wife they maintain a chaste union. These faulty interpretations of the Law of Chastity are all condemned by the church.

It will never be known how Travis felt about breaking his sacred covenant. What is known, however, is that it was out of character for Travis. Close friends of Travis do not believe he took his vows lightly. Instead, they say he was just human—with human weaknesses and failings. It was likely that he continuously strove toward celibacy but was simply not infallible.

"Travis wasn't perfect—none of us are—but he was a really incredible human being," Chris Hughes said. "But when you know where he came from, how he grew up, you couldn't help but admire him and be in continual awe of all that he accomplished in his short life."

If Travis decided to repent for his mistakes he would have been required to admit his sexual indiscretions privately to his bishop, a leader of the ward or congregation.

In situations where grave transgressions have been made, the church has several protocols for disciplinary actions. Members who confess serious sins may lose leadership positions in the church, face disfellowship, or be excommunicated. In addition, their temple recommends may be revoked for a period of time. To be allowed inside the Mormon Temple, an LDS member must be "temple worthy," which means they are in good standing and living by the covenants.

For a period of his life in 2004, Travis and Deanna both lost their temple recommends when they confessed to their respective bishops about their sexual indiscretions. After repenting they did not break the Law of Chastity again in their relationship and were eventually allowed back into the temple.

Years later, in late 2007 or early 2008, Travis was once

again banned from temple, according to his friends. Travis had told several people that he had "gone too far" with a woman, although many believed he had stopped short of actual intercourse. Travis had also mentioned being in a disciplinary council, which is convened to decide the consequences for any transgressions—including sexual relations.

Sometime later Travis's temple recommend was reinstated, something that would only happen if he had repented for his mistakes. To Taylor Searle, this indicated that Travis had admitted his transgressions, had been forgiven, and was working to better himself.

"People make mistakes and get back on the path, choosing the right life," Taylor said. "I believed he was working to get back on the right path."

By the time he turned thirty, Travis would have a change of heart about marriage—deciding he was ready to find a wife. He would feel so strongly about starting a family, in fact, it would become his main priority.

But in the fall of 2006, he was content being a bachelor. During this period he would be drawn to a woman who was looking for a much deeper commitment.

Ultimately, their union would derail the course of his life.

In September 2006, Travis attended a Prepaid Legal conference in Las Vegas. Walking around the MGM Grand, he saw her—a gorgeous blonde with almond-shaped brown eyes, pouted lips, and a single dimple on her right cheek.

Like an arrow, Travis shot straight toward her, his gaze unflinching.

"Hi, I'm Travis," he said, his hand outstretched.

The woman smiled, glancing up at Travis. She placed her hand in his. "I'm Jodi."

CHAPTER 8

Three hundred and fifty miles north of Riverside—where Travis Alexander was born and raised—lies the scenic city of Salinas, California.

Located on the Central California coast, Salinas is a sunny suburb with a booming agriculture industry. Surrounded by fruit groves and vegetable patches, the city's 150,000 residents live in modest homes with grassy front yards.

Jodi Ann Arias was born in Salinas on July 9, 1980. She was the first child of Bill and Sandra Arias. Her birth would be followed by brothers, Carl and Joseph, and a sister, Angela. In addition, Jodi had an older half-sister, Julie, from her father's prior marriage.

Jodi was a pretty child with a naturally tan complexion. She was of mixed heritage—her mother was Caucasian, her father Mexican American. A natural brunette, even as a toddler she wore her hair long with thick bangs.

Childhood photos show a happy girl with an impish grin. In one photo, Jodi was dressed in floral print overalls, her hair in pigtails tied with pink ribbons. She was being cradled in her father's burly arms.

Jodi Arias would later testify about her own life story in court, describing her early upbringing as wholesome.

"Until about age seven it was a pretty ideal childhood," Jodi said. "I have predominately positive memories."

Her parents worked in the food service industry and, over the years, owned several restaurants across California. When Jodi was young, her mother worked as a server at the family diner. Later, Sandra became a dental assistant.

In Salinas, the family lived in a house at the end of a cul-de-sac, with a spacious backyard where Jodi and her brother Carl, who was two years younger, would climb trees and play with the other neighborhood children. She grew up roller-skating, riding bikes, and playing hopscotch and four square.

The family traveled frequently, often taking camping trips and visiting theme parks around California. Throughout her childhood, animals were a very central part of Jodi's life. They owned many pets, including dogs, cats, fish, birds, and a pet rat.

Naturally soft-spoken, Jodi was described by family members as sweet and sensitive. She took piano lessons and played the flute. Early on, she was extraordinarily creative and showed a talent for art and enjoyed coloring and drawing.

"When I was younger I liked to color with Crayolas," Jodi recalled. "I began to get into art . . . I would see art and it would fascinate me. I slowly began to practice doing that."

While she was generally a bright child, when it came to academics, Jodi initially struggled and was held back in kindergarten. For the first three years of her education, she attended private school, eventually transferring to public school.

When Jodi was eleven, the family relocated to Santa Maria, a city about 150 miles northwest of downtown Los Angeles. There, Jodi completed middle school.

Three years later, they moved again to Yreka, a quaint community on the Oregon-California border with a population of less than eight thousand people. Nestled in the northernmost corner of the majestic Shasta Valley, Yreka boasted panoramic views of three mountain ranges. At the heart of the city was a historic district, featuring a well-preserved gold rush-era town.

The Arias family purchased a modest single-story house

painted grayish blue with dark trim, at 1021 South Oregon Street. A chain-link fence surrounded the yard to the north and east of the residence, boxing in a backyard basketball court.

Jodi attended Yreka Union High School. Friends remember her as fairly intelligent, articulate, and vivacious. Others describe her as a quiet person who didn't really open up to many people. In large groups, she was known to be shy and quiet.

Jodi would later say the frequent moves were taxing on her early upbringing. Moving every few years to a new city made sustaining friendships difficult.

"I had a few friends, but I didn't really make a lot of close friends. It just seemed like I was constantly making friends and then moving away," Jodi recalled. "I had a large circle of friends but no one I was really close with."

Throughout high school, Jodi studied Spanish, which was among her favorite classes. When she wasn't in school, she worked part-time at her family's diner.

As a teenager, Jodi's talent for art blossomed. She began experimenting with oil paints and colored pencils. In art class, she quickly mastered all artistic mediums and was usually the first student to complete an assignment.

"She was very conscientious, very smart, very hard working, and very skillful," said a former art teacher, Richard Rangel. "She was very quiet and always seemed more mature than the rest of the kids. She had a maturity about her that was noticeable."

When Jodi was ten, she received her first camera, and developed a lifelong passion for photography. A lover of nature, Jodi often took pictures of the mountains surrounding Yreka, and was rarely seen without her camera.

But when it came to her art, Jodi didn't find much support at home. While she was praised by classmates and art teachers, her parents were largely indifferent.

"They didn't discourage me by any means, but they were lukewarm," Jodi said. "They weren't really moved by it. They never went out of their way to display it."

* * *

While her childhood appeared normal, from a young age Jodi's parents recognized there was something unusual about their daughter.

As a child Jodi was disobedient—defying her parents' rules and often running away from home. But as she approached her teens, Jodi's rebellion escalated toward emotional instability. She was prone to extreme irritability and bouts of anger, her moods shifting to an extent beyond that of a typical adolescent. When mad, she grew enraged; if sad, she became inconsolable and many times threatened suicide.

While Sandra Arias seemed aware her daughter's behavior was dysfunctional, she wouldn't truly understand the extent of Jodi's issues until years later.

"Jodi has mental problems," Sandra told a detective in 2008. "Jodi would freak out all the time. I had quite a few of her friends call me and tell me I needed to get her some help. In fact, I had one call me in the middle of the night and tell me I needed to get her some help."

To control her misbehavior, Jodi's parents became strict and sometimes used physical discipline. It began with spankings as a form of punishment, but as she got older, Jodi claimed it became increasingly brutal.

"My parents would spank or hit us as discipline. It seemed like at age seven, it started to get a little more intense," Jodi said. "That's the first year my dad started using a belt."

Both her mother and father punished her and her siblings physically, according to Jodi. Large and imposing, with graying hair, Bill Arias practiced martial arts, frequented the gym, and could bench-press more than five hundred pounds. He used his strength to push his daughter into the furniture or walls.

Sandra Arias, a plump woman with a round face and wavy brown hair, carried a wooden kitchen spoon in her purse, which she used to whack Jodi and her siblings when they misbehaved, according to Jodi. When the spoon wasn't available, Sandra would grab anything nearby to use as a weapon, at times leaving bruises and welts.

In her early teens, Jodi began responding to the discipline by inflicting violence on her parents. Sandra received the brunt of her daughter's rage. She and Jodi argued constantly, and at times, Jodi would hit or slap her mom for no discernable reason.

When Jodi was fourteen, Bill and Sandra discovered something else disturbing: their daughter was using drugs. On the roof of their house they found marijuana plants growing out of Tupperware dishes. Alarmed, her father called the sheriff's department. Following the discovery of the drugs, her parents searched her room for the first time.

To Bill, the incident seemed to spur a deep rift in their relationship. Jodi became distrusting and developed a habit of lying and hiding things from her parents.

"After that . . . something turned in her head," Bill said in 2008. "We were nosy parents and we're going to search everything that she had so she hid everything from us. She's never been honest with us since then."

As another form of punishment, they tried grounding their daughter, sending her to her room for weeks without television or the phone. In rebellion, Jodi snuck out of the house. On the night she moved from Santa Maria to Yreka, she was caught out of the house past curfew. The next morning, in anger, her father confronted her.

"My dad asked where I had been. I sat up and I was disoriented," Jodi testified. "I didn't give him a satisfactory answer, so he hit me across the face and I fell back down. And then he sat me back up and asked me again and I didn't give him a satisfactory answer so he hit me again."

While for Bill and Sandra the discipline was driven by concern, Jodi considered herself to be abused. She felt confused, betrayed, and grew bitter toward her parents. The contempt Jodi felt toward them would stay with her most of her adult life.

"As I got older it would really make me mad. I understood why I was being punished, but I was just mad at them all the time because it hurt," Jodi said. "It put a strain on our relationship."

CHAPTER 9

Jodi would grow from being a cute girl to a gorgeous woman. With high cheekbones, olive skin, and full lips, she was an exotic beauty with a coy smile and long dark hair. Her figure was slim but curvaceous. In her twenties, she would bleach her hair platinum blond. It appeared unnatural against her complexion, yet it somehow suited her.

Her striking good looks attracted a slew of male attention. When Jodi began dating in her mid-teens, like many young girls, her relationships with men became her primary interest.

Over the course of Jodi's dating life, however, a disturbing pattern emerged. Jodi tended to lose herself in a relationship. Whoever she was dating at the time became her identity. While she had few friends, Jodi seemed to need a partner to complete her and was rarely without a man in her life.

Friends say she had a way of picking "bad boys," and described her boyfriends as generally controlling.

"From a young age, she started picking guys that were just not the best choice for her," said Tina Ross, a high school friend. "And she was such a beautiful girl."

Jodi met her first boyfriend when she was just fifteen.

In the summer of 1995, Yreka hosted the State Fair, which Jodi attended with a few friends. In the crowds, she noticed a thin man with long, dark curly hair and deep-set brown eyes. He was dressed in the eighteenth-century Gothic style, in a black suit with a high-collared shirt. At the time, he was hobbling along on crutches.

"I remember seeing him walk by and I didn't approach him, but I noticed him," Jodi recalled. "He just seemed intriguing to me."

Jodi wanted to talk to him but was too shy. Later that night, while her friends were on one of the rides, Jodi saw him again. He motioned for her to come talk to him.

"Would you like to ride with me?" he asked.

Jodi smiled. "Yeah, sure."

They rode the Zipper together and chatted briefly. But that night they parted ways.

Months later, during her freshman year in the fall of 1995, Jodi was at the school's football homecoming game when she saw him again. This time she mustered the courage to approach him.

Jodi learned the boy was an eighteen-year-old senior named Robert Juarez, who went by Bobby. Jodi gave Bobby her phone number, they began talking, and soon they were a couple.

Each day on her lunch break, Jodi would leave campus and meet Bobby at the nearby USA Gasoline station, which included an indoor arcade. Bobby would play video games and he and Jodi would hold hands.

A Goth with an interest in the occult, Bobby was something of an oddity in the small California town. Early on, Jodi discovered he had some atypical beliefs.

"He had all sorts of wild ideas. He entertained the belief in vampires," Jodi testified. "He thought let's go to San Francisco and see if we can find some real vampires . . . so we could live together forever and be together forever."

After only a few months of dating, Bobby grew very serious. But while Jodi initially liked the idea of spending her life with him, she eventually began to withdraw.

"At age fifteen, I thought the relationship was getting very intense. He was talking about being together forever," she said. "I loved him, but I didn't feel like I was in love with him."

In early 1996, she called Bobby and broke up with him over the phone.

"He didn't take it well," Jodi testified. "I learned a few years later that he slit both of his wrists and tried to kill himself."

Bobby was committed to a mental institution in Citrus Heights, north of Sacramento. He and Jodi didn't speak for years.

In the summer of 1997, just before her seventeenth birthday, Jodi spent three weeks abroad in Costa Rica, as part of a student exchange program. For the trip, she stayed with a family who, coincidentally, also had the last name Arias. They had a daughter and two sons, the older of whom, Victor, was close in age to Jodi.

Jodi felt an attraction to Victor Arias, who was tall and muscular with short black hair and a strong jawline.

"We kind of clicked and got to know each other, and a romance sort of blossomed," Jodi said. "It was my first experience with the warm fuzzies—someone that I felt I really cared for."

When she returned to Yreka, her romance with Victor continued long-distance. They spent the summer exchanging flowery love letters, which he wrote in Spanish. Jodi wrote so often, the post office workers knew her by name.

Later that summer, Victor flew to Yreka and stayed with Jodi for two weeks. During the trip, he gave her a promise ring. But Victor was also jealous. He didn't like the idea of Jodi talking to other men or associating with male friends.

"He wanted me to come live down there and start a family," Jodi said. "I couldn't see myself moving to Costa Rica and having that kind of life."

By October 1997, Jodi ended her relationship with Victor Arias.

* * *

From an early age, Jodi explored spirituality and religion. She grew up believing in Christ, but rarely attended church. She considered herself a nondenominational Christian, but when it came to religion she was easily influenced.

When Jodi was seventeen, she worked part-time in her family's restaurant. One of the regulars was an old man who always carried his Bible and quoted scripture. Many times, he told Jodi he had deciphered the puzzles of the Bible and had predicted the second coming of Christ would occur on September 23, 1997.

"I was kind of naive and I believed him," Jodi said.

Faced with a religious quandary, Jodi's thoughts drifted back to Bobby Juarez. During their relationship he hadn't been religious. To Jodi, it was important for Bobby to be told about the possible rapture.

The first two times she called him, Bobby hung up on her. Eventually, he called her back and Jodi explained the reason for her call.

"I reached out to him for spiritual reasons," Jodi said. "I felt kind of silly, explaining to him why I was calling him. I kind of expected him to laugh at me, but it was important to me."

After she informed him of the old man's prediction, Bobby thanked her and, over the next few weeks, they rekindled their friendship.

Around the time Jodi ended her relationship with Victor Arias, her feelings for Bobby returned.

"I had begun to develop feelings for him right before Christmas," she said. "He had feelings for me too, so we decided to give things another try at that point."

By early 1998, Jodi and Bobby's relationship became romantic. Then twenty, Bobby was still an eccentric with unusual beliefs.

"I was still drawn to that. And part of that was fascinating to me," Jodi said. "I thought he was beautiful on the inside and out."

Bobby lived with his adopted grandparents, who were in

their seventies, in a dilapidated house in the neighboring town of Montague. The Juarez family home was dirty, with boxes of junk cluttering the living room. Cigarette tar coated the walls; the linoleum tiles peeled from the floor.

As Jodi grew closer with Bobby, she spent more time away from home, distancing herself from her parents. From Jodi's perspective, Bill and Sandra were negative, judgmental, and abusive. Jodi began to grow weary of their rules and physical discipline.

One night, during a heated argument Jodi had with her mom and dad, Bill pushed her into the doorframe, briefly knocking her unconscious, Jodi testified. Following that incident, Jodi began making secret plans to move out.

At the time she was working as a hostess at a diner called Grandma's House. Her parents' restaurant had since closed and her dad had given her boxes of plates and silverware for when she was on her own. Slowly, Jodi began packing her possessions into boxes and taking them to Bobby's house to store in his shed.

In April 1998, Jodi's parents were called by the school after she skipped a class. Driving around Yreka, Bill found his daughter in a parking lot off campus. Incensed, he grounded her for three months, until she turned eighteen.

Unable to fathom being grounded for such a long time, and anxious to be on her own, Jodi decided to move in with Bobby.

That night she stayed up late, packing her belongings and loading them in her car. At 7 A.M. her mom woke up and asked her what she was doing.

"Nothing," Jodi said, as she grabbed her cat and left the house for good.

For the next year Jodi lived with Bobby and his grandparents in the tiny house in Montague.

After Jodi's abrupt departure, her parents grew increasingly troubled by their daughter's behavior.

"After she left the house she just kind of got a little strange," Bill told the police in 2008. "She was really friendly sometimes, she'd call and be real sweet. Ten minutes later she'd call in a rage and just screaming."

Her fits were so erratic that her mom was often concerned Jodi would try to hurt herself or commit suicide. After one conversation with his daughter, Bill confronted Jodi about his suspicion of her mental problems.

"She called me and started yelling, and I said, you know, 'Have you ever thought of yourself as being bipolar?'" Bill said in 2008. "'Oh my God,'" she cried hysterically and then she called back and I hung up on her and she called up and kept calling and kept calling and kept calling until I could tell her, 'No, I'm just kidding.'"

Jodi would later claim that she suffered from depression and low self-esteem, beginning in her teenage years. Her issues seeped into her adult life, although she largely hid her emotional instability from others out of concern about how she would be perceived. Jodi's public persona was something she deeply valued and it was important for her to be viewed as "calm and collected," she wrote in her journals.

In her relationships with men Jodi would occasionally "scream and vent," but for the most part suppressed her emotions. When upset, as the anxiety inside her grew, she would tremble in anger. Later, she would privately unleash her fury, Jodi confessed in an e-mail to a friend.

"My anger is very destructive," Jodi wrote. "I've kicked holes in walls, kicked down doors, smashed windows, broken things."

After moving in with Bobby, Jodi was forced to support herself financially. Because Bobby didn't have a job, she began working full-time, stopped attending classes, and completed her junior year with mostly failing grades. She decided not to return for her senior year.

"Toward the end of the year I just let it all fall apart," Jodi said.

In August 1998, she found work as a waitress at Denny's. For a while she also worked part-time busing tables at a restaurant called the Purple Plum.

For a while her relationship with Bobby was good. Months

after she moved in, Bobby's grandparents relocated to a nursing home. When Jodi switched to the graveyard shift at Denny's, she and Bobby began sleeping during the day and staying up all night.

But unbeknownst to Jodi, while she spent nights at work, Bobby was chatting with a woman he met through a party line. In the late 1990s, before chat rooms, 900 numbers provided a forum for people from around the world to converse. Bobby became addicted to the party line and formed a relationship with a woman in Louisiana. He sent her romantic e-mails and they spoke every day by phone.

Jodi knew about the woman but was under the impression that she and Bobby were just friends. But when her boyfriend became distant, Jodi grew concerned and decided to investigate by reading his e-mail. For Jodi, this would develop into a pattern. In her relationships if she became jealous or suspicious of cheating she would pry into her boyfriend's private correspondence for information.

One day, before her shift at Denny's, Jodi secretly logged onto Bobby's Hotmail account and discovered the love letters.

"I clicked the back button to see what was really going on with her because I had suspicions," Jodi said. "I found a whole bunch of love letters that he was writing her."

Jodi was heartbroken.

"I was not well, emotionally. It didn't make me feel good. He was very loving and poetic with this person, and I could tell he had real feelings for her," she said. "I felt jealous a little bit. My heart was pounding. I guess I felt very deceived."

After calling in sick to work, Jodi printed out the letters and confronted Bobby. He apologized, begged her to forgive him, and swore he would never again stray.

Eventually, Bobby convinced Jodi to stay, but their relationship was never the same. Perhaps partially due to Jodi's issues with anger, their union became tumultuous. Over the next few months they argued frequently and broke up numerous times.

"I was advised over and over to get away from him because it was not healthy," Jodi said. "But my heart still cared for him."

Once during an argument in early 1999, Bobby became violent, Jodi testified. As the fight escalated, Bobby grabbed her and placed her in a stranglehold. Jodi fell to her knees, gasping for air. After a few seconds, he let her go.

"I said something to the effect that my family would be very upset if they found out what you just did," Jodi testified. "He began to describe in detail how he would kill each member of my family. He knew a lot about my family so these were all very personalized details about how they would die."

Jodi snatched the phone and dialed 911. Bobby grabbed her arm, nearly breaking it. Prying the phone out of her hand, he screamed at Jodi, "Shut up!" When the operator called back, Bobby explained it as a misdial.

After the fight, Jodi moved in with her grandparents in Yreka. They lived at 352 Pine in a small home painted white with blue trim, just a mile from her parents' house. Jodi was close with her grandparents Carlton and Caroline Allen, and especially with her grandma, whom everyone called Wilma.

Despite the physical abuse, Jodi continued to talk to Bobby. She rationalized that it was a one-time incident and that he had never been violent in the past. But Jodi knew she had to get away. In 1999, she took a week-long vacation to Costa Rica to clear her head.

"I spent a lot of time just reflecting and healing from that. I felt in a lot better place by the time I got back," she said. "I needed to just remove myself from the situation so I could allow my heart to move on a little. So that break from him had helped me a lot."

By the time she returned, Jodi had created some much needed space between her and Bobby. They continued on and off for the next few months until Bobby moved to Medford, a large Oregon metropolis, about fifty miles north of Yreka.

In Oregon, Bobby found work and rented an apartment with a man named Matt McCartney. Tall and trim, Matt was handsome with dark blond hair.

Through Bobby, Jodi became friends with Matt and his family. After she and Bobby separated for the final time, Jodi and Matt became a couple.

"Matt and I began to hang out more and we developed feelings for each other," Jodi said. "We became romantic, and then we were boyfriend and girlfriend."

In early 2000, Jodi moved to Medford and she and Matt rented a one-bedroom apartment together. Jodi worked as a server at an Applebee's restaurant; Matt was a manager for a Subway sandwich shop.

With Matt, Jodi felt she had found a healthy relationship.

"I see that period of my life as one of the best times in my life," she said. "He treated me very well. He was very kind, he was very respectful . . . I was in love with him."

Like Bobby, he also had a fascination with the occult, only Matt's interest was more spiritual. When she first met him, Matt had several books on Wicca, a modern pagan religion that involves the practice of magic. Matt explained to Jodi that he had been turned off from the Christian religion and was on a spiritual journey.

Although she never belonged to a witch coven or cast spells, Jodi felt a fleeting attraction to Wicca's spiritual basis in nature. For Wiccans there is no written creed that the orthodox must adhere to, nor do they build stone temples or churches in which they worship. They practice their rituals outdoors: in parks, gardens, forests, yards, or on hillsides.

Moreover, Jodi liked the Wiccan belief in karma. The Wiccan creed is: "What ye send out, comes back to thee." To a witch, there is no sin and therefore no need for forgiveness or salvation. Instead they believe an individual's actions in life will come back to them three-fold. If a person harms another, they must be willing to accept the karmic consequences.

Jodi's interest in Wicca was brief. With Bobby, she studied various spiritual beliefs including Hinduism and Buddhism. Periodically, the couple attended new age seminars in subjects like transcendental meditation.

"Our relationship took a lot of spiritual turns and twists," she said. "We sort of explored together, and opened up to other beliefs."

In the summer of 2000, Jodi and Matt both found seasonal work at a lodge in Crater Lake, Oregon. Located in the south-central region of Oregon, Crater Lake was a national park with a deep caldera, famous for its clear blue water. For the next few months Jodi and Matt worked and lived at the lodge in the staff quarters.

At the end of the season they returned to Medford, where Jodi resumed working at Applebee's.

By the spring of 2001, however, Jodi and Matt began to argue more frequently. That summer he returned to Crater Lake to work at the lodge, and Jodi stayed behind. Each week-end Matt would drive down from Crater Lake to spend time with Jodi. But over the next several weeks, she began to feel he was withdrawing. At Matt's father's house, she discovered photos of him with another young woman. She suspected he was cheating.

"I felt we were distancing," she said.

In September 2001, while working her shift at Applebee's, Jodi walked past a table and two people stopped her.

"You're Jodi, right?" one of them asked.

They told her they worked with Matt in Crater Lake and had driven down to reveal a secret: Matt was seeing another woman. Jodi was crushed.

"I was reeling," Jodi said. "Of all the boyfriends I had I would have expected him to not be the one to have cheated on me. He was very loyal. I trusted him completely."

Leaving work, Jodi went home, changed her clothes, and made the hour-and-a-half drive to Crater Lake.

"I decided I wanted to find out if it was true," she said. "I didn't want to continue in the relationship if that was the case."

When she arrived at the lodge, a friend directed her to the cottage where the woman was staying. Jodi knocked on the door of the cabin and confronted the woman—a pretty bru-nette from Romania named Bianca.

Bianca informed Jodi she had been seeing Matt for weeks.

She had been under the impression that Matt and Jodi were no longer a couple.

Jodi was devastated. Because it was too late to drive, she stayed the night in a friend's cabin. At sunrise, she drove back to Medford and found Matt at his father's house.

"I confronted Matt and he confirmed it. At that point he was honest about it," she said. "And basically our relationship was over. It was kind of sad."

CHAPTER 10

Following her breakup with Matt McCartney, Jodi Arias decided to move away from Oregon. Every street in Medford reminded her of Matt; each place they used to visit brought back fond memories.

"I wanted to leave the area because Matt and I had a lot of experiences, mostly all good, in that whole southern Oregon area," Jodi said. "Every street that I drove, it was sentimental."

Through a friend, Jodi learned about a job opportunity in Big Sur, a tourist destination on California's central coast where the Santa Lucia Mountains rose from the Pacific Ocean. Nestled in the mountains above the sea was a ritzy, four-star resort called the Ventana Inn and Spa.

In the fall of 2001, at the age of twenty-one, Jodi drove to Big Sur and applied for a server job at the resort's restaurant. She was hired by the food and beverage manager—a man named Darryl Brewer—who would become her direct supervisor.

Around this time, she resumed speaking to Matt.

"Our feelings were tender. And it was just a sticky situation. He was really ashamed of his behavior," Jodi said. "Eventually we began to talk again."

When she told Matt about the job at the Ventana, he also sought out employment there and was hired as well.

Because the staff quarters were occupied at the time, for the first few weeks of their employment, Jodi and Matt shared a tent at the lodge's campground. During that time they had sex one more time.

"There were blurred boundaries because we were familiar with each other and comfortable with each other," she said. "I considered it platonic. I still had some feelings for him, but we were not really together and we were just friends."

As an adult, Jodi didn't have many friends, but Matt would remain one of the few people close to her throughout her life.

A few weeks after they were hired, Jodi and Matt were transferred into staff housing. For the next three and a half years, Jodi worked and lived at the Ventana Inn. It was one of the best jobs of her life.

In the summer of 2002, after the staff wedding coordinator died suddenly from pancreatic cancer, Jodi temporarily worked in the position, assisting brides and grooms in the planning of their nuptials.

Over the course of her employment, Jodi worked closely with Darryl Brewer. Twenty years her senior, Darryl was a recent divorcé and single father with a son named Jack. Darryl was athletic with a full head of salt-and-pepper hair and sharp features.

Despite their age difference, Jodi began to develop feelings for Darryl. But because he was her direct supervisor, the hotel's rules forbade them from dating.

"I began to develop a crush on him," Jodi said, "but he was my boss so I didn't let that on."

In the fall of 2002, after Darryl resigned from his management position, they began dating. Jodi was twenty-two; he was forty-two.

"He was older but attractive, and we had a lot of similar interests," she said. "I think he was more concerned about the age gap than I was, because he was concerned about how people may view him for dating someone so young."

To celebrate stepping down from his position, Darryl and Jodi went on a trip to San Francisco, where they toured the city and attended a 49ers game. That night, they had sex for the first time.

"We began to spend a little more time together and became intimate and fell in love," Darryl testified in court. "It was a happy relationship."

For the next year they lived in separate quarters in staff housing at the resort. A year later, when Darryl moved to Monterey, about thirty miles away, their relationship continued.

As they grew closer, Darryl introduced Jodi to his son. Jodi and Jack got along well, and she became like a big sister.

But as their relationship progressed, Jodi discovered a few aspects of Darryl's personality she found disconcerting. Darryl was a smoker and an admitted alcoholic, although he later stopped drinking. And because he had just gone through a nasty divorce, he had no interest in remarrying or having more kids. He told Jodi he liked her, and was attracted to her, but didn't see himself remarrying.

"He didn't want to get married, so he made that very clear right off the bat," Jodi said. "I was young at the time so it didn't bother me. I figured I still had many years left and I enjoyed being with him so that's what I did. I enjoyed the time we had together."

Years later, however, Jodi would have a very sudden change of heart.

By 2005, Jodi and Darryl had been dating seriously for three years.

Financially, Jodi was in a good place in her life. She had saved more than $10,000 and had earned good credit. With her savings, she had even been able to pay for breast implants, which she had wanted to enhance her figure.

But Jodi yearned for a future beyond being a waitress. She saw herself as a future real estate investor. She began taking real estate classes at Monterey Peninsula College, as well as following trends in the housing market.

Because the housing market was taking off at the time, she wanted to buy a home as an investment. Darryl, too, thought it was wise to purchase property.

In June 2005, Darryl and Jodi bought a house in Palm Desert. Approximately eleven miles east of Palm Springs, in the heart of Southern California's famed Coachella Valley, Palm Desert was a small resort community surrounded by hotels, shopping boutiques, and dozens of hilly golf courses. A popular retreat for snowbirds, each winter the city's population practically doubled with seasonal residents.

Darryl and Jodi cosigned on the property, which they purchased for $357,500. Located at 76572 New York Avenue in Palm Desert, the house was a 1,482-square-foot single-family home with three bedrooms, two bathrooms, and an open floor plan. Built in 1981, the house sat at the end of a long driveway. It had a terra-cotta roof, grassy front yard, and tall hedges that blocked the front windows from the street. The backyard pool was encircled by mature fruit trees.

For the first year they lived in the house, their mortgage was $2,200 a month, which Darryl and Jodi split down the middle. Because they each had a full set of bedroom furniture, Darryl and Jodi kept separate rooms, although many times they slept in the same bed.

By then, Jodi had left her job at the Ventana Inn and was working as a waitress at an Italian restaurant called Piatti, as well as tending bar at a California Pizza Kitchen location inside the local mall.

For the first few months, the arrangement worked out fine, even though Jodi was unsure of their future. But by the following summer, Jodi had begun to rethink many of her life's aspirations. She realized she wanted to marry and have children.

"At the time, my goal was marriage and children, at least someday," she said. "I became a little more disenchanted in the relationship. . . . We were going in different directions. We had different visions for our future."

At the time her relationship with Darryl was deteriorating, the economy was also faltering. Housing prices had peaked and home values in the area were stagnant. Even more disconcerting, Darryl and Jodi had signed on for an escalating house payment. In the summer of 2006, the mortgage climbed to $2,800.

At first, Jodi was able to pay it by dipping into her savings, but soon, she was forced to make payments on her credit card. As she struggled, Jodi began to feel discontent with her unplanned future. She had spent her early twenties aimlessly drifting from one waitress job to the next. Without a high school diploma and with limited job experience, however, she found few career opportunities.

"I was looking for other ways to get on my feet financially so I could invest in real estate, and could do other things I enjoy such as photography," she said.

While she was working her shift at the California Pizza Kitchen her manager asked her a question: "What do you plan to be doing in five years?" He continued, "Because I plan to be retired."

The manager had recently signed up to be an independent associate with Prepaid Legal and was attempting to recruit Jodi as an associate.

The man gave Jodi a DVD and encouraged her to learn more about the business opportunity. For months that DVD sat in the corner of a room collecting dust. Then, in early 2006, Jodi was cleaning out her room when she came across the DVD. She was about to throw it away when something compelled her to watch it.

On the video she heard speeches about several people just like her who had become independently wealthy through Prepaid Legal. She decided to call and learn more. In March 2006, she signed up to be a Prepaid Legal associate.

Soon after, she met up with her representative, Michelle Hagen, who provided her with marketing materials.

But while Jodi had been initially excited, she couldn't envision herself approaching family, friends, and strangers to sell legal insurance. For months, the marketing materials sat in a closet.

In the fall of 2006, she got a call from Michelle Hagen,

who informed her about the upcoming Prepaid Legal convention in Las Vegas. Although Jodi was initially reluctant, after some convincing she decided to attend.

"I didn't know what to expect," Jodi said. "I wasn't looking forward to going, but I figured I should give it an honest shot."

In September 2006, Jodi, Michelle, and another associate carpooled to the convention at the MGM Grand hotel in Las Vegas.

There, Jodi Arias would meet a man who would change her life forever.

CHAPTER 11

J odi and her two traveling companions had just finished dinner at the Rainforest Cafe and were standing outside the restaurant at the MGM Grand. Across the hotel, from a small group of Prepaid Legal associates, a handsome young man in a dark suit emerged. It was Travis Alexander.

"Out of the corner of my eye, I saw someone walking toward me, pretty fast-paced," Jodi recalled. "He stepped right in front of me, and stuck his hand out and introduced himself."

Travis and Jodi chatted briefly and he explained his position with the company. As the entire group made their way back to the lobby of the hotel, Travis stayed focused on Jodi. Wandering through the labyrinth of slot machines and blackjack tables in the casino, Travis made a point of walking next to Jodi, keeping her engaged in conversation.

After they parted ways, Jodi thought little about the encounter. She had a boyfriend, and Travis was just another Prepaid Legal associate with a name she had to remember. But for Travis, Jodi left a lingering impression.

The next day he called and invited her to the Prepaid Legal Black and Gold Ball, a special event reserved for high-level executives and their guests. Initially, Jodi was hesitant. It was a black-tie affair and she hadn't packed anything appropriate. She eventually agreed to attend, granted she could find a formal dress. As she searched a local department store for something suitable, Travis called once again.

"I found you a dress," he said.

Travis had informed Sky Hughes about the pretty girl he wanted to take to the ball. Because Sky was always eager to assist her friend in matters of the heart, she offered to loan an extra dress she had packed for the trip.

"She's about your size," Travis told Jodi. "It should fit you."

Sky provided Travis her hotel room key and Jodi met him outside the Hughes' room to change. Dressed in the borrowed gown, Jodi looked stunning. She strutted into the ball on Travis's arm. That night Travis and Jodi talked, laughed, and dined.

For Jodi, the experience was intoxicating.

As part of the banquet, various Prepaid Legal associates gave presentations about their financial success with the company. Jodi began to realize it was a legitimate business opportunity, one that could transform her future.

"It definitely made a big impression on me," she said. "It stuck out in my mind."

Throughout the weekend conference, Travis continued to pursue Jodi. During the presentations, he invited her to sit with him in the executive level seating. On Saturday night they went out for dinner.

At first, Jodi was unsure about Travis's intentions. He was friendly, but not overly flirtatious. But by Saturday night, it became clear that his interests were romantic. She decided she needed to make it clear to him that she had a boyfriend.

Late on Saturday night, she asked to speak to Travis privately, and they took a walk around the hotel.

"I like you," she told him. "But I'm in a relationship."

Jodi went on to explain the crumbling status of her and Darryl's relationship. She said she wanted to get married and have kids, but Darryl did not. "I'm not sure where it's going, but he is my boyfriend."

Strolling around the lobby, Travis and Jodi found a bench where they sat and chatted for hours. Throughout the conversation, Travis spoke about Mormon values, including the importance of marriage and children.

At dawn, Travis escorted Jodi to her room. Inside the elevator, he leaned close to her, licked his lips, and stared at her mouth. Just when it seemed he was about to steal a kiss, he withdrew.

"I wish you didn't have a boyfriend," he said softly.

When the elevator doors opened, Travis put his arm around Jodi, and walked her back to her hotel room.

The following morning they had brunch together and she escorted him to the lobby, where he checked out and left in a taxi for the airport. At the end of the weekend, Jodi returned to Palm Desert, not knowing if she would ever see Travis again.

When she arrived back home, however, Jodi began to question her relationship with Darryl. Just one chance meeting with Travis had caused her to reevaluate her life.

"Leaving the convention was painful. I knew there was a lot of change on the horizon at that point," Jodi recalled. "The idea of change was uncomfortable. I really liked Darryl, but I could not continue."

That realization was further solidified the day after the conference when Travis called. Over their subsequent conversations, he encouraged Jodi never to settle for mediocrity.

"The things he said made a big impression on me," she said. "He made me think about the direction of my whole life, where I stood and where I was going."

Now in her mid-twenties, Jodi wanted more than anything to get married.

Travis was young, attractive, and financially successful. A future with a man like him was alluring.

Four days after meeting Travis, Jodi sat down with Darryl and explained her recently realized life goals.

"I know we're not getting married," she said. "But I'd like to have kids someday, and I think I'd like to pursue that goal."

Meanwhile, Darryl was dealing with his own life change. His ex-wife had remarried and wanted to take his son to Monterey, about a ten-hour drive from Palm Desert. For Darryl, living so far from Jack was not an option. He told

Jodi he was looking for a job in Monterey and was making plans to move.

Later, Darryl would say he was unclear that their relationship had ended at that point. But for Jodi, she now considered herself a single woman and had every intention of pursuing a budding romance with Travis Alexander.

That Friday—five days after the convention—Jodi met Travis at the house of Chris and Sky Hughes. The Hughes lived in Murrieta, an upscale city in Southern California, about an hour-and-a-half drive from Palm Desert.

For Travis and Jodi, it would be the first of many visits at the Hughes' house. Over the next six months they would visit the Hughes every couple of weeks.

At first, Chris and Sky were impressed with Jodi. While she was soft-spoken, she was extraordinarily friendly. And Travis was clearly enamored with her.

"We liked her when we first met her," recalled Sky. "She was very charming, excellent eye contact. She seemed to be really well-read and intelligent. She was almost overly nice."

That first weekend, Chris and Sky hosted a party, which Jodi attended. Both she and Travis stayed the night, assigned to separate bedrooms in the house.

On Sunday morning, Travis and Jodi attended church with the Hughes family. It was Jodi's first visit to a church since she was eleven, and her only visit to a Mormon church at that point in her life.

After church, Jodi drove back home to Palm Desert.

Three days later, as Travis was heading back to Mesa, he met with Jodi at a Starbucks in Palm Desert. There, he presented her with a gift—a copy of *The Book of Mormon*.

"I challenge you to read it," he told her.

Jodi took the challenge very seriously. After that she was rarely seen around Travis without the book.

Although Travis and Jodi lived in different states, over the next few weeks they got to know each other through lengthy late-night phone conversations. They kept in almost daily contact, exchanging thousands of e-mails, text messages, and instant messages.

On their respective MySpace accounts, Travis and Jodi also publicly posted flirty comments.

"I wonder how much you raise the hotness level of Yreka all by yourself, factoring in its per capita hot stats before you came, I am sure it has raised exponentially," Travis wrote.

Scrolling through Jodi's online photo album, he complimented many of her photos. "What a knockout," he posted on a photo of her smiling.

Jodi responded by commenting on many of Travis's pictures. In one, Travis had his nose playfully stuck inside a flower. Jodi wrote: "You look so innocent—very much what Adam must have looked like in the Garden of Eden."

Travis would grow to have a significant impact on Jodi's life. As they got to know each other, Travis spoke often about his passions, ambitions, and methods for staying motivated. As he did with everyone he met, he also discussed his faith and how the gospel guided his life.

With Travis, Jodi seemed receptive and genuinely interested in the Mormon faith, asking thoughtful questions. Many of their conversations focused on religion.

To educate her further on his faith, Travis arranged for Mormon missionaries to stop by Jodi's house once a week. Jodi began studying *The Book of Mormon* and attending church each Sunday.

In addition to his religious influence, Travis would also encourage Jodi on her career path. He recommended inspirational books, which Jodi quickly bought and consumed.

Jodi began to get heavily involved in Prepaid Legal, attending regular business briefings and events. Unlike Travis, however, Jodi found limited success. While she was very active in the company, she failed to thrive in sales. For a few months she earned more than a thousand dollars in commissions, but the business would never grow to become a substantial income.

Jodi explained to Travis that her true passion was photography, and he encouraged her to pursue it professionally. In 2006, Jodi launched a photography business she called J Fine Art & Photography. She later created a Web site and online portfolio, with portraits of her brother and sister, and a few weddings.

During their many inspirational talks, Travis explained one of his motivational tools was a dream board, a collection of images and words used to visualize goals. In his office, Travis kept a poster board filled with images to reflect his life's dreams. Soon after, Jodi created her own dream board. On it she posted a picture of a sports car, a private jet, and the words "Explore the World." In the corner of the board was also an image of a large diamond engagement ring—a reflection of her deep desire to marry.

On MySpace, Jodi made a blog of inspirational quotes of many of Travis's favorite motivational authors. Included on the page was a quote Travis himself often used.

> *"The difference between a stumbling block and a stepping stone is the character of the individual walking the path." —Travis Alexander.*

She began talking in the same vernacular as Travis, referring to motivational techniques like "limitless thinking" and the "power of attraction." Jodi began to mimic Travis's own personality traits, presenting herself as a driven young professional.

The changes in Jodi were so abrupt that for many people in Travis's life, they would go unnoticed. Travis's friends, not knowing Jodi prior to her involvement with the young Mormon, assumed that they just had a lot in common.

Jodi herself would later say that she and Travis were drawn together because they were both inspired visionaries.

"He shared a lot spiritually with me—his wisdom, his insight, his philosophy, his creeds," Jodi recalled. "I adopted a lot of them."

Prior to meeting Travis, however, Jodi had not been an

exceptionally driven entrepreneur who wanted to change the world. And she was not particularly religious. With Travis she seemed to transform herself into what she believed would be his ideal mate.

At first, Travis seemed to believe he shared a strong connection with Jodi based on their mutual drive to succeed.

"You are as enlightened as you are beautiful," he wrote on her MySpace page.

While still living with Jodi in Palm Desert and preparing to move, Darryl Brewer noticed the changes in Jodi.

Unaware of Travis Alexander or his influence, Darryl thought it was Prepaid Legal that spurred the changes. As Jodi got more involved in the company, she seemed less responsible and stopped paying bills.

"I saw a lot of changes in Jodi. She became a bit of a different person than I had known previously," Darryl said in court. "It seemed she wasn't as logical and rational as she was prior."

Jodi explained the Prepaid Legal business model to Darryl, but he was skeptical. As she grew more focused on Prepaid Legal, their relationship seemed to further deteriorate.

"I think she had thoughts of succeeding in Prepaid Legal and being able to support herself through those efforts, and it didn't quite seem to be the case," Darryl testified. "There was an almost magical thinking that if we only believed and worked hard enough that Prepaid Legal would come through."

Even more peculiar was Jodi's sudden spiritual awakening. Over the four years they had been dating, he had never known Jodi to be actively religious. Her newfound interest in the Mormon faith seemed out of character.

Jodi told Darryl she was making changes in life. She claimed to give up coffee and said she no longer wanted to cuss inside the house. In addition, she informed her live-in boyfriend that she no longer wanted to have sex.

"I want to save myself for my future husband," she told him.

Darryl adhered to her wishes, and he and Jodi kept to their

separate bedrooms. Through it all, he never knew about Travis. He had no idea another man had stolen her heart.

All he knew was this wasn't the woman he had fallen in love with.

In October 2006, Travis and Jodi met for a rendezvous in Ehrenberg, a tiny ghost town on the border between California and Arizona, and a midway point for the couple.

During their two-day stay at a motel, they watched game shows, studied *The Book of Mormon,* and Travis made music CDs for her on his computer. Driving to the neighboring town of Blythe, they had dinner at Sizzler and saw a movie. On their last day, they got breakfast at a local truck stop before parting ways.

Weeks later, in November, Travis surprised Jodi at her house in Palm Desert. He was on his way to a Prepaid Legal conference and stopped at her house specifically to see her. Darryl was away at work and unaware of the visit.

By then, Jodi had developed strong feelings for Travis.

"I felt like I began to love him early on," she said. "And as I got to know him, my love for him grew."

But by late November, Travis seemed a bit distant and preoccupied. Jodi worried that he may be losing interest in her. Around this time she told him she was ready to convert to Mormonism.

Jodi claimed she felt a strong connection to the Mormon faith. Beyond the spiritual beliefs, she seemed drawn to the religion's view on family values.

"The more that I discovered about the church, the more I discovered it did not conflict with my beliefs and was more in line with the values I had," Jodi said.

In mid-November, Jodi asked Travis to be the one to baptize her. Travis was thrilled. On November 26, 2006, Travis baptized Jodi into the Mormon faith. The ceremony took place in Palm Desert. Jodi had invited Darryl and her family, but none of them attended on her behalf. Perhaps because they viewed her decision as hasty and impulsive, Jodi's parents did not support her sudden religious conversion.

The baptism—the first ordinance of the Mormon faith—was meant to be symbolic of Jesus' death, burial, and resurrection. Dressed in white jumpsuits, Travis and Jodi were photographed together, flanked by two missionaries in suits.

Travis stepped into a large baptismal font filled with water. Reaching out, he took Jodi by the hand.

"Jodi Ann Arias: Having been commissioned of Jesus Christ, I baptize you in the name of the Father, and of the Son, and of the Holy Ghost. Amen," he said.

Jodi took a deep breath and closed her eyes, as Travis submerged her entire body beneath the water. When she re-emerged, Jodi's past sins were forgiven in the eye of the church.

After her baptism, Travis seemed more attentive toward Jodi, and they resumed talking daily.

By all appearances, Travis and Jodi's union seemed pure. But while they both preached Mormon virtues, their relationship was secretly steeped in sin.

CHAPTER 12

There was an undeniable physical attraction between Travis and Jodi, and very early on in their relationship, the two became sexual.

In court, Jodi would testify about their many erotic encounters. Their first intimacy was that first weekend together at the home of Chris and Sky Hughes, according to Jodi. After everyone had gone to bed, Travis slipped into Jodi's room. They sat down on the bed, and without uttering a word, he began to passionately kiss her. Travis removed Jodi's pajamas and performed oral sex; she reciprocated.

Weeks later, during their rendezvous in Ehrenberg, they spent most of the weekend having sex. When she arrived, Travis led her to the bed, which took up most of the length of the cramped motel room. He pulled her body to his chest, his lips meeting hers for a sensual kiss. Locked in an embrace, they lay down on the mattress and peeled off each other's clothes. Once naked, Jodi writhed on top of him, while he caressed her body.

But at that motel, in between sexual encounters, Travis seemed disconnected. On the phone they spoke for hours, but in person it seemed purely sexual.

"The whole time he was checked in he was kind of distant," Jodi said. "There wasn't much of a mental or emotional connection like there was over the phone. It was just primarily physical."

After they parted ways Travis didn't call her for two days. Not hearing from him, even just briefly, caused Jodi to panic. She had begun to feel foolish for letting herself be so sexual so early on in the relationship and feared he was no longer interested.

Jodi left two voice messages and sent a text before Travis called her back. When he did, their long-distance relationship resumed.

In the beginning, they never progressed to the extent of vaginal intercourse. Instead they had oral sex and "outercourse"—physical stimulation without penetration. According to Jodi, Travis led her to believe oral and anal sex were less sinful than intercourse.

Prior to her baptism, Jodi was interviewed by officials in the church concerning the Law of Chastity. Although she had been sexual with Travis, Jodi claimed to be chaste. Later, she said she believed she had been following the law by restraining from intercourse.

"My understanding is that vaginal sex was off limits but all other sex was more or less okay," Jodi said. "I didn't feel like we were sinning."

By defining sex only as intercourse, they seemed to justify their actions, cheating the Law of Chastity. Although Jodi was no virgin, she claimed she wanted to adhere to the law, if only by restraining from intercourse, because she believed it would enhance their relationship.

"I wanted to conform with that Law of Chastity because I believed our relationship would be blessed if we did that," she said.

In court, Jodi claimed Travis was the one who pursued her sexually. Travis's friends, however, say she was more likely the aggressor. While simultaneously presenting herself as a devout new Mormon, Jodi was also a temptress.

"She would always be sucking on his ear, kissing his neck—while we were sitting there talking to them," Sky

Hughes said. "She was glued to him. If he moved or shifted, she shifted."

At the Hughes' house, Jodi followed Travis from room to room, chasing after him like a lost puppy. When Travis sat on the couch, Jodi would sit on top of him or lay her head on his lap.

"It was beyond the cutesy new relationship. She was all over him, on top of him," Chris Hughes recalled. "Travis was embarrassed. It clearly made him so uncomfortable. He was literally pushing her off of him."

While the Hughes were initially impressed with Jodi, during her subsequent visits to their home, some unusual aspects of her personality began to emerge.

When Travis left his phone unattended, Jodi would grab it and scroll through his messages. If Travis stepped out of the room to take a call, Jodi stood just out of sight, eavesdropping on the conversations. On more than one occasion, Chris and Sky caught her standing outside of Travis's room.

"I was about to knock," Jodi would say quickly.

"She would literally stand outside the bathroom and wait for him," Chris Hughes said. "When she heard that he would flush or that he was off the phone, she would walk away."

During one visit, the Hughes took Travis and Jodi for a drive in a nearby ritzy neighborhood to view some of the multi-million-dollar homes in the area. Sky drove, with Chris beside her in the passenger seat. Travis sat next to Jodi in the backseat. As she was driving, Sky caught Jodi's reflection in the rearview mirror. Jodi was gazing at Travis, while he stared out the window.

"She is making goo-goo eyes at Travis, and he wouldn't look at her," Sky recalled. "Jodi was going berserk because Travis wouldn't look into her eyes. They almost fought because he wouldn't gaze into her eyes."

Around the Hughes' house, Jodi would carry her copy of *The Book of Mormon*. On occasion, while Travis played with the Hughes' children, Jodi sat upright in an adjacent chair with the book on her lap. At times she appeared to be studying it, at others her gaze drifted to Travis, as if she wanted to ensure he saw her.

The Hughes found this odd. Although they were LDS, they didn't make a habit of studying *The Book of Mormon* among the chaos of playing children. To the Hughes it seemed that Jodi was acting how she believed Mormons behaved.

"Jodi would study the scriptures at the strangest times," Sky recalled. "She would sit there and pretend she was having a Mormon experience. It was all just for show."

By the date of her baptism, the Hughes had begun to believe Jodi's interests in the Mormon faith were entirely disingenuous. To them, it seemed Jodi was using Travis's religion as a perverse form of courtship.

Jodi knew Travis wanted to marry a Mormon, and appeared to believe she had a better chance at becoming his wife if she joined the church. The Hughes began to suspect Jodi was presenting herself as someone she was not.

"She is a chameleon. It was a hundred percent fake. It was theater from top to bottom," Chris recalled. "She was acting when she got baptized; she was acting when she read the scriptures. It was all about manipulating Travis."

Soon after meeting Travis, Jodi fell deeply in love. She seemed enchanted with him, engraining herself in every aspect of his life.

"It's kind of like I was swept off my feet," Jodi recalled. "He came at me really strong in a positive way. It was like nothing I had experienced before."

While Travis liked Jodi, and was attracted to her, he knew her feelings were stronger than his. Travis wasn't in the phase of his life where he wanted to be in a serious relationship, something he made Jodi aware of.

Over the next few months, Jodi seemed frustrated by Travis's lack of commitment. Throughout their visits to the Hughes', Jodi often talked privately with Sky, while Chris and Travis were in another room discussing business. With Sky, Jodi expressed her concerns about her relationship, agonizing that Travis would not commit. But the more questions Jodi had about Travis, the more concerns Sky began to have about her.

Tears in her eyes, Jodi would often say: "Why won't he commit?" "Why won't he ask me to move to Arizona?"

On more than one occasion, Jodi told Sky she wanted to marry Travis.

"I actually had a dream that we were getting married," Jodi said.

By the end of 2006, Jodi began showing up at the Hughes' house by herself, often unannounced. During these times Jodi talked to Sky about Travis, consulting with her for advice.

"She would show up and talk to us about him," Sky recalled. "The more she did it, the more odd we thought she was."

Concerned, Sky later mentioned it to Travis. In a later conversation, Travis also admitted to Sky that Jodi had no friends, aside from her ex-boyfriend, Matt McCartney. As Jodi explained, "All girls are jealous of me and all guys want to sleep with me."

"You know what she told me, Sky?" Travis said. "She said you were her best friend."

Sky was taken aback. She hardly knew Jodi and did not consider her to be a close friend, much less a best friend.

To Sky it didn't make sense. "Is she really this nice or is she a psychopath?" she asked.

"No." Travis laughed. "She really is that nice."

In late 2006, Jodi was working part-time at an upscale restaurant called Bing Crosby's in Rancho Mirage, a few miles outside Palm Desert.

As she grew close to Travis, Jodi's coworkers noticed a change in her. Jodi had become consumed with her relationship with her new boyfriend.

Many times before her shift, she would show up in the parking lot, but wouldn't come inside the restaurant. The other servers would find Jodi in her car talking or texting Travis, refusing to work until she heard back from him.

"I just need to know where he is," Jodi explained.

In between waiting tables, she spoke constantly of her relationship with Travis. She told her coworkers she had met her future husband and the father of her children.

"I'm just so in love," Jodi said. "I want to be with him all the time."

It was beyond the intense infatuation of a new relationship. Jodi's attachment to Travis was obsessive, said one of her coworkers.

"Jodi never knew what she was going to do with her life, or where she was going," said a former coworker. "When she met Travis, it was like she found her purpose."

Throughout the end of 2006, Travis and Jodi saw each other frequently. In addition to the trips to the Hughes' house, Travis would visit her in California about once a month. In return, she drove to Arizona every few weeks to see him.

In December 2006, Prepaid Legal was hosting an event in Arizona. In preparation, Travis had invited dozens of friends from Utah and California to stay at his house. When Jodi learned of the event, she told Travis she would be attending. Since there was no room at his place, she said she would stay with other friends.

But the night before the event, Jodi showed up at Travis's doorstep. Entering the house she announced herself as his girlfriend.

"She's not my girlfriend," Travis quickly corrected. "We've been dating."

Travis reminded Jodi that there was no room at his place. "I'll see you tomorrow at the event."

But as the hours passed, Jodi lingered, her attention focused on Travis, as she followed him from room to room.

That night Travis slept in his office, while two female friends stayed upstairs in his bed. But Jodi never left as planned. Curling up on the living room floor, she slept underneath the Christmas tree.

Later, Jodi would say that during the trip she began to notice that Travis treated her differently in front of certain groups of people.

In front of strangers, he was affectionate. With his LDS friends in Arizona, Travis acted as if they were just friends. Jodi would try to hold his hand, or grab and kiss him, but he would push her away.

Perhaps Travis wanted to keep the true nature of their relationship secret, because he knew they were sinning. Or maybe he didn't want to appear committed to Jodi because he intended to date other women. Whatever the reason, their sexual relationship continued, only in secret.

While Jodi was aware they weren't exclusive, for the first few months they were seeing each other, she believed she was the only woman in Travis's life.

After the December trip to Mesa, however, Travis admitted he had been seeing other women. He reminded Jodi that they were not committed, and encouraged her to date as well.

In December 2006, Jodi went on two dates with men she met through Prepaid Legal. One of those men was Abe Abdelhadi. A muscular man with bright blue eyes and a shaved head, Abe had met Jodi at a Prepaid Legal conference in Pasadena. The two exchanged phone numbers and when they saw each other at business events would sit together and go out to lunch.

They went on just one date, dining together in Anaheim. After dinner, they stopped by a Barnes & Noble bookstore, where they ended up in the spiritual section. As Jodi perused the books, she asked Abe about his religious background and explained her newfound interest in the Mormon faith.

"I'm dabbling in Mormonism," she said.

Abe gave her a curious glance. Mormonism was highly restrictive—no caffeine, alcohol, or premarital sex, he told Jodi.

"Wow. That's a very tough religion if you're going to jump into religions," he said.

At the end of the night, Abe walked Jodi to her car. They began to kiss, and Jodi pressed her body against his. Abe embraced her and, touching the waist band of her jeans, he could tell she was wearing thong panties.

"That's not magic underwear," he said, joking about the temple garments worn by Mormons.

"No." Jodi gave a seductive smile. "But there's magic in them."

She's a fun girl, Abe thought. *This is going to be exciting.*

Abe was surprised when, weeks later, Jodi called him and told him she could no longer see him.

"She explained to me that she was getting back together with her ex and that she felt guilty," Abe recalled. "She felt like she was cheating on him with me even though we really only got together the once."

After the date, Jodi would talk to Travis about Abe, attempting to elicit a jealous response.

"Abe won't stop calling me," Jodi told Travis. "He keeps asking me out."

Eventually, Travis grew contemptuous of the other men in Jodi's life and began making disparaging comments.

In court, Jodi admitted that Travis became jealous when she discussed her dates with other men. But not because she was dating, she said. According to Jodi, he was angry the other men were not Mormons.

After December, Jodi rarely dated anyone else. She only wanted to be with Travis.

"I would go on dates occasionally with other people but there was no spark there because Travis had my heart," she said. "There wasn't making room for anyone else."

The more time the Hughes spent with Jodi, the more peculiar they began to find her behavior. While she said all the right things, there was something off about her. She seemed bizarrely unemotional, her affect flat. She never got mad, even when she should.

Even stranger, Jodi seemed desperate to appear desirable. When Travis wasn't around, Jodi spoke constantly about the men who "wanted her."

At Prepaid Legal conferences, Jodi would lay her head on a married man's shoulder and then tell the Hughes that he wouldn't leave her alone. Later, they learned it was typically Jodi who had initiated the contact. Other times Jodi fabricated stories about the guys who were "pursuing her." It became evident to the Hughes that Jodi wanted them to relate these stories to Travis.

"She went to the seminars with us and we got to watch her in action. She was always trying to get a guy's attention," Sky recalled. "We would watch her as she manipulated these men."

Later, Jodi called Travis and told him about the encounters.

"He asked me on a date," Jodi said. "He actually tried to kiss me."

If at first he wasn't bothered, Jodi escalated the behavior, coldly toying with Travis. She claimed these men wouldn't stop calling her, wouldn't take no for an answer. Eventually, Travis grew perturbed.

The Hughes weren't the only ones wary of Jodi. When Travis first began bringing Jodi around his friends, many expressed concern. Clancy Talbot, an executive director with Prepaid Legal living in Utah, was in her forties, with long blond hair and a dark tan. She considered Travis like a "little brother."

When she first met Jodi, Clancy said she could quickly tell something was "off about her." Travis's friends tolerated Jodi's presence, but no one really liked her, she said.

"When you looked at Jodi, it was like she was empty. She never talked about her life, her past, her family, any friends. No one really knew anything about her—ever," Clancy said. "She just kind of morphed into whoever she was around. She just took on the personality of whoever else was in the room."

As word spread among Prepaid Legal associates about their relationship, an acquaintance of Travis's also delivered a warning.

"She is bad news," the friend said. "She is going to ruin your business. She will ruin your life."

In late December 2006, Darryl Brewer found a job in Monterey and moved out of the house in Palm Desert, officially ending his four-year relationship with Jodi.

"We parted at this point," Darryl said. "I didn't feel the

relationship had ended, but it had definitely changed. We both saw our paths going different ways."

Their plans for the house were initially unclear. For the next few months, Darryl continued to pay his portion of the mortgage. But by February, neither could afford to keep up with the payments.

Their loan slipped into default. Jodi would continue to live in the house for several more months. By the end of the year, she would lose the first home she ever purchased to foreclosure.

By early 2007, Jodi's desire for a commitment with Travis had become all-consuming. For Sky, it seemed like Jodi was constantly crying and complaining that Travis wouldn't ask her to move to Mesa, wouldn't give her a commitment.

For a period in January Chris and Sky started to feel sympathetic toward Jodi. The Hughes knew Travis had a reputation as a womanizer and a flirt. Jodi appeared so in love and, according to her complaints, it seemed that Travis was mistreating her.

At one point Sky e-mailed Travis and reprimanded him for using Jodi sexually without giving her a commitment, calling him a "heart predator."

"Jodi was being treated horribly, you weren't beating her physically, but you were emotionally," Sky wrote. "She has given you everything, all control, and you give her 3 A.M. calls and make-out fests."

It was clear to the Hughes that Travis and Jodi weren't right for each other. During one of her unexpected visits to their house, the Hughes took Jodi aside and encouraged her to stop seeing Travis for her own good.

Soon after, Travis found out about the encounter, firing off an angry e-mail to Sky. "You crossed the line."

He rebuked Sky for causing "irreparable damage to mine and Jodi's relationship," and denied being more than a "jerk" to her.

"I adore Jodi," Travis wrote. "In fact, I don't know if it has ever been easier to be nice to someone as it is with Jodi."

Any sympathy the Hughes briefly felt toward Jodi, however, quickly vanished as Jodi's behavior became increasingly strange.

Weeks after the e-mail exchange, Travis was with Sky in the kitchen of the Hughes' house when he received an e-mail from Jodi. The message concerned a mysterious, anonymous e-mail that Jodi claimed she received from a male stalker.

"I watch your every move," the e-mail read. "I will have you."

It went on to describe Jodi as beautiful and talented.

"Travis doesn't deserve you," the e-mail continued. "He's too far away to protect you."

Jodi called Travis and told him more about the message.

"I wasn't going to say anything," Jodi said. "But I was scared, and it mentioned your name, and you deserved to hear about it."

Alarmed, Travis read the e-mail out loud to Sky. When she heard it, Sky burst out laughing.

"Travis, Jodi wrote this," she said with a chuckle. "This is totally fake. She wants you to ask her to move to Arizona."

Travis became defensive. "This is serious and very scary."

As much as Sky tried to convince him it was a ploy, Travis wouldn't listen.

"Jodi would never do something like that," Travis insisted. "She's not like that."

In early February, Jodi showed up unexpectedly at Travis's home in Mesa. She had left Palm Desert after work in the evening, arriving at his place at 2 A.M.

As Jodi got out of her car, she began to have second thoughts, worried how Travis would react to the late-night visit.

Just as she was about to get in her car and head home, she noticed a blue light flickering in the second-story window. She could tell Travis was in his room awake, watching TV. Before she could change her mind, she went to the front door and rang the doorbell.

When Travis opened the door and saw Jodi, a wide smile spread across his face. They spent the next few days in his house, watching movies, reading books, and surfing the Internet.

At one point they were sitting on the oversize chair in Travis's bedroom scrolling through pictures from an exhibit that had recently come to the Phoenix museum called Body Worlds, which features preserved human bodies and body parts that reveal their inner anatomical structures.

Travis got out of the chair, leaving Jodi with his computer. Jodi began clicking the back button until she was in his MySpace account message inbox.

"The temptation got the better of me so I clicked on his e-mail," Jodi admitted.

In it she found sexual e-mails from Travis to other women. Most disturbing, she claimed, was an e-mail exchange with a married woman in the Mormon church. Most of these exchanges had taken place weeks and months prior.

Jodi made no mention of the e-mails to Travis. More than anything she still wanted an exclusive relationship with the man she adored. During her stay at his house Travis and Jodi had a discussion about their relationship. Perhaps because he was concerned about the other men in Jodi's life or the apparent stalker terrorizing her, Travis decided he was ready to commit.

On February 2, 2007, they became a couple, much to Jodi's delight.

"When I became what I believed was exclusive, I believed it was the natural next step," Jodi recalled. "Things began to develop a little more rapidly."

By late March 2007, Sky Hughes began to sense that Jodi was not simply strange, but that she may be dangerous. Her fixation with Travis was bordering on scary.

During a visit, Jodi asked to talk to Sky privately. They took a walk around the property and Jodi revealed to Sky what she found on Travis's computer.

"I know he's talking to other women," Jodi said.

Jodi admitted that she had logged into his MySpace account and said she had e-mailed those messages to herself.

Later, Sky spoke with her husband, and they agreed they needed to tell Travis that they didn't feel Jodi was the right girl for him.

Travis and Jodi's final visit was in April 2007. As Chris was showing Travis something in his office, Jodi sat in the kitchen talking to Sky about her relationship.

By then, Sky had little patience for Jodi. As Jodi spoke, Sky slyly reached for her phone and typed a text message to Chris.

"She's driving me crazy," Sky wrote. "Get her away from me."

Sky sat her phone on the counter, out of Jodi's line of sight.

In the office, Chris got the message. Before Chris could hide the phone, Travis's gaze fell to the screen.

As Travis read the message, his face contorted. "What's that supposed to mean?"

"We need to talk to you later, bro," Chris said. "We have some concerns."

For the next few hours the Hughes pretended everything was normal. After dinner, Sky pulled her husband aside. "We need to talk to Travis."

Around 10 P.M. Jodi went off to bed and the Hughes sat down with Travis for a private talk in their master bedroom.

"Travis, there's something major wrong with her," Chris began the uncomfortable conversation.

They listed instances of her weird behavior, including her unannounced visits, reading his e-mail, eavesdropping on his phone calls, her flirtations with other men and apparent calculated manipulations.

Travis appeared hurt, repeating over and over, "Really?"

Sky said they wanted to like her, but she was manifesting some disturbing behaviors. Travis, however, was unconvinced.

"Travis, don't you get it?" Chris said. "There's something wrong with her."

"She's just trying to be friends with you guys," Travis said.

"I'm really uncomfortable with Jodi," Sky told Travis. "Something's not right."

"She's a nice girl," Travis insisted.

"Dude," Chris said. "You can't see it. But we can see it."

"She scares me," Sky added. "I'm afraid we're going to find you cut up inside her refrigerator."

Travis laughed.

"I'm serious," Sky exclaimed. "There's something not right with her. Travis, I'm really worried."

Travis shook his head. His friends were wrong about Jodi, he told them. The conversation went on for nearly two hours as they cautioned him about the relationship.

From downstairs Sky heard the faint sound of a door creaking. A moment later, a chill traveled down her spine. She was suddenly overcome by a sense that they were being watched.

Sky changed the conversation—talking loudly about something else. A few minutes later, there was a knock. Travis opened the door and found Jodi standing there.

"When are you going to sleep?" Jodi said.

"When we're done," Travis told her. "I'll come say goodnight before I go to bed."

Jodi went downstairs and they continued to talk. About a half hour later, Sky got that cold, dark feeling once again. Silently, she mouthed to Travis, "She's out there."

Travis whispered, "No way!"

Quietly, Travis approached the door. Jerking it open, he found Jodi standing there, glaring at Travis. Her face was flushed, her jaw tight.

"What do you want?" Travis asked.

Jodi's glare darted between Sky and Chris.

"Is there a problem?" Jodi asked.

"Nope," Travis said.

"Is this a private conversation?" she asked.

"Yeah it is," Travis said.

Years later the Hughes would recall the fear they felt that night.

"She had this look on her face that gave us chills," Chris said. "She had so much rage."

"It was like pure evil," Sky added. "She was emanating, pulsating this terrible energy."

Jodi left the room. Soon after, Travis headed downstairs and met with Jodi in her room, where they talked until the early-morning hours.

Sky was terrified. "Do we need to get our kids and bring them in our room?" she asked Chris.

For ten minutes they debated getting their kids. They asked themselves how they had allowed someone in their home that made them feel so unsafe.

"I don't want her here ever again," Sky told Chris.

"Neither do I. I'll tell Travis in the morning," Chris said. "He is going to hate us."

Eventually, they decided to go to sleep. Sky checked on her kids throughout the night.

The next morning, they spoke with Travis. "She's absolutely not welcome in our home anymore," Chris said.

"Fine," Travis said. "Then you tell her that."

In an awkward, two-hour conversation, Sky spoke to Jodi alone, informing her they did not feel comfortable with her anymore.

Toward the end of their talk, Jodi asked incredulously, "Are you going to tell Travis not to date me?"

"Yes," Sky said. "I don't think you are good for him."

That afternoon, Jodi left. The Hughes never let her back inside their house again.

"We made it very clear to Travis that if you continue with this relationship, you're going to have to do it at a distance from us," Chris said. "Because she is not coming around our kids, she's not coming around our house. This is not going to be your meeting ground anymore."

The decision put a strain on the Hughes' relationship with Travis.

Although Travis and Jodi no longer met at the Hughes' home, neither was willing to end their romantic entanglement.

Yet, now the couple had a big obstacle to overcome—
the thousand miles of open road separating them. Over-
coming that hurdle, Travis and Jodi took their relationship
on the road.

CHAPTER 13

Travis Alexander spent the last full year of his life living as if he were dying. For Travis, that meant challenging himself to explore new experiences, seizing new opportunities, and broadening his long-term perspective.

It was a life philosophy inspired, strangely enough, by a country-western song.

In March 2007, Travis was driving, with Jodi by his side, to a Prepaid Legal convention in Oklahoma City when he first heard the song he made his anthem. Passing through the wide open plains on the outskirts of the city, his car radio lost reception. He tuned the dials, but the only stations he could receive were country music stations.

"It's Oklahoma, what did I expect?" he told Jodi.

Travis hated country music, but since he had no choice, he left the station on. He preferred it over silence. A particular song caught Travis's attention: Tim McGraw's "Live Like You Were Dying."

Travis turned up the volume, paying close attention to the lyrics. The song was powerful, inspiring—and it ignited something in Travis.

The song was about a man in his early forties who, after learning he had a terminal disease, decided to live life to the fullest. The song's chorus listed all the things that the man decided to do with his remaining time on earth, including sky-diving, climbing the Rocky Mountains, and riding a bull.

At that moment the song spoke to Travis. He decided to quite literally live the next year as if it would be his last.

Later that spring, Travis went skydiving. During a trip to Colorado, he hiked the Rocky Mountains. The song includes the line, "I finally read the Good Book." As part of his goals Travis started reading the Bible and was determined to finish it by the end of the year.

For the rest of the year, he put his career on the backburner and began traveling the country. Around this time he came across a book called *1,000 Places to See Before You Die: A Traveler's Life List*. The guide listed a thousand exotic places around the world, including sacred ruins, grand hotels, wild-life preserves, hilltop villages, castles, hidden islands, and museums. Each location included a description of the destination.

Later, he mentioned the book to Jodi.

"There's this great book I found," he said.

Travis told Jodi he wanted to spend his life crossing off all the places on the list. Jodi seemed to echo his enthusiasm and together they began taking weekend trips, checking off the destinations one by one.

"He thought it would be a cool goal to have, maybe a life-time goal, to check off as many places as you could. I began to join him on that pursuit," Jodi said. "We began calling it 'the list.' And we were checking places on 'the list.'"

While touring many of these destinations in the travel guide, the pair also visited significant Mormon sites, including places mentioned in *The Book of Mormon*. With her during every trip, Jodi had her camera, snapping hundreds of photos.

"I've always had my camera, always," she said. "So it goes everywhere I go."

On several weekends Travis also drove to California to see Jodi and they toured nearby beaches and museums. In Los Angeles, they went to the Getty Center, a museum special-izing in pre-twentieth-century European paintings, draw-ings, and sculptures, and nineteenth- and twentieth-century American and European photographs.

In the spring of 2007, they spent a day at Disneyland and Disneyland California Adventure. Together they posed for a picture on the teacups ride.

On another trip as they were passing through Amarillo, Texas, they drove an hour out of their way to visit the famed "Cross of our Lord Jesus Christ" monument. Viewed by more than ten million people each year, the memorial features a 190-foot freestanding cross that can be seen from twenty miles away. The base of the cross is surrounded by life-size bronze statues depicting twelve scenes from the life of Jesus.

Jodi snapped a picture of Travis posing, his arm around one of the Jesus statues like he was having a conversation with a close friend.

On their trip to Oklahoma, they stopped outside the Oklahoma City Temple, the ninety-fifth operating temple of the Church of Jesus Christ of Latter-day Saints. They also drove to Nauvoo, Illinois, where they toured the historic town that was first established in the early 1800s by members of the Mormon church.

During the trips, Travis and Jodi shared a hotel room and were often intimate. As they walked around the tourist destinations, they were openly affectionate and acted as if they were a couple.

But when they were at Prepaid Legal conferences, Jodi noticed a change in their interactions. In front of his friends, Travis was distant. He ignored Jodi and sometimes wouldn't hold her hand.

At out-of-town Prepaid Legal events, which were attended by many of Travis's Mormon friends, they kept separate rooms. As part of the Law of Chastity, single Mormons are discouraged to share a room with members of the opposite sex.

"I knew it was a church standard," Jodi said. "I knew we were going against the church standard when no one else knew about it."

The disparity of affection was disconcerting for Jodi. Over the course of their relationship, Jodi began to feel like she was Travis's dirty secret.

* * *

After they officially became a couple, Jodi's resolve to marry Travis strengthened.

It was beyond an infatuation; Jodi strongly believed Travis was "the one." She told many people that she could not imagine marrying anyone else or for some other man to be the father of her future children.

"I began to fall in love with him," Jodi recalled. "I felt pretty intense as far as being in love with him."

Her adoration of Travis was a devouring, consuming sort of love. She loved and adored him with an almost selfish intensity. It was almost as if she wanted to inhale him—absorb his soul.

Jodi had altered her life for Travis and converted religions. In doing so, it seemed she believed there was an unspoken agreement that they would one day walk down the aisle.

While Travis liked her, he did not feel the same. He appeared to compartmentalize his relationship with Jodi as a completely separate aspect of his life. While his associates with Prepaid Legal all knew about Jodi, most of his LDS friends in Mesa knew nothing about her.

Jodi sensed something was wrong. When he introduced her to a new friend or acquaintance in Mesa, she noticed that no one seemed to know he had a girlfriend—something she found alarming. Travis was apparently keeping her away from his inner circle.

Jodi seemed jealous of anyone in Travis's life. Anytime he mentioned the name of another female, she became quiet and her expression would darken. When she asked about the women, Travis maintained they were just friends and denied he was seeing anyone else.

"I can be flirtatious, but there's nothing going on," Travis told her repeatedly. "I'm not dating anyone else."

Over the course of their relationship, however, Jodi's jealously took a toll.

At the Prepaid Legal event in Oklahoma that March, Clancy Talbot was among the dozens of his friends from the company who were in attendance. On the night of the executive ball, Clancy had a little too much to drink, and at one point staggered over toward Travis and laid her head on his shoulder. To brace her, Travis grabbed her by the waist. At the sight of her boyfriend even touching another woman, Jodi fell apart.

"I just got this feeling inside like my stomach flip-flopped," Jodi recalled. "I couldn't believe he was doing that, especially in front of our friends. I felt like I wanted to cry, but I didn't want anyone to see that."

Jodi slipped away into the women's bathroom. She locked the stall door, put her feet on the toilet seat, and wept for an hour.

The next day, Jodi followed Clancy into the bathroom.

"She cornered me in the bathroom, she was shaking and upset," Clancy said. "She just kept saying the same thing over and over."

Jodi explained that she was now with Travis.

"I am more upset with Travis than I am with you," Jodi said, trembling. "But I wanted to let you know Travis and I are official now. We are together now."

After several minutes, a friend of Clancy's came into the bathroom and she was able to escape. Years later, Clancy would look back on the encounter.

"It was just so strange, so weird, so creepy," Clancy recalled. "Jodi was so possessive. She didn't want anyone anywhere near Travis."

For the next few days, Travis and Jodi fought about the incident. But even after they made up, doubt and suspicions continued to plague her.

Jodi would later admit she was jealous in their relationship, but it was only because she believed she was being two-timed.

"There's sort of a distinctive feeling that comes when you have that sneaky suspicion that somebody might be not so monogamous," Jodi recalled. "I had a suspicion."

By the spring of 2008, Jodi's financial situation had worsened. Her savings had been depleted and she owed thousands on her credit cards.

In May, Jodi moved out of her house in Palm Desert, just months prior to the pending foreclosure. To try to get back on her feet financially, she resumed working as a waitress at the Ventana Inn and Spa in Big Sur. Because she could live and work at the resort for the season, Jodi was able to save money.

When she wasn't working, Jodi spent much of her time in Mesa, where she often attended Prepaid Legal sales conferences and LDS gatherings with Travis's friends. Jodi always seemed polite and pleasant, yet highly possessive. She would follow Travis from room to room. At social gatherings, if he were to speak with someone else, Jodi kept one eye on him, monitoring his every move.

Embedding herself into his life, Jodi attempted to form friendships with many close to Travis. Jodi used these new friendships to fish for information about Travis and his whereabouts.

"She intentionally tried to get as close as she could to anyone Travis was close to," said Sky Hughes.

One Sunday after church Travis invited several friends, including Taylor Searle, back to his house to make cookies. When Taylor first saw Jodi strutting around Travis's house like she lived there, he was taken aback.

"When I met Jodi, she kind of announced herself as his girlfriend," Taylor said. "And that was a surprise to me at the time because I know he had interest in other girls."

On another occasion when Jodi was in town, Travis's neighbor, Dave Prusha, attended a Prepaid Legal briefing. While he was there, Dave had a casual conversation with Jodi, where she brought up her relationship with Travis.

She made it clear to Dave—a practical stranger—that she wanted to marry Travis. Dave felt pity for Jodi. He knew Travis did not feel the same and wasn't ready for marriage. Later, Dave spoke privately with his neighbor. Travis confided in him that he knew he had to break up with Jodi.

"I know I need to end it," Travis said. "It is unfair to continue the relationship with Jodi when I don't feel the same."

CHAPTER 14

While Travis had always been content being single, as he approached thirty, his perspective began to change. While he was accomplished in every other aspect of his life, a wife and family had eluded him.

As he did some soul searching, a quote from David O. McKay, the ninth president of the Church of Jesus Christ of Latter-day Saints, troubled him: "No other success can compensate for failure in the home."

Travis realized he was lonely. Although he had been dating Jodi for five months, he didn't see a future with her. Travis recognized he didn't have a true partner in life, something he yearned for.

"I have become renowned for being single, unfortunately," Travis wrote on his blog in 2008, months after his birthday. "I used to imagine myself as some dangerously handsome tycoon in *Time* magazine, as one of the world's most eligible bachelors. I had a bit of a swagger because of it—a smirk on my face, a pep in my step. Then I turned thirty."

As a thirty-year-old unmarried Mormon, Travis would be in the minority, especially among his friends. As a core LDS teaching, the church encourages young adults to marry soon after returning from their mission. Most marry in their late teens and early twenties.

"Most of my peers have been married for years and have several children," he wrote. "As you can imagine from friends and family alike, I am constantly getting grilled and lectured over my solitary status. I have countless scouts that, out of love and concern, are diligently looking underneath every rock and tree for a mate to get me hitched to."

Travis wanted his future wife—his eternal companion—to be a moral Mormon woman who was spiritual, worthy, and pure. He decided he was finally ready to shift his focus toward finding a wife.

"I realized it was time to adjust my priorities and date with marriage in mind. Not to ask someone on a date because I planned on marrying them, but to date someone to look for the possibility of marriage with them," he wrote on his blog. "This type of dating to me is like a very long job interview and can be exponentially more mentally taxing—desperately trying to find out if my date has an axe murderer pent up inside of her and knowing she is wondering the same thing about me."

Beyond a legal marriage, Mormons believe in a divine union known as a celestial marriage, which lasts beyond the grave and through eternity. If a couple is married only by a civilly recognized authority, Mormons believe the marriage will end at death.

For a celestial marriage, also known as eternal marriage, to occur the couple must be sealed in the Mormon temple. A temple sealing is considered one of the very highest ordinances that Mormons can receive. Not only do Mormons value a temple marriage as something highly desirable and extremely sacred, they also believe it is a prerequisite for the highest degree of being in the afterlife.

It's possible Travis felt he and Jodi were just too different for such a marriage. Maybe he was turned off by her extreme jealousy and obsessive behavior. Or, perhaps, the fact that she slept with him before marriage tarnished Jodi in his mind. Whatever the cause, he did not consider Jodi marriage material.

Travis decided it was time to end his relationship with Jodi.

* * *

While Travis was contemplating ending the relationship, Jodi began to have her own reservations. She believed her boyfriend was unfaithful.

"I had been getting my suspicions about things. He was treating me a little differently—a little more distant, a lot more flirty with other women, and it just made me uncomfortable," Jodi said. "When I tried to talk to him about it, he blew up and got very defensive, even though I didn't accuse him of anything. So it was kind of a red flag."

Jodi tried to convince herself that Travis was not cheating, and that she was reading into things that were not there because of the past infidelity of her prior boyfriends. But she continued to express doubts.

In June 2007, Travis and Jodi were visiting friends in Utah. Travis went to his room to take a nap, leaving his phone in the living room on the couch, wedged between two cushions.

Quickly, Jodi snatched the phone, darted into the back room, and shut the door. Clicking around the phone, Jodi found Travis's text messages and began to read them.

As she read the messages, Jodi began to tremble. She knew Travis had a lot of female friends, but he always maintained the relationships were innocent. On his phone, however, Jodi discovered more than just flirty messages. In many of the messages Travis discussed making plans with other women.

"Where do you want to meet," one message read.

"Wherever would be best to make out," Travis had replied.

Jodi's stomach sank—Travis was cheating on her.

"I was devastated when I discovered that he wasn't being faithful to me," Jodi wrote in her journal.

For the next two weeks she kept the information to herself, not revealing what she had discovered on the phone. Travis and Jodi had a vacation scheduled in a couple of weeks and she decided to wait to expose Travis's infidelity until after they returned.

But while Jodi tried to act like everything was normal, behind the facade she was brokenhearted.

On June 18, 2007, they left for a week-long vacation, beginning in New York, where they toured significant Mormon sites as well as checking destinations off on their list.

Among their first stops was Niagara Falls. While in New York, Travis and Jodi also traveled to see the Finger Lakes—a series of long, narrow lakes resembling fingers.

In addition, they also drove to the Sacred Grove, a forested area near the border of western New York State, across from the former home of Joseph Smith, the prophet founder of the Latter-day Saints movement. The Sacred Grove was the location where Joseph Smith had his first vision, which led him to the golden plates that he was later said to translate into *The Book of Mormon*.

After leaving New York they stopped in Cleveland, Ohio, where they toured the Rock and Roll Hall of Fame, a massive museum containing thousands of artifacts from the history of rock music.

On the second part of their trip, Travis and Jodi flew into Huntington Beach, California, for a free Prepaid Legal trip Jodi had won through the company. They spent five days relaxing on the beach and soaking up the sun at the resort's pool.

Throughout the entire trip, Jodi was cold and aloof. Cursed with the knowledge that her boyfriend had been cheating, Jodi spent most of the vacation sulking.

"What's wrong?" Travis asked repeatedly.

"Nothing," Jodi answered, trying her best to seem normal.

At one point, while Travis was sleeping, he received a text message from another woman. Jodi grabbed his phone and read his messages once again.

"Sorry I didn't get back to your last text message," the other woman wrote. "What time is it there?"

Jodi scrolled through the phone to read the message Travis had last sent, which read: "I really miss you . . ."

Because the woman had asked about the time in Huntington Beach, Jodi sent a reply.

"Cuddle time with Jodi," she wrote. "Good night."

"Then I deleted the message, went to sleep, and never mentioned it to him," Jodi later told a friend.

In Huntington Beach, Jodi also spoke with her friend Leslie Udy. Jodi first met Leslie in September 2006, at the same Prepaid Legal convention where she had met Travis. They struck up a conversation and discovered they had a mutual love of photography and other things in common.

With blond hair with brown streaks and bangs that framed her face, Leslie was a few years older than Jodi. Despite the fact that Leslie lived in Utah, she and Jodi became good friends. To Leslie, Jodi confided her suspicions about Travis.

"She mentioned that she was concerned he might be seeing someone else, some other girls," Leslie said in court. "I asked her why she would think that? She said she had seen some texts on his phone."

On their last day together, Travis and Jodi stopped by Anaheim, where they spent the day at Disneyland and Disneyland California Adventure.

For a few fleeting moments on the trip, Jodi felt connected to Travis, which was even more painful because it reminded her of how much she truly loved him.

"I knew the relationship couldn't continue like that," Jodi recalled. "I was kind of waiting for the right moment to tell him."

While Jodi planned to end the relationship at the end of the trip, she couldn't quite bring herself to look in Travis's eyes and tell him they were over. Instead, she confronted him days later by phone.

"There's some things I want to talk to you about," she told Travis.

Jodi confessed about seeing the messages from other women. Travis apologized, but to Jodi he seemed only mildly remorseful. He did not grovel for the transgression.

"I don't think either of us is ready to be in this kind of relationship," Jodi told Travis.

The trust was broken. They both seemed to agree it was better that they were no longer a couple.

"I don't think I could trust him fully to be monogamous," Jodi later told detectives. "And I didn't think he thought he could trust me to not get into his phone again."

On June 29, 2007—about a month before his thirtieth birthday—Travis and Jodi officially ended their relationship.

While Jodi was crushed, Travis seemed relieved. He was ready to start the next chapter of his life and was optimistic about finding true love.

"This life is a beautiful life. A life that is all the more beautiful when we find someone of like mind, heart and spirit to share it with," he wrote on his blog. "Genesis is right, 'It is not good that man should be alone.' Certainly the synergy, that comes from a marriage of two equally yoked people yields limitless potential."

Travis did not mourn the loss of Jodi. In early July 2007, days after their breakup, Travis began dating a girl from the singles ward. Her name was Lisa Andrews.

Lisa was wholesome and spiritual—the exact type of girl Travis was looking for in an eternal companion. An Arizona State University student, she was intelligent and funny, with a bubbly personality. On her blog, she described herself as a person who enjoys "a healthy conversation, with maybe a hint of debate," and someone with a "love for all things Disney, Kevin Costner, and Karaoke."

Travis had first seen Lisa during the summer of 2006, one year prior. Eleven years younger than Travis, Lisa was just nineteen at the time.

It was a Sunday and Travis was at church. Services had just ended and the congregants were trickling out of the building. As usual, Travis was going room to room collecting the trash.

He entered the Relief Society Room, which is designed and tailored for female congregants to gather for class. Decorated with tablecloths, flowers, and curtains, the room was the most feminine in the meeting house.

Chatting with a group of friends was a beautiful girl with long blond hair, soft blue eyes, a sun-kissed tan, and a bright smile. Travis stopped for a moment, watching her. Lisa turned and left the building, never noticing Travis.

"I don't remember this encounter, but he swore it was the

first," Lisa Andrews recalled. "To be honest, I don't remember ever seeing or talking to him until months later."

That fall the ward hosted a campout. On the drive to the campground, Travis rode in the same car as Lisa and five others, including Lisa's boyfriend at the time, Steve Bell, and her sister, Allyson.

During the drive, Lisa learned much about Travis, including the fact that he loved to play Six Degrees of Kevin Bacon and hated body hair. Travis referred to himself as a "man-scaper," and thought hygiene was important.

"I brought extra toothbrushes," Travis told Lisa. "I know at least one person will forget."

Later, he mentioned that only one person admitted to forgetting their toothbrush, but he knew there were others.

"During all that, he still found the time to make fun of me and Steve, saying that we were too mushy, and why didn't we just start making out already," Lisa recalled. "I could not believe the nerve of this guy."

After the campout, Travis mercilessly teased Lisa about the way she snorted when she laughed. Perhaps Lisa didn't consider at the time that Travis was teasing her the way a schoolboy does when he has a crush on a girl. To her he was just "the old guy in the ward" who would show up at church events dressed in his flashy suits.

Throughout 2007, while dating Jodi, Travis and Lisa spoke more often, eventually becoming good friends. Several times she went over to his house to make cookies. On another occasion, Travis threw a hip-hop-themed party at his house, which Lisa attended.

The more she got to know Travis, the more he impressed her. She began to see him as a "spontaneous, caring, driven individual, who loved faux-paint and sang show tunes."

Over time, Lisa, who had since broken up with Steve Bell, began to have feelings for Travis. So when Travis asked her out in early July, she said yes. Lisa and Travis began spending much of their time together. Soon they were a couple.

While Travis had been sexual in his past relationships, with Lisa he portrayed himself as a virgin. And by all accounts their union remained chaste—Travis and Lisa never had a sexual relationship.

While he began building a relationship with his new girlfriend, Travis and Jodi seemed unwilling to move on from each other.

The day after their breakup, Travis called Jodi. On the phone, she claimed he begged for another chance. The conversation turned intimate, then sexual, according to Jodi. By the end the tension had vanished and Jodi found herself once again hopelessly in love.

Although they were no longer a couple, they resumed their regular routine. He could call late at night, sometimes at 4 A.M., and they would talk for hours. Jodi began to leave her phone at her bedside so she would not miss a call from Travis. At the time, she seemed hopeful they would reunite.

"I believed he had the potential to change," Jodi said.

Two weeks after the breakup, Jodi made the astonishing decision to leave California and move to Mesa. Despite the fact that they would no longer be a couple, Jodi would later say Travis strongly encouraged the move. She claimed he loaned her money to relocate and let her store her possessions in his garage.

"Travis painted a nice picture of the benefits of moving to Mesa," Jodi said. "He said we could hang out more and figure things out."

But those close to Travis say he strongly objected to Jodi's plans and that they fought about the decision. In mid-July, Travis was on a fourwheeling trip with friends from Prepaid Legal, including Mike Bertot, a burly Prepaid Legal associate in his thirties, with dark hair and a goatee.

During the trip, Travis was largely distracted, talking and texting with Jodi about her decision to relocate.

"He was not thrilled about her moving to Mesa by any means," Mike said. "He was arguing with her over the phone and by text most of the time."

Throughout their arguments, Mike overheard portions of their conversation.

"You have no reason to be in Mesa," Travis said. "You have no friends here. It didn't work out with us. I don't want you that close to me."

Toward the end of the conversation, Travis said, "I'm hanging up now."

Afterward, Travis complained to Mike that Jodi only decided to move after they broke up.

"I just told him, 'watch your back,'" Mike said. "That's some crazy, stalker stuff. A normal person wouldn't do anything like that."

Either way, in late July, Jodi relocated to Mesa. She had planned to rent a room in a house owned by a Mormon woman. When those plans fell through, she wound up renting a room from a person she had never met who she found through a Mormon housing Web site.

The house was just four miles away from Travis—a ten-minute drive—at 9634 East Nido Avenue in Mesa. The 2,000-square-foot home was a spacious one story, with three bathrooms and three bedrooms—one of which Jodi rented.

But when Travis discovered how close she would be living to him, he was upset, Jodi admitted.

"Travis found out it was so close to him he freaked out about it," Jodi later told detectives.

Not only was it very close to Travis, Jodi was also in the boundaries of his singles ward. To avoid any conflict, Jodi said she decided to attend a different ward.

Jodi soon found work as a waitress at Mimi's Cafe and later at P.F. Chang's Chinese restaurant. In addition, she continued to sell Prepaid Legal insurance.

In Mesa, Jodi also pursued her passion for photography—registering her photography business through the Arizona Corporation Commission in 2007. She booked some photography jobs, but business was slow and she struggled for money.

To help her financially, Travis paid Jodi $200 a month to clean his house twice a week.

For a while, Travis and Jodi got along fine with her living in Mesa. Because she did not have many friends locally,

Travis focused much of his attention on helping her become acclimated.

On July 28, 2007, Travis turned thirty. Jodi celebrated her ex-boyfriend's birthday—baking a square cake with chocolate frosting. On the cake she wrote in green icing, "Happy Birthday T-Dogg." She lit the green candles, his favorite color, and snapped a photo, posting it on his MySpace page.

It would be Travis's last birthday. He wouldn't make it to thirty-one.

CHAPTER 15

Late at night, Jodi slipped into Travis's house through the unlocked front door. Creeping quietly up the stairs, careful not to disturb his roommates, she stepped into his bedroom. Stripping off her clothes, she crawled into his bed, stirring him awake with a lustful kiss.

Night after night, this became a routine for Travis and Jodi. Despite their breakup, they continued their lurid sexual affair throughout the time she lived in Mesa. Only now, their encounters were even more clandestine.

Behind the double doors of Travis's bedroom, they slept together in secret—getting together for sex three to four times a week.

Late at night, after his roommates had gone to bed, Travis would text Jodi. "I'm getting sleepy . . ."

"That became like his code word for I'm going to sleep so come over here now," Jodi recalled.

At other times, Jodi enticed Travis with graphic and erotic text messages. By tempting him sexually, her grip on Travis remained firm.

"I want to grind you," she sent in text messages. "My pussy is so wet."

According to Jodi, by this point there was no longer any pretense of finding loopholes in the Law of Chastity. They were now having regular vaginal intercourse, in addition to other sexual acts.

"By then we were engaging in all sorts of activities without any boundaries," Jodi said.

Travis and Jodi's sexual relationship continued throughout 2007, unbeknownst to Lisa Andrews.

But it was lust, not love that drew Travis to Jodi. Although they remained intimate, he told many friends he had no intention of marrying Jodi.

With Travis, Jodi appeared content with the "friends with benefits" relationship. But Jodi's attachment was much deeper. While she tried to keep the encounters casual, she was still madly in love with Travis and remained sexual with him, in part, because it gave her a chance to remain close.

"We were blurring boundaries because we were still sleeping together," Jodi said. "It kept my heart more involved than maybe it should have been."

Travis and Jodi had a fiery relationship. When they weren't being intimate, they argued frequently.

During their fights, at times Travis lost his temper, spewing angry, hate-filled words. Jodi would later claim he was jealous and controlling, and when enraged, terrifying.

During their fights, as she attempted to suppress an emotional outburst, Jodi would tremble, tormented by her inner turmoil.

"When he got mad at me I would visibly shake," Jodi testified. "I would feel some sort of trepidation or apprehension or unsettled."

With her own ongoing issues with anger, however, it was Jodi who often initiated or escalated their feuds. She intentionally did things to raise Travis's ire, including snooping on his phone and hacking into his e-mail.

Over the next few months, Travis would grow weary of Jodi. His frustration became evident in multiple text messages he sent to her throughout 2007 and 2008.

"I'm sick of you playing stupid, and dealing with childish tactics."

"It's just always something, Jodi. It just gets old. You don't care about anything that doesn't involve you. Just give me a pardon from any madness. I don't need it. It was wearing me out."

"Just forget it. I know how you operate."

"If you're tired of me, leave me alone."

A vicious cycle began where Travis and Jodi would argue, make up, and have sex.

As their feuds escalated, so did their sex life—becoming increasingly kinky. While in the beginning they didn't progress to the point of intercourse, they now began acting out their most raunchy fantasies.

"Sometimes when we got together he was very loving and romantic. Sometimes it was just very animalistic," Jodi said. "Afterwards when he was done he was done for a while."

At times, Travis seemed at war with himself. He seemed to realize the relationship was unhealthy and was aware he was compromising his beliefs while at the same time presenting himself as an icon within the church. But the temptation was just too great.

During this period of his life Travis had several late-night, in-depth talks about his relationship to Jodi with his friend Dave Hall. Travis confessed to Dave that his relationship with Jodi had spiraled beyond his control.

"He told me they had messed around way too much and he had told his ecclesiastical leader and he was on probation with the Church because of that problem. He was working his way back through the process of repentance," Dave said. "Jodi was his Achilles' heel. He thought he had enough strength to tell her no but she kept coming over and throwing herself at him."

During these talks Travis never alluded to the fact that they had sexual intercourse, only that they had "messed around way too much physically."

Travis explained his relationship with Jodi as hot and cold. During the day they could fight, but at night their relationship would turn sexual. This was something that caused Travis great remorse, according to Dave.

"After she leaves I feel guilty, I feel horrible," Travis told Dave. "I hate myself for letting her back in my life."

"Why do you even talk to her?" Dave asked.

"It's hard to say 'no,' when someone throws themselves at you," Travis explained.

Most of the people in Travis's life, however, did not know the truth about Jodi. As far as anyone could tell, they were just friends.

The back-and-forth with Travis kept Jodi on edge. When Travis was loving, he was the man of her dreams. If they were fighting, she was dejected. Her emotions hinged on the status of her relationship with Travis.

And as her desperate desire for a future with Travis slipped further and further away, Jodi grew depressed and talked about killing herself.

Throughout 2007 and 2008, Jodi kept a journal where she regularly wrote passages about her life and relationship with Travis. The pages were filled with love and pain, hope and despair, dreams of building a future with Travis and plans to commit suicide if that future never came to pass.

On August 26, 2007, she wrote of her overwhelming love for Travis.

"I love Travis Victor Alexander so completely that I don't know any other way to be," she wrote. "I wish I didn't because at times my heart is sick and saddened over all that has come to pass. I don't understand it and, at times, I still have a hard time believing it. He makes me sick and he makes me happy. He makes me sad and miserable, and he makes me feel uplifted and beautiful."

Even after their breakup, Travis and Jodi continued to travel the country together. Throughout 2007, he maintained his goal of checking off destinations listed in *1,000 Places to See Before You Die*.

While he was dating Lisa, he never asked her to accompany him on his trips. Just as he did with Jodi, Travis kept Lisa compartmentalized in a separate aspect of his life.

In the summer of 2007, Travis and Jodi took several trips.

With them during two of these excursions were Travis's friends Dan Freeman and Dan's sister, Desiree. Dan was lanky, with short brown hair, a neatly trimmed beard, and deep-set blue eyes. Desiree was pale with a round face and stick-straight brown hair.

While living in Mesa, Jodi had befriended Dan Freeman and often went to his family's home for Sunday dinner.

In front of Dan and Desiree, Travis and Jodi acted like a couple. While the siblings witnessed several fights between Travis and Jodi, both were under the impression that the couple generally enjoyed each other's company.

For their first vacation the foursome toured the Grand Canyon. There, they hiked down a remote trail on the edge of a cliff passing through tunnels and steep descents.

After touring the Grand Canyon, they stopped by Sedona, a city in the northern Verde Valley region of Arizona, where they explored the Red Rocks and a stunning array of red sandstone formations. The Red Rocks form a breathtaking backdrop to the small city. When illuminated by the rising or setting sun, the formations appear to glow in brilliant orange and red.

Throughout the trip, Jodi snapped several photographs. In one picture, Travis posed with his hands on his hips standing in front of the Painted Desert. In the background the bright blue sky met the horizon of the red rock plains, resembling a postcard.

Later that summer, Travis, Jodi, Dan, and Desiree planned a weekend trip to Havasupai, an isolated Indian reservation featuring spectacular waterfalls.

As they were preparing to leave for the trip, Travis and Jodi got into an argument. Jodi had overpacked her luggage and when Dan tried to take some items out of the bag, Jodi burst into tears and ran upstairs. Travis chased after her, and in the bathroom they argued loudly, until Dan came upstairs.

Eventually they all got in the car and left for the trip. For half an hour Jodi stared vacantly out the window, not saying a word. By the time they made it to Havasupai, however, they had made up.

That night they camped, sleeping in hammocks. The next morning, hiking around the plains, they came across a hidden oasis in the arid desert—the Havasupai Falls.

Located in a remote canyon of Havasupai, the spectacular waterfalls are called paradise on Earth. The tallest of the waterfalls is Mooney Falls, its water tumbling 190 feet into a large blue pool.

Staring up at the waterfalls, Travis was in awe. As he looked on, Jodi snapped photos of him from behind, the entire falls in view. Later they stripped off their clothes, changed into their swimsuits, and swam in the natural pool.

In one photo, Travis and Jodi were in their swimsuits at the base of the falls. The water foaming around them, Jodi was seated on Travis's lap, both arms wrapped around his neck. In her left hand, she held Travis's chin.

In the picture Jodi was smiling wide and bright. Travis, however, looked uncomfortable. The corners of Travis's mouth were upturned slightly in a contrived grin.

While adventurous, these trips were costly. Jodi and Travis split their expenses, with Travis funding his portion with the money he had withdrawn from the equity of his house. Over the course of 2007, however, Travis noticed his business began to suffer. The more time Travis spent with Jodi, the less time Travis devoted to Prepaid Legal.

Soon, Travis's wealth was depleted.

While Travis continued to be sexual and take trips with Jodi, he was simultaneously attempting to build a more virtuous future with Lisa Andrews.

Several times he tried to end it with Jodi. But the more Travis pulled away, the more Jodi seemed to cling to their relationship. She called Travis constantly and spent much of her time at his house. She seemed to be reliant on Travis for daily advice, spiritual questions, and moral dilemmas.

When Travis was home he rarely locked his front door. Jodi would often show up, unexpectedly, and let herself inside.

When Lisa first began coming by Travis's house, she noticed how often Jodi was around. Travis explained that Jodi was just his friend. As time went on, however, Jodi's constant presence made Lisa uncomfortable, creating discord between the new couple.

In the beginning Travis wasn't forthcoming about Lisa, explaining to Jodi that she was just a friend. But based on what she had learned through reading his text messages and e-mails to Lisa, Jodi knew the relationship was much more serious.

"He swore they were just friends and he wasn't in the least bit interested," Jodi later wrote to a friend. "But the feeling persisted . . . he said I was crazy to think that, so I left it alone."

On one occasion, after her shift at P.F. Chang's, Jodi went to Travis's house unexpectedly. She later said she thought Travis was not at home, and was bringing over food for his roommate.

Jodi entered through the front door where she encountered Travis standing near the kitchen island with another woman—Lisa Andrews.

"I was mortified. I immediately turned back and walked straight out the front door," she said. "I was really embarrassed because I thought he wasn't home."

Jodi got in her car and drove away. Travis jumped in his car and chased after her. When he caught her he told her that Lisa was just a friend and that he was showing her his house.

On another night, Jodi went to Travis's house unexpectedly to retrieve an item from the boxes she left in his garage. She tried entering though the side door of the house, but found it was locked. Walking through the backyard, she headed straight to the porch's sliding glass door. Inside, she could see a blue glow flickering from the TV.

Peering through the glass door, Jodi could see two people kissing passionately on the couch. The woman appeared to re-hook her bra. The man stood up and wiped his mouth. He turned toward the door and Jodi saw it was Travis.

Ducking quickly out of sight, Jodi burst into hysterical sobs. Seeing the man she loved kissing another woman was overwhelmingly painful. The next day Jodi went to Travis's house, finding him in the laundry room painting the walls.

"If you're dating someone, it's okay," Jodi told Travis. "You can tell me. I won't freak out."

Travis dropped his paint brush, slamming his palm against the wall in frustration. He left the room and went upstairs.

"I heard this thud, this banging. It was like something was hitting something over and over and over," Jodi would later claim. "I went upstairs and went to the bedroom. He's banging his head repeatedly on the linen room closet."

She called Travis's name and he stopped, eventually calming down.

Later, Jodi asked Travis again about Lisa, but he became angry. Once again Travis lied—telling her he was not seeing anyone else, according to Jodi. By this point, Jodi knew he wasn't being truthful. Jodi wanted to tell Lisa everything, but didn't want to lose Travis.

"The whole time we were seeing each other after we 'broke up' he had another girlfriend. I had no idea. He didn't tell me about her," Jodi recalled. "I felt so bad. This time I was the other girl."

Jodi continued to snoop for information, checking Travis's phone whenever possible and reading his e-mails. In court Jodi would later claim Travis gave her the passwords as a way to reestablish trust.

But Travis was disturbed when he caught her reading his correspondence. At times he sent himself e-mails directed as a message to Jodi. In the subject he wrote: "Jodi, you're caught!"

"Stay out of my e-mail," Travis wrote. "We will talk about this later."

In 2007, Travis signed up for a Facebook account where he posted photos, videos, and regular updates on his life. By this time Facebook had been growing in popularity, overtaking MySpace as the leading social networking site.

Gradually, Travis stopped logging into MySpace as often and instead posted mainly on Facebook. Jodi used Travis's Facebook page to keep tabs on him—checking on which girls he was speaking with and what he was doing.

When Jodi learned his password, she started logging into

his account to read his messages. If she heard that he talked to another girl, Jodi would friend the girl on Facebook.

For Travis, juggling two women must have been difficult. He was committed to Lisa, but at the same time continuing to sleep with Jodi. In public with his friends, especially those who knew Lisa, Travis became openly disdainful of Jodi, claiming she was "obsessed" and a "stalker."

In late 2007, a man named John Hepworth was renting a room from Travis. He came to realize that Travis was two-timing both women. At one point, John tried to explain the situation to Jodi, pulling her aside at Travis's house.

"You know, he's dating other women," John said.

"I know he's been on dates," she replied.

"No, he's really trying to date," John said. "He's desperate to get married."

Later, Jodi told Travis what she had learned.

"That night I confronted him and we had a really big fight," Jodi later told detectives.

But John also saw how Jodi would use sex to keep a hold on Travis. When Travis would distance himself from Jodi, John witnessed her often calculated behaviors.

"I talked with Travis on a number of occasions trying to convince him to not let her back in the house," John recalled. "I knew what was going on between them. I was there for a couple of their fights. I saw how manipulative she was."

If sex didn't work, Jodi would make other threats. During their fights, if Travis told Jodi it was over, Jodi would threaten to commit suicide.

"She would always tell him that if he broke up with her she'd kill herself," said Sky Hughes. "I told him if she did something like that he wouldn't be responsible but he just said, 'I could never live with myself if that happened.'"

In court Jodi would later testify that during the fall of 2007 she had, in fact, become suicidal.

After a particularly vicious fight with Travis, Jodi called her ex, Matt McCartney, and asked to borrow a gun. She told Matt about her deep depression and he urged her to call a suicide hotline.

In her journal she would write about her suicidal thoughts connected to her relationship with Travis.

"I just wish I would die. I wish suicide was a way out. But it is no escape," she wrote. "I wouldn't feel anymore pain though if I could just stop existing and have my consciousness dissolved into nothingness and my energy recycled into something else useful for I am of little use to the world right now through no fault but my own."

After a few months of dating, Lisa began to suspect her new boyfriend wasn't being entirely truthful. Travis was always talking about Jodi and when they were together Jodi seemed to call and text constantly. It was almost as if Jodi knew when Lisa and Travis were together—like she was watching them.

Lisa felt it was inappropriate to be in a committed relationship but remain so close to an ex. Anytime she brought it up to Travis, however, he insisted the relationship was innocent. Jodi was still in love with him, Travis told her, but he made it clear that they were no longer romantic.

"We're just good friends," he said repeatedly.

In mid-September, John Hepworth told Lisa's sister the truth: Travis was still intimate with Jodi. To Lisa it made sense why Travis was always talking about Jodi.

"I came to the understanding that he was cheating on me," Lisa later said in court.

Lisa promised not to reveal to Travis how she received this information. Instead, she decided to end the relationship.

On September, 23, 2007, Lisa sent Travis a lengthy e-mail.

In it she wrote that she thought they were not headed in the right direction. She laid out all her concerns over the past few months: she thought he was too focused on sex and it made her feel used and dirty. Throughout their relationship Travis had been self-consumed and was inconsiderate of her feelings.

More than anything, Lisa was mad about Jodi.

"I'm sick of hearing about Jodi Arias," Lisa wrote. "What woman would hold on for so long without some sense of reassurance? If you really cared, you would tell Jodi to back off, regardless of your past."

She told Travis not to respond to the message and simply to respect her wishes and leave her alone. Lisa felt betrayed.

"I didn't feel I could trust him," she recalled. "I felt cheated and lied to and didn't want to hear anymore."

A few days later, Travis called her and told her he still cared about her. If given the chance, Travis swore he would make it up to her. Eventually, he learned the reason for the breakup. Travis convinced Lisa that he had never really cheated with Jodi. And a few weeks after the breakup, Travis and Lisa resumed their relationship.

"I understood that he had not cheated and that I had received faulty information," Lisa said in court.

After they got back together their relationship was much better. Travis seemed to take the words in Lisa's e-mail to heart. He was more attentive to her needs and concerns.

When it came to sexual relations, he was almost too restrictive. When they made out, he would pull back before things went too far. On several occasions Lisa had to be the one to encourage him to continue kissing her.

In October 2007, Travis and Jodi attended the Albuquerque International Balloon Fiesta, the largest hot air balloon festival in the world. For years it had been a goal of Travis's to attend the festival and he had planned the trip for months.

The weather that week was chilly, and Travis and Jodi were both cold and tired when they arrived at the Balloon Fiesta Park on the northern edge of the city.

When Travis first saw the sea of colorful balloons, he was speechless. Some were uniquely shaped—like a floating castle or eagle. Others were massive in size.

Thousands of people gathered on the field to watch the balloons launch. The highlight of the event was the mass ascension, with hundreds of balloons rising at once, filling the sky with bright colors and shapes.

Throughout the trip Jodi snapped dozens of photos. In one

photo Travis and Jodi were side-by-side, their faces touching as a rainbow-checkered balloon was inflated behind them.

While in New Mexico, they stopped by the Carlsbad Caverns, which includes one of the deepest limestone caves in the world. In addition, they toured the UFO Museum in Roswell and the Cumbres & Toltec Scenic Railroad in Charma, where Travis had his first train ride.

They spent the trip trying new foods and enjoying new experiences together. For Jodi, it felt as if they were bonding. But when they returned to Mesa and Travis resumed his relationship with Lisa, Jodi was crestfallen.

Late in the fall of 2007, strange things began happening to Travis. He would return home and find his computer had been used, his property out of place. Once he found his personal journals were stolen. As he searched through his valuables, he discovered an engagement ring he had once purchased for an ex-girlfriend was also missing.

On one occasion he arrived home and found Jodi inside his house. The front door had been locked. When he confronted her about how she got inside, she reluctantly admitted that she broke in through the doggie door. She claimed she had left something inside his house and came in to get her property.

Then, in late 2007, Travis and Lisa were at her house, upstairs, when they heard a beeping noise. The house was equipped with a security alarm that chimed when someone opened the front door.

Travis and Lisa went down to see who may have come through the door, but no one was there.

"Hello," Lisa hollered. "Is anyone home?"

When she found the house was empty, Lisa became scared. She asked Travis to stay the night. That night he slept in one of the spare bedrooms. Nothing happened the rest of the night.

Some weeks later, on the night of December 6, 2007, Travis was at Lisa's house when there was a knock at the door. But when he answered, he found there was no one outside.

He stepped out onto the porch, glanced around the property, but found no trace of anyone. Travis went back into the house. That night he fell asleep at Lisa's, as they watched a movie together on a LoveSac.

The next morning Travis discovered the tires had been slashed on his BMW. He went back into the house and told Lisa about the incident. They both assumed it must have been a random act and Travis had his tires replaced.

The very next night Travis was at Lisa's house again when there was another knock at the door. Travis bolted off the couch and whipped open the front door. Again, he saw no one. Rushing to his car, he discovered the tires had once again been slashed.

Travis called the Mesa Police Department to report the incident and file a criminal damage report. Afterward, he called a tow truck and had the tires replaced again.

The following morning at 8:52 A.M., on December 8, Lisa opened up her laptop to check her e-mail. One message stood out. It was addressed from a "John Doe." As she read it, Lisa was aghast. It referred to her relationship with Travis.

"You are a shameful whore. Your Heavenly Father must be deeply ashamed of the whoredoms you've committed with that insidious man," the message read. "If you let him stay in your bed one more time or even sleep under the same roof as him, you will be giving the appearance of evil. You are driving away the Holy Ghost, and you are wasting your time. You are also compromising your salvation and breaking your baptismal covenants. Of all the commandments to break, committing acts of whoredom is one of the most displeasing in the eyes of the Lord. You cannot be ashamed enough of yourself."

The message went on to urge her to repent of her sins.

"Think about your future husband and how you disrespect not only yourself, but him, as well as the Lord and Savior Jesus Christ," the message read. "Be thou clean, sin no more. Your Heavenly Father loves you and wants you to make the right choices. I know you are strong enough to choose the right. Your Father in Heaven is pulling for you. Don't ignore the promptings you receive, because they are vital to your spiritual well-being."

Lisa was sickened by the e-mail. Perhaps the sender of the message was under the notion that Mormons were daft—that faith in the Lord would lead them to believe a mysterious e-mail was a message from God. Lisa, however, was no fool. Immediately, she thought of Jodi Arias.

Weeks later, when Lisa was at Travis's house, the tires on her car were slashed as well. She told her boyfriend she thought Jodi was responsible. For a while Travis couldn't conceive that his soft-spoken ex-girlfriend would be capable of such destruction.

Eventually, he would come to believe that Jodi Arias was a very dangerous woman.

Despite Jodi's invisible presence, Travis and Lisa's relationship became increasingly serious. Travis began to talk about marriage.

Perhaps Travis was in love only with the idea of Lisa. She may have represented the wholesome, true love that he so desperately desired. He seemed to believe she was the one.

But in early December, as he discussed marriage, Lisa began having reservations about their relationship. Lisa was still just nineteen and not ready for such a serious commitment.

"He started talking about marriage earlier than I was comfortable with at the age of nineteen," she later said in court. "I felt I was too young and too immature and wanted to live my life before I got married."

She told Travis it was better if they ended their relationship. She thought that if he was at the point in his life where he felt he should be married, then he should explore other options.

But Travis and Lisa continued to talk. A few weeks after she broke it off, Travis convinced her to take him back and their relationship resumed.

Even in the midst of this twisted love triangle, Travis continued to devote much of his life to spiritual and personal development.

Travis spoke to Lisa about how he had been inspired to live 2007 as if he were dying, and she admired his determination for self-improvement.

"Throughout the time I knew Travis, he was constantly trying to better himself. He considered mediocrity a sin. He refused to accept it from himself or from anyone else that was around him," she recalled. "He didn't care what kind of background you came from because he said that anyone had the potential to make of themselves whatever they put their mind to. He pushed us all to be better."

Always striving toward self-improvement, Travis had developed a method to help him achieve his goals each year. Instead of creating a New Year's resolution, he did something different that he credited with making all the difference in becoming a better person by the end of the year. Travis wrote about this principle, "auto suggestion," or vocally exclaiming what one wants to do, be, and have.

For the past three years Travis had practiced this devotedly.

"I take the month of December and do a huge self evaluation of me for the good, the bad and even the ugly, and based on all that, I get busy being ambitious and create the accomplished individual I want to be on paper," he wrote. "I will read it and adjust the wording several times until I can feel the power of the words internally."

On January 1, while listening to music, typically the songs of Enya, he read it "out loud and animated." At least once a day for the rest of the year he would recite this mantra.

"After a few months with no effort it is memorized and becomes part of my regular daily thoughts and in consequence the person I am becoming is always at the forefront of my mind," he wrote. "My daily actions are based upon the words I speak daily and my life becomes what I want it to be."

In December 2007, Travis spent the month reflecting on how he could improve himself during the following year. Among his goals for 2008: to have a thirty-two-inch waist and be his personal pinnacle of health, earn a six-figure

Prepaid Legal ring, become a published author, succeed at real estate, and create multiple streams of income from his other entrepreneurial endeavors.

Perhaps most important to Travis, he was ready to get married and start a family. He wrote, "I will find an eternal companion that enhances me exponentially."

As 2007 was winding down, however, even as he created his goals for the next year, Travis still had not completed his last aspiration for his year of living like he was dying. He had gone skydiving and climbed the Rocky Mountains but he still hadn't ridden a bull. Taylor Searle's father owned a ranch for troubled youth and Travis had discussed going there to complete his ride. As the days slipped away, he realized he wouldn't have time. He was disappointed in himself for not creating the opportunity.

On New Year's Eve 2007, Lisa had made special arrangements.

"I knew he was disappointed in himself for not conquering one of his biggest fears of riding a bull," Lisa said. "But little did he know I had a surprise all lined up for him."

She took Travis to a Walmart in Apache Junction, a suburb of Phoenix. Inside, toward the front of the store, was a toy mechanical bull designed for kids to ride for a quarter. At 10:45 P.M. on New Year's Eve Travis mounted the bull, holding on to the plastic handle with one arm. "And he made it eight seconds," Lisa said.

After riding the bull Travis rushed home to read the last few pages of the Bible. He finished just before midnight. Travis had accomplished each of his goals for living 2007 as if he were dying.

"I can honestly say that Travis did 'love deeper and spoke sweeter' the more I got to know him," Lisa recalled, in a reference to the lyrics of the song that inspired Travis. "He became a better individual by working on things that he knew would also better a relationship."

CHAPTER 16

T his year will be the best year of my life," read Travis's affirmation for 2008. "This is the year that will eclipse all others. I will earn more, learn more, travel more, serve more, love more, give more and be more than all the other years of my life combined. This is a year of metamorphosis, of growth and accomplishment that at previous was unimaginable. A year where the impossible becomes common place and the unachievable become effortlessly achieved. Where I raise myself to heights only visited by the great men and women of this world and by doing so this year will be the best year of my life."

Each day of 2008 Travis read this affirmation. Despite his best intentions, his dreams would not be realized. Instead, the year would end in an unimaginable tragedy. Though there was no way he could have known it then, Travis Alexander had just six months to live.

In early 2008, the country was on the brink of a recession. The housing bubble had burst and property values were plummeting. The mortgage crisis had chilled consumer spending and layoffs were mounting. Banks and other creditors, burned by the sub-prime crisis, had tightened lending regulations, making it more difficult for everyone—from small business owners to private equity firms—to secure capital.

Although Travis remained positive, like most Americans he was facing financial hardships. Recently he had taken more time off from work than usual—traveling with Jodi and developing his relationship with Lisa. Consequently his income had plummeted.

With Prepaid Legal making money had come so easily to Travis. Now, it was not so effortless. Americans were holding on to their savings and were less willing to take on extra expenses, including legal insurance.

For Travis, the prospect of financial failure was frightening. Evaluating his finances, he realized he needed to tighten the budget or face serious debt. He created a plan.

"What will I do to improve my finances?" he wrote in his affirmation. "I will work harder, yes, but more importantly I will work smarter and learn to leverage myself and get more out of one day than I previously got out of a month. . . . The money I earn I will not waste frivolously, but instead invest wisely so that my wealth will beget more wealth."

Travis's largest monthly expense was his mortgage. The equity he had taken out of his house just two years prior was mostly gone—having been spent on home improvement and travel. Because he had refinanced at a higher price, his monthly mortgage was now beyond what he could afford. In early 2008, he refinanced his house a second time to lower his interest rate. Because his house value had dropped, he had to put some money back toward the principal to help lower his payment. His new mortgage: $332,500.

To save money he had been renting out the extra rooms in his house to a few different male roommates. At least one, who stayed for a short period, had been a nightmare. After some seedy details surfaced about the roommate's character, the man was evicted from Travis's house and subsequently the church ward.

Travis wanted his next roommate to be a friend. Several times he asked Taylor Searle to move in with him. For months he tried to convince his friend that living together would help motivate them to further pursue their clothing business and other entrepreneurial efforts.

"This is the place to be," Travis told Taylor. "Just move in. We can more efficiently get a lot of crap done in our lives."

Taylor, however, told Travis he needed to pay off some debt before he considered moving.

When Taylor declined to move in, Travis asked around and found a twenty-two-year-old Mormon named Zachary Billings, who was looking to rent a room. A waiter at McGrath's Fish House, a seafood restaurant in Tempe, Zachary was tall and athletic, with wavy blond hair and blue eyes. On January 29, Zachary moved into a spare bedroom on the second floor of the house on East Queensborough Avenue. He paid $450 a month for the room with full access to the rest of the house.

At the time Zachary was in a serious relationship with a woman named Amanda McBrien, a twenty-year-old petite brunette with pale skin and deep brown eyes. Spending a lot of his spare time with his girlfriend, Zachary was rarely at home.

As the country slipped toward recession, Jodi too continued to struggle financially. Living in Mesa, she had been consistently broke. Her credit cards were canceled and she could no longer afford the payments on her Infiniti. In 2008, she stopped making the car payments, knowing the bank would soon repossess the car.

Emotionally, Jodi was also teetering on the edge. Despite the pain caused by Travis's infidelity, Jodi was still desperately in love. And they continued to have sex—delving further into carnal temptations. Jodi introduced him to sexual lubricant to make anal sex more enjoyable for her. They began to incorporate skimpy lingerie, sex toys, and even candy as they acted out each fantasy.

On January 20, Jodi skipped a friend's baptism to spend the night having sex with Travis. "We explored every naughty fantasy we could conjure up in our fruitful imaginations that we haven't already fulfilled with one another," Jodi wrote in her journal. "I love him, I really do."

Four days later, she wrote about her feelings for Travis. Although she knew he was seeing other women, she was still fixated on him.

"Well speaking of Travis, he frustrates me and thrills me. I love, love, love him. And he sings to me, goes out of his way to display a massive amount of love for me. I'm almost haunted by it," she wrote in January 2008. "It stays with me. I can't get it out of my mind and my heart, but it still remains that I cannot marry him."

By this point Jodi knew they were not meant to be. Over time she was becoming increasingly uncomfortable with a sexual relationship that was going nowhere. She had hoped that their sexual connection would reignite their relationship. Slowly, she began to realize that it was not to be. She knew she was in an unhealthy situation and needed to escape.

Meanwhile, Travis had encouraged her repeatedly to move back to California. She was making his life unlivable. When they fought, he told her he wanted nothing to do with her.

Jodi grew depressed by the constant back-and-forth with Travis. In the spring she decided to move back to Yreka. But because she was broke, Jodi couldn't afford the move. She called her parents and her mom loaned her money.

"It was miserable, I wanted to leave," Jodi testified. "My relationship, the circumstances, and how things were going. The roller coaster we were always on. . . . The ups were great and the downs were horrible."

By February 2008, Travis's economic conditions had not improved. He had not fallen behind on his bills, but he found himself relying more and more on his credit cards. Around this time, he borrowed money from several friends, including almost $1,000 from Jodi, which he quickly paid back.

To save money, Travis decided to sell his BMW. When he mentioned the idea to Jodi, she said she wanted to purchase it.

Because her car would soon be repossessed and her credit was poor, they created an arrangement where Jodi agreed to make monthly payments directly to Travis. He sold her the car for $6,000, with an agreement that she would pay at least $100 a month, more when she landed a better job.

"He gave me very easy terms to pay for it," Jodi recalled. "I was a little bit leery about getting that car. I was reluctant, but his idea made sense to me because I had to give my car back."

Travis purchased a used 2004 black Toyota Prius hybrid. Trading in his car was largely a financial decision, but he also felt good about helping the environment, which had always been one of his passions. Whenever possible he would recycle, reduce waste, and use cloth grocery bags. The Prius was one more way he could live greener.

Travis was somewhat embarrassed by his financial problems. While his close friends were aware of his money troubles, he kept them well hidden from others. When asked about why he traded in his BMW, he told some friends that it was entirely driven by concern for the environment. With others he admitted it was economically motivated.

Travis's money problems bled into other aspects of his life, too, including his relationship with Lisa Andrews. Travis always planned on being financially stable by the time he got married and had kids. His debt was now preventing him from moving forward with that plan, he believed.

Analyzing his situation, he decided to end the relationship with Lisa and focus on his finances. In February, he broke up with Lisa. For Lisa, the breakup was abrupt. When she asked why the sudden change of heart, Travis stammered. He couldn't explain—he was ashamed to admit he was going broke.

"Lisa was confused by Travis's breakup. He was prideful and didn't want to explain," recalled a friend of Travis's. "She was upset and confused because he didn't explain the cause for the breakup."

Later, even Travis seemed unsure of the real reason he ended the relationship. Was he looking for excuses? Did he still have a fear of commitment? Was he just not ready for marriage?

"I don't know if he had a real honest reason for breaking up with her other than it was time for a real commitment," Taylor Searle recalled. "They were getting real close and he freaked out, as they were on the precipice of getting married."

While Travis was breaking up with Lisa, Taylor was also ending his relationship with his girlfriend. Because they were both going through breakups, Travis and Taylor formed an even closer kinship, spending hours several nights a weeks commiserating over their shared relationship woes.

In later online chats with Taylor, Travis admitted that one of the factors in his breakup with Lisa was his attraction to another girl at the church singles ward, twenty-nine-year-old Marie Hall.

Petite, with an olive complexion and dark brown hair, Marie, who went by the nickname Mimi, was a natural beauty, although she sometimes played down her looks with thick-framed glasses. A lifelong Mormon, she was intelligent and well-traveled, having visited France, Austria, Germany, London, Italy, and many places in the United States. She worked in finance and had ambitions to serve as a justice of the peace.

After graduating from college in Provo, Utah, in 2007, Mimi returned to Mesa, where her family lived. She first met Travis that summer, when she began attending the Desert Ridge singles ward. For months Travis and Mimi saw each other at church activities where they chatted casually about their families and jobs. One Sunday she gave a presentation to the congregation, after which Travis complimented her. Beyond that, they did not associate.

"Realize I never spoke to her other than, 'Hi,' before I broke up with Lisa," Travis told Taylor in an online chat. "But I couldn't hang with Lisa and figure it out with Mimi."

In February 2008, shortly after breaking up with Lisa, Travis asked Mimi out. She said yes.

Travis became enamored with the idea of Mimi. She was beautiful, smart, and successful. He decided she was his perfect match.

After his breakup, Travis finally admitted to Jodi the truth about his relationship with Lisa. By then, Jodi had been aware of his deception for months. When she reacted with seeming indifference, Travis started being more honest with Jodi about his feelings toward other women. And once he began dating Mimi, Travis told Jodi he thought she was "the one."

He explained to Jodi that he was receiving signs from God that Mimi would be his future wife. Over the next few weeks, Jodi became convinced Travis and Mimi would soon be married.

On their first date, Travis and Mimi went to dinner. Then, they walked to a Barnes & Noble, where they perused the bookshelves, chatted, and sipped on hot chocolate. Throughout the date, however, Mimi seemed uninterested. She was concerned that members of their church ward would find out they were dating, and she didn't want to be the subject of rumors. Travis, however, felt he was receiving contradictory signals from Mimi. He wanted to get to know her better but she seemed closed off.

"I thought he was a really nice guy but I didn't have any sparks," Mimi later said in court. "I acted like the way you act with someone when you're not really into someone."

At the end of the date Travis brought Mimi back to her place, where they exchanged a hug.

"I had a great time," Mimi told him. "Thank you very much."

A week later, Travis asked Mimi out again, but she declined. She had begun dating another Mormon at the church.

"He was sweet and respectful and understood," Mimi said.

In late February, after Mimi stopped seeing the other man, she agreed to another date with Travis. For their second date Travis took Mimi to As You Wish, a paint-your-own pottery store.

That night they chatted casually as Mimi painted a bowl. Although she still didn't have romantic feelings for Travis, she was intrigued.

"He was a really fun guy. I was trying to get to know him," Mimi recalled. "I didn't want to write him off too soon."

On their third date, on leap day 2008, Travis took Mimi

to the Phoenix Rock Gym in Tempe, where they spent a few hours indoor rock climbing.

During the date, Mimi was so aloof that Travis found himself overcompensating. He was awkward and self-conscious, which was out of character. Typically he was the confident one. With Mimi, he felt befuddled.

Although their relationship wasn't progressing as quickly as he would have liked, Travis remained optimistic.

When he arrived home from the date, Travis found Jodi in his house sleeping on the LoveSac upstairs in his loft. She told Travis she had laid down for a while and accidentally fell asleep, but Travis believed Jodi was waiting for him to return from his date.

Over the next few weeks, Travis continued to notice personal possessions missing from his house. On one occasion, he came home and discovered pages of his new book were missing. By this point he suspected Jodi may be responsible.

In early March, Travis picked up Jodi and they went out to breakfast. On the way home, she told him of her plans to move back to Yreka. Once she moved, she would no longer take part in Prepaid Legal, she said.

For a few minutes, they stayed talking in his car. Jodi was able to tell Travis some of the things she had wanted to reveal for months. She wrote about this conversation in her journal, in an entry dated March 2, 2008.

"This will help us both move on and close the gap," Jodi wrote. "It was the beginning of bitter sweet closure. He is my best friend in the whole world. It is so unimaginable to live without him, but it has to be this way. It will be better for both, I think."

At the end of their conversation, Jodi leaned in to give him a hug. He turned his head so their lips met.

After Jodi told Travis she was moving, they began to argue more frequently. During this time, Travis's roommate Zachary witnessed many of these encounters with Jodi. To Zachary, Travis seemed exasperated by Jodi's conduct.

Consumed with his feelings for both Mimi and Lisa, Jodi was simply a nuisance.

Despite the turmoil, Jodi would later claim they continued to have sex. At this point, however, the interludes were less frequent. "It eventually became just about sex," Jodi said.

But if Jodi felt used, she did not express it. Perhaps she wanted so badly to be close to Travis, she tried to appear accepting of a purely sexual relationship. Over time, however, it seemed to cause deep resentment.

"It was kind of like old habits die hard," Jodi said. "There was still some chemistry or attraction to a degree. I knew it was unhealthy but I wasn't making healthy choices at that time so I continued to sleep with him."

In March 2008, Travis threw a nineteenth birthday party for his friend Michelle Lowery. For her birthday, she had just one request: a piñata filled with candy. Without hesitation, Travis nailed a hook in his living room ceiling to hang it for her.

That night Travis's house was packed with people. Among the guests: Michelle's new boyfriend, twenty-year-old Dallin Forrest. Lanky, with spiked brown hair and a boyish face, Dallin lived with his parents and worked at a printer press.

Michelle had just begun dating Dallin and her birthday party was one of the very first occasions they spent time together. When Dallin arrived, Michelle brought him directly upstairs to the loft, where they stayed for most of the party.

At one point, Michelle pointed out Travis to Dallin. Because Travis was busy mingling with guests, however, he didn't formally meet Dallin that night.

Several weeks after the birthday party, Dallin, Michelle, Travis, and Mimi went out together on a double date to dinner and a comedy club.

Michelle was close friends with Mimi. Over the next few weeks, Travis often consulted with Michelle about his relationship with Mimi, to get a female perspective.

"I would always get the '411' on his dating ups and downs, his problems and successes," Michelle recalled. "And since

I happened to be friends with all the women he was interested in, he dubbed me his 'wingman.' As his 'wingman,' my job was to talk him up. And every time I happened to be talking to one of the girls, I had to figure out a way to bring him into the conversation."

Any time Michelle spoke with Mimi, Travis would call her or send a text message.

"What did you say?" he would ask. "Did you bring me up?"

Jodi spent most of late March planning and organizing to prepare to move to Yreka. But separating from Travis was complicated.

"I knew I was making the right decision about moving back, even if it was difficult," Jodi said.

While she was looking forward to spending time with her family, she wanted to stay connected to Travis. On March 2, 2008, she wrote an entry in her journal about her pending move.

"I wish I could turn back the clock and make some different decisions," she wrote. "I have anxiety about moving. This is going to be the period of my life when I will need to breathe deeply and flow."

Throughout March, Travis and Jodi argued habitually. By this point, Travis seemed largely unconcerned about Jodi. He was getting over Lisa, while at the same time preoccupied with chasing Mimi.

As he pursued Mimi, Travis found himself missing Lisa's companionship. He had had a real connection with Lisa, something lacking on his dates with Mimi.

Travis began to regret the breakup. He realized he had made a mistake. Yet, when he saw Lisa at church functions, she completely ignored him.

"Lisa has an effective, yet heartless method of moving on," Travis told Taylor in an online chat. "Complete excommunication. I am dead to her."

Travis had wanted to marry Lisa and now she was out of

his life. He was miserable. While in the midst of pining after Lisa, he found himself having less and less patience for Jodi's antics.

"He was in hell because Lisa wouldn't talk to him," Taylor Searle recalled. "Through all this, Jodi was just driving him crazy. She was a thorn in his side."

From Lisa's perspective, she wasn't bitter or angry with Travis. In fact, she still loved him. She felt she needed to create distance so that they both could heal.

"I knew we couldn't remain close after the final breakup or else I would end up back with him," Lisa recalled. "We didn't speak for months."

On March 31, Travis and Lisa were both at the same house for Family Home Evening. Just seeing her, he caught himself welling up in tears. Later that night, he sent Taylor a text message.

"Dude, I've been missing Lisa lately," he wrote. "It's getting to me."

"How's 'Project Mimi' going?" Taylor asked.

"It's not," Travis wrote. "She has showed zero interest lately. I thought no action would be the best action."

Travis wondered if the fact that he hadn't been as occupied as usual allowed his mind to drift back toward Lisa.

"So what do you want?" Taylor asked. "Do you want Lisa?"

"I don't know. I know that I miss Lisa. I'm not sure what I want other than to not be lonely," Travis wrote. "The past couple weeks loneliness has gotten me. It's very unusual for me."

On April 6, Travis tried contacting Lisa, sending her a text message. She did not respond.

Throughout the spring, Travis and Mimi continued to talk.

"I would hear from him almost every day by text, e-mail or phone," Mimi said. "I knew he liked me a little more than I liked him."

When she started a film and book club, Travis offered his loft as a meeting place.

That coming summer, Travis was invited to be part of an upcoming Prepaid Legal trip to Cancún. The company was paying to send its top four hundred leaders to Mexico, and both Travis and Chris Hughes were on the list.

Travis had originally invited Jodi to accompany him on the trip, according to several of his friends in Prepaid Legal. At one point the trip's organizer even had Jodi Arias's name recorded as Travis's Cancún companion. But after Travis started dating Mimi, he decided he wanted to bring her as his guest, although he was unsure if they had progressed to the point in their relationship where an out-of-town getaway would be appropriate. He asked Taylor's advice.

"I'm trying to figure out if I should ask her to go to Cancún," Travis said. "It's in two months but I have to put a name on the ticket pretty soon. So the timing is risky."

"That's pretty heavy," Taylor responded. "A bit risky."

Travis decided to "play it cool," and see how the next few weeks went with their relationship.

In April 2008, Jodi was preparing to leave Mesa. She rented a U-Haul truck, loaded Travis's old BMW on the back of a dolly, and drove away.

Glancing in the rearview mirror, she saw white smoke billowing up from the BMW. She pulled the truck over to the side of the road. Later, she learned she had left the car in "drive," causing extensive damage.

"There was black oil and white smoke all over the place," Jodi said. "It was completely ruined."

The car was towed to a Mesa auto shop. For the next few weeks Travis and Jodi worked with their respective Prepaid Legal attorneys to figure out who would be responsible for the damage.

Jodi later said that Travis was understanding about the incident, and she agreed to pay for the damage.

"I trashed his car and he took it so well," Jodi later told detectives. "We were trying to figure it out through our lawyers. That was a debt I promised to pay. He never had any doubt I would pay him back."

In early April, Jodi spent her last week in Mesa at Travis's house, sleeping in his bed, having sex.

That week, Travis and Jodi continued to argue. At one point, she got in the truck to leave, but came back and stayed for two more days.

Their final fight that week was ugly. In anger, Jodi stormed out of the house. Travis followed her out on the porch, yelling.

"He went over to the front porch and he turned around and flipped me the double bird and then walked in the house and shut the door, so I just drove away crying," Jodi said. "It hurt my feelings. I didn't want to leave things like that."

After the incident, Travis told his neighbor Dave Prusha about Jodi's foolish error with his BMW. He said it was further confirmation that Jodi was nothing but trouble.

"You won't be seeing her around anymore," Travis told Dave.

When Jodi left Mesa, Travis seemed relieved. He thought he could finally move forward with his life and get back on the right spiritual path. His entire mood seemed to lighten.

"When she moved back to California, he was rejoicing, just jumping for joy," Taylor recalled. "He was like, 'I feel like I have the biggest burden lifted off my back and I can live my life again.'"

With Jodi a thousand miles away in Yreka, Travis's friends thought he was done with her for good. But as it would turn out, the story of Travis and Jodi was far from over.

CHAPTER 17

More than a decade had passed since she dropped out of high school and moved out of her parents' house, and Jodi Arias had little to show for her life.

In 1998, she was broke, working as a waitress, drifting along with a directionless future. Now twenty-seven, she was back in Yreka, no closer to her goal of becoming a wife and mother.

Because she didn't get along well with her parents, she stayed in the cramped spare bedroom of her grandparents' house, which was filled with boxes containing her meager belongings. Soon after moving, Jodi found work as a waitress at a Mexican restaurant called Casa Ramos, and later at a diner, the Purple Plum. She also furthered her fledgling photography business, booking a few wedding gigs.

Living so far away from Travis, Jodi felt both relief and despair.

"I started feeling after I moved to Yreka like this cloud was lifting off of me," Jodi said. "I was still depressed, but I felt better than I did in Mesa."

Despite everything that had happened between them, Jodi and Travis continued to communicate through text messages, e-mails, phone calls, and instant message chats. And Jodi's mood remained dependent on Travis. If they were getting along, she was upbeat and positive about the future. When they argued, her depression worsened. Still, she couldn't imagine her life without Travis, couldn't let him go.

"I still had feelings for him and I still wasn't making the best choices for myself. I would still call him and I would still answer his calls when he called me," she said. "We almost continued the same thing except from far away."

On his unending quest of self-discovery, Travis often wrote down his thoughts. His writing was intuitive, introspective, and highly idealistic.

In addition to his book and journals, in April 2008, Travis started a blog. This wasn't something he was too serious about. "I don't care too badly if anyone reads this, I guess it is just more for me," he wrote.

He called it *Travis Alexander's Being Better Blog,* describing it as "just a bunch of random thoughts, excerpts from a book I am writing, or me being stupid."

In the blog, he wrote about his life philosophy, religion, motivational tools, and his quest to find an eternal companion. His first post, dated April 14, 2008, concerned the importance of living a purposeful life.

"We only live once; we don't get another shot if we screw it up. Why not live life to the fullest?" he wrote. "On our death beds, none of us will wish they watched more TV or read more tabloids or listened to foul music, and they certainly won't wish that they blamed their lives on someone else a little more."

In Yreka, Jodi paid close attention to Travis's new online endeavor. Reading his blog, she posted complimentary comments.

"This is my favorite post," she wrote on an entry about finding the meaning of life. "It's loaded with inspiration, humorous sarcasm and fresh perspectives, love it!"

For Jodi, the blog seemed to be another way for her to stay connected to his life. Thirteen days after Travis started his blog, Jodi created her own blog. She called it *Something to*

Think About, describing it as "random musings, observations and insights regarding everyday life and beyond."

In it she never mentions Travis or any relationship. Instead, her writing seemed to closely mimic Travis's own philosophical and introspective reflections. The similarities were eerie.

It appeared that she was trying to prove to Travis, through her writing, that she was as much of a visionary as he was.

Days after each of Travis's entries, Jodi would post her own blog on the same topic. On April 14, in a religious post titled "Why We Are Here," Travis wrote about accountability and making a difference in the world.

"It is my prayer that we live all the days of our lives," he wrote. "That we will be brave enough to unplug from the matrix and let the greatness within us manifest to all the world."

Fifteen days later, Jodi wrote an oddly comparable posting titled "Awakening," even using the same terminology: "unplug from the matrix."

"How you are defined by others has no relevance when you finally wake up and unplug from the matrix. Open your eyes and realize who you already are—a child of the Divine."

In a posting about limitless potential, Travis quoted spiritual activist and author Marianne Williamson.

"Our deepest fear is not that we are inadequate. Our deepest fear is that we are powerful beyond measure. It is our light, not our darkness, that most frightens us. We ask ourselves, who am I to be brilliant, gorgeous, talented, fabulous? Actually, who are you not to be? You are a child of God. Your playing small doesn't serve the world. There's nothing enlightened about shrinking so that other people won't feel insecure around you. We are all meant to shine, as children do. We were born to make manifest the glory of God that is within us. It's not just in some of us; it's in everyone."

Two weeks later Jodi quoted that exact same passage. Introducing the quote, she wrote: "The following is borrowed from Marianne Williamson's book *A Return To Love,* and has made the rounds on the Internet since its initial publication over 16 years ago. It doesn't just bear repeating, but it is in harmony with the theme of this post, and couldn't be more well-written."

On April 16, Travis wrote about the impact of the "law of attraction."

"The more intensely we focus on the achievement of something the more 'the law of attraction' works in our favor," he wrote.

Just eighteen days later, Jodi wrote her own posting about the law of attraction.

"About six months ago I stopped believing in the law of attraction or at least the accuracy therein. And do you know what I found out? I found out that even when you don't believe in it, it still continues to work with perfect precision."

In Jodi's final post, she wrote about her deep yearning for internal gratification and fulfillment.

"I want to search it out in evergreen forests, fields of tall, golden grass, desert sands, moonlit nights, in the eyes of other children of God, in the eyes of every living creature. It is in all of these things, yet it is fleeting. It has the power and potential to move me to tears in a matter of seconds," she wrote. "Yet somehow, I don't believe that all of the wandering in the world will lead me to its attainment. Somehow, I know it's right here inside of me."

Meanwhile, Jodi also had a new man in her life.

In April 2008, she had attended another Prepaid Legal conference in Oklahoma City. At the conference she was briefly introduced to a man named Ryan Burns.

Brawny, with dark hair and a chiseled face, Ryan vaguely resembled Travis. Ryan lived in Utah, had a bachelor's degree in psychology, and worked for Prepaid Legal under the management of Dave Hall.

Like Travis, Ryan was a rising star in the company. As an executive director, Ryan earned upward of $10,000 a month selling legal insurance.

By sheer coincidence, Ryan had been inspired to succeed by Travis Alexander. When Ryan first started selling Prepaid Legal in 2007, he initially struggled. After three months he had considered leaving the company. Then, he attended a Pre-paid Legal seminar where Travis had been hired to speak.

"I was struggling, not doing so well. I was even thinking about quitting. And then at some point Travis Alexander was flown into town as a guest speaker," Ryan later recalled. "I attended that training and I was inspired by him. It kind of changed my business around."

Like Travis, Ryan was also a Mormon. Ryan, however, had not been active in the LDS community nor had he been to church for more than a year.

Ryan and Jodi's conversation that first meeting was brief. Although they talked for a few minutes, he was instantly at-tracted to her.

In late April, at the encouragement of friends, Ryan called her.

"Hey, do you remember me?" Ryan asked.

That night they talked for about half an hour. The next day they spoke again. Over the next few weeks they talked three to five times a week, mostly around 10 P.M., when their days were done.

With Ryan, Jodi presented herself as a devoutly religious Mormon convert and a driven entrepreneur. Jodi told him about books she enjoyed, including *Atlas Shrugged, Think and Grow Rich, How to Win Friends and Influence People,* and *The Greatest Salesman in the World,* all of which were Tra-vis's favorite books.

Ryan saw Jodi as a beautiful woman and a driven young professional.

"When I initially met her she was a businesswoman at a national convention for entrepreneurs, so I thought that was an attractive trait," Ryan testified. "We had a lot of the same interests. She was a really good conversationalist on the phone. We just had a lot in common."

Jodi also spoke about going to church, reading the scrip-tures, and the importance of the gospel. When she learned Ryan hadn't been to church in more than a year, she encour-aged him to return.

"She would often tell me about her religious beliefs—*The*

Book of Mormon, and how she felt," Ryan said. "She was trying to bring me close to God."

By late April 2008, Travis had gotten nowhere with Mimi. On Saturday, April 26, they had a date, but Mimi called at the last minute to cancel, saying she was sick.

As a gesture of affection, Travis went to the store and bought her an herbal remedy, juice, apple cider vinegar, and two Shel Silverstein books. He arranged it in a wicker basket and left it on Mimi's doorstep. Afterward, he sent her a text message to look outside her front door.

Later, he told Taylor about the encounter in an online chat.

"I was gonna try to turn lemons into lemonade and just make a push. Take a risk," Travis wrote to Taylor. "I was sick of getting put off. I was making my intentions obvious. I was dejected by the date falling apart and needed to gain some ground."

Ten minutes after leaving the basket on her doorstep, he received a text from Mimi, "You shouldn't have."

"Why not?" Travis asked via text message.

"Thanks a ton, but don't be so nice to me," Mimi wrote.

"What's wrong with being nice to you?" he replied.

Travis waited twenty minutes but got no reply. He sent another text.

"Listen I had no ulterior motives in doing the basket thing. I think when someone is sick, it helps to have stuff like this to make you better, just like chicken soup," he wrote by text. "However it is no secret that I am interested in you. I have no idea if the feeling is mutual. You are a hard one to read. But I need to know if I am going to ask you out again, because I don't want awkwardness when I ask if you want to go out. I don't want you to feel obligated and I don't want to waste either of our time. So I need to know if you are at all interested or curious, if you are, we will reschedule, if you are not, that's totally cool."

All night Travis waited for a reply, which he never received.

The next morning he saw Mimi at church. She approached Travis and asked if he received her text. Travis told her he had not.

"Let's chat later," Mimi told him.

That evening they spoke on the phone. She told Travis she was "interested and curious," but wasn't sure as to what degree.

"I don't know either but I know I want to take you out still if you want me to," Travis told Mimi. "And time will tell for both of us."

The uncertainty with Mimi set Travis off kilter. He told her he had a hard time being himself around her.

"You'd like me more if I could have more confidence but the environment makes that hard," Travis told Mimi. "I think too much, but it's because it's hard to know what you are thinking."

Mimi told him to stop overthinking the situation. When she was ready, she had no problem making the first move.

"Just relax. Don't worry about it," Mimi said. "Time will tell."

After that discussion, Travis felt more secure about their future relationship. He decided to invite Mimi to Mexico.

"I thought what the hell, no guts no glory, and so I asked her a few days later," Travis told Taylor.

On May 1, he called Mimi.

"Hey," Travis said. "Do you want to go to Cancún with me?"

At first Mimi was reluctant, but Travis assured her that it would be innocent and that they would be staying with an LDS family in separate rooms. All expenses would be paid so she wouldn't be obligated to Travis in any way.

Mimi giggled. "Yeah, sure." She decided she would go.

Later, Travis called the trip's organizer with Prepaid Legal. Because the tickets had not yet been purchased, he was able to change the name on the reservations from Jodi Arias to Marie Hall.

Travis was thrilled—he felt things were finally progressing in his relationship with Mimi.

"Mimi is going to Cancún with me. She told me today," Travis told Taylor. "This is good for a lot of reasons."

Travis was excited for Mimi to see him speak at a Pre-paid Legal conference, where he was completely in his element. In that environment, Travis knew he would shine.

In Yreka, Jodi learned about the change in Travis's vacation plans. As Travis explained it, however, he was going to Cancún alone. He told Jodi that he was paying off a debt to a friend by bringing the family's babysitter as his guest, so they would have someone to watch their kids.

With Travis, Jodi seemed understanding but disappointed. Cancún held special significance to her. Approximately one hour inland of Cancún were the ancient Mayan ruins of Chichen Itza and Tulum, Mexico's most visited archaeological sites. The highlight of Chichen Itza was the Kukulkan Pyramid, an eighty-foot-tall step pyramid.

Rated as one of the "seven wonders of the world" in 2007, the ruins of Chichen Itza were also noted in the book *1,000 Places to See Before You Die*.

While in Cancún, Travis made plans to see Chichen Itza. But he would not be with Jodi. For this trip he would be with another woman.

Outwardly, Jodi seemed to be moving forward with her life. Her long-distance relationship with Ryan Burns appeared to be progressing.

They had been speaking several times a week, often for hours at a time. They also exchanged flirty text messages, e-mails, and instant messages.

"Hey hottie-biscotti. What's new?" Jodi wrote in one instant message.

In text messages, Ryan encouraged Jodi to come up to Utah for a visit.

"Just come and stay," he wrote.

On May 3, he sent another text. "So I'm getting close to talking you into it?" he wrote. "What do I have to do to seal the deal?"

In another set of messages, Jodi talked about being a "snuggler," and wanting to cuddle up with Ryan while they watched movies.

"You promise not to play hard to get when you get here," Ryan wrote.

By mid-May, Jodi agreed to come see him and began making plans to travel to Salt Lake City, Utah. There was a Prepaid Legal business briefing in June, and Jodi told Ryan she was making plans to attend.

In subsequent conversations, Jodi discussed her dating history with Travis. She admitted she had "trust issues," stemming from the relationship.

"Do you mind me asking what it is that caused the trust issues?" Ryan asked.

Jodi explained how she discovered Travis was talking to other women while they were dating. For weeks she did not mention the infidelity to Travis, she told Ryan.

"So he probably never figured it out that you knew," Ryan wrote. "He was getting away with it."

"But it got to the point where I couldn't keep it in anymore," Jodi replied. "And I told him and we broke up and I kind of wish that was the end of the story. But we continued to see each other even though we were no longer boyfriend and girlfriend."

"Oh man, that is intense," Ryan wrote.

While their sexual relationship continued, Jodi said she believed Travis was not dating anyone else. Then, she learned about Lisa.

"I asked him gently about it and he got really angry and it led to an argument," Jodi told him.

Jodi also admitted to Ryan that she had spied on Travis.

"Gosh, I'm making myself look so bad," she wrote.

When she discovered the text messages from Lisa, she knew Travis had been lying. She said she was so upset she was trembling.

"I'm sorry you had to feel that. It hurts me to think you were so hurt you were shaking," Ryan wrote.

"I wanted to tell her but that would have caused a lot of unnecessary drama," Jodi said.

"I love how honest you are," Ryan said. "You did not hide anything."

Despite the pain, despite the lies, Jodi seemed to harbor no hatred toward Travis. In fact, she said she was still fond of him.

"He's a great person. I wouldn't want to say anything else. We all have our character flaws," Jodi wrote. "We have seen each other at our worst and at our best. We are just fundamentally different."

Even with the progress he had made in the relationship with Mimi, Travis missed the companionship he had with Lisa, who still wanted nothing to do with him.

While Travis lamented her loss to his friends, he also knew it would be inappropriate to pursue her during his blossoming relationship with Mimi.

"It would be unfair of me to try and go after Lisa right now, if I could get her or not, if I am still going to be hung up on Mimi," he told Taylor in an online chat. "Because eventually I would come back to the same line of thinking that led to our breakup. It would take the complete death of the Mimi option or any other 'Mimiesque' option for us to have a fair chance."

Still, he longed for her friendship.

"My goal with Lisa is to somehow become friends again," he told Taylor. "I wish I had at least an open door with Lisa. Nothing to push just an open door."

Meanwhile, Travis continued speaking to Jodi. He even began discussing a possible visit to Yreka, during which they planned to drive up the Oregon coast to check places off "the list."

On May 10, Travis and Jodi had a conversation, which she recorded, and that would later be played in court.

"Are you coming up here before Cancún?" Jodi asked. "We'll go up the Oregon coast and to Crater Lake."

"Yeah, that's my plan," he said. "You're at the top of my list."

On the phone they were flirty, speaking like a couple. They talked about songs and superhero movies. At one point they sung to each other.

Travis complimented her like a boyfriend.

"You are pretty. You're just so attractive," he said. "Seriously I've never seen you look bad in all my life."

"Yes you have, when I have puffy eyes and I've cried off all my makeup," Jodi said.

"You don't look bad then, you just look miserable," Travis responded.

In the conversation, Jodi made reference to the fact that they would not end up together. When she married, she wanted to find someone equally as sexual as she was, she said.

"Eventually we're both going to marry other people," Jodi said. "I'd really like to marry a return missionary but like you someone who can be freaky. I feel like I may feel like a wilting flower that may not blossom to my full potential, sexually."

As they began to reminisce about sexual encounters, Jodi and Travis's flirtations turned erotic.

"You have the most incredible stamina that I've ever dreamed of," she said.

"We've had more than two-hour sessions many times," Travis replied.

The conversation evolved into phone sex.

"Are you touching yourself? I am already," Jodi moaned. "You make me so horny. I seriously think about having sex with you every day."

While her reasoning for taping the phone call remained unclear, Jodi kept a copy of the recording. It was possible she wanted a memento from their relationship. Or perhaps she planned to use the tape to expose Travis's secret sexual life.

Or maybe her motives were even more malevolent.

Even long distance, Jodi and Travis continued their familiar pattern of fighting and then becoming sexual. In addition to the phone sex, Travis and Jodi sent sexually charged text messages.

At times, his messages were vulgar.

"You are the ultimate slut in bed," he wrote in early May.

"It is my only desire to be your muse designed for your most vile and lustful pleasures," he wrote in another.

Despite the physical separation, Travis and Jodi could not seem to create distance. Jodi later admitted in court she knew it was an unhealthy situation.

"It's complicated. I still loved him," Jodi said. "I was making a string of bad choices during that time in my life."

Meanwhile, Jodi felt tortured. When he was sexual, Travis paid her a lot of attention. In between encounters, he was withdrawn. When they were not being intimate, they argued. Only now, their fights seemed more vicious.

"He got meaner after I moved," Jodi said.

On May 10, Travis caught Jodi logging onto his Facebook page. Furious, he confronted her through text.

"You have no respect for people's privacy and you dare insult me of all people," Travis texted. "Someone you show through your actions you hate more than love by denying me a human right of privacy countless times. You have a lot of freaking nerve."

In mid-May, a second roommate moved into Travis's house. Enrique Cortez was an acquaintance of Travis's from church. He was a twenty-seven-year-old Mormon with dark eyes and closely cropped black hair. Like Zachary Billings, Enrique had a serious girlfriend, named Kim, with whom he spent most of his free time.

Enrique moved into the room next to Zachary's—down the hallway, off the loft on the second floor of the house. Under the same roof, the three lived very separate lives. They didn't talk much or socialize, basically keeping to themselves.

The roommates came and went as they pleased. Travis hardly ever locked his front door and neither roommate had a key. When the doors were locked, they entered using the keypad on the garage door.

There weren't any set cleaning duties in the house, and all just cleaned their own messes. Each did their own laundry and dishes. Enrique and Zachary cleaned the upstairs bathroom, while Travis cleaned the downstairs guest bathroom.

With the addition of Enrique's rent money, Travis's finances began to improve.

On May 15, a few weeks before the Cancún trip, Mimi called Travis. She told him she felt they were better off remaining friends.

"He understood," Mimi later said. "He actually thanked me for telling him directly."

As for the upcoming trip to Cancún, Mimi said she thought it would be fair if he wanted to take someone else on the trip.

"There is no one else I want to take," Travis told her.

It was too late to change the reservations—the trip was in less than four weeks. They discussed it and decided they would go to Mexico together as friends. They were scheduled to depart at 9:25 A.M. on June 10.

After the breakup, Travis was deflated. He sent Taylor a text message.

"Mimi just gave me the 'I just want to be your friend talk,'" Travis wrote. "I want to kill myself. I have f'd up my life."

Travis's relationship with Mimi did not end with a bang, it had simply fizzled out. Part of the reason for the breakup with Lisa was the prospect of a relationship with Mimi. Now, Travis had lost them both. He felt foolish.

For the next few weeks, Travis was depressed over losing both Lisa and Mimi. He seemed to be lacking a bit of his usual vigor, as if something were weighing heavily on him. When he spoke with friends, they heard the sorrow in his voice.

After the breakup with Mimi, Travis's thoughts drifted once again back to Lisa. He checked her relationship status on Facebook to ensure she was still single, which she was.

On May 19, he sent a text message to Taylor. "I think I want Lisa back. I need to figure out a plan."

* * *

On May 18, Travis wrote his last blog entry. The post, humorously titled "Why I Want to Marry a Gold Digger," concerned his personal quest to find an eternal companion.

In it, he lamented his single status. His thirtieth birthday—eleven months prior—had been a turning point, he wrote.

He described the qualities he was looking for in a future wife: spirituality, mutual physical attraction, the ability to communicate effectively, and the desire to have children.

"But there is one thing that I have come to appreciate as much or more than all the others. I don't know how to label this quality except to say that it is the quality to appreciate the qualities in me," he wrote. "I want someone to fall in love with me because I am a man of ability and achievement."

In other words, Travis wasn't looking for someone who loved him for his money, but because of his drive, ambition, and ability to earn a lot of money. He didn't want to find someone who was attracted to his accomplishments, but because he was a person who worked to achieve great things out of life. He believed this so strongly, in fact, that he wrote that he wouldn't want to be with a woman if these weren't at least some of the reasons she loved him.

"There is a phrase with a stigma attached I find interesting, 'gold digger.' Now, I obviously don't like the stereotypical gold digger," he wrote. "However, I couldn't think of a better phrase to describe what I desire in an eternal companion. I want someone to love me for the gold that is within me and is willing to dig with me to extract it."

To attract such a woman, Travis needed to be "worthy of such a woman," he wrote.

Appraising his life, Travis made a list of qualities he was looking for in a future spouse. Then, he rated himself on a scale of one to ten on how he was doing in those categories.

"It is an eye opener. I realized the reason I wasn't married wasn't because the type of person I was looking for doesn't exist but that the type of person I wanted wouldn't be interested in me," he wrote. "Doing this has given me more purpose in my personal development. It has given me a stronger 'why' for the things I do every day. It has also helped me to weigh in opportunity costs on the decisions I make and how it affects the person I am and the people I attract. It really has in my biased opinion, made me a better person. Or in other words has increased the goldmine inside of me."

Reading Travis's public posting about his future wife must have been torturous for any woman in love with him. Travis was ready to find his eternal companion. Whether it was Mimi or Lisa or someone he had yet to meet, it was not Jodi Arias.

If Jodi had checked her calendar after reading that post, she would have surely realized that Travis had dumped her right before he turned thirty—the age he started dating with marriage in mind.

Reading between the lines, it seemed to imply Travis had never been serious about their relationship—she was just someone to keep his bed warm until he met his true love.

Jodi had done everything possible to become Travis's ideal woman. When she learned he would not marry outside his religion, she converted to Mormonism. When the distance between them strained their relationship, she moved to Mesa. Nothing she did was enough.

All the while, Travis had no intention of ever marrying her.

In Yreka, Jodi's behavior abruptly shifted. For nearly a year after the breakup, she had been consumed with Travis. Now, Jodi was chillingly quiet.

If she was bothered that Travis was taking someone else to Cancún, she told no one. If she felt used, she didn't speak of it.

In considering a plan to win Lisa back, Travis weighed his options. He knew that Lisa would be skeptical because of the timing of his breakup with Mimi.

He wanted to go big—to make a grand gesture—rather than waiting patiently. But he worried that if he presented it as win or lose, he might never get a second chance.

"I need a foot in the door," Travis told Taylor.

"I think I might be a fan of just calling her up and telling her everything, start to finish," Taylor said. "See what she says."

Travis decided to mull it over. But by May 19, he couldn't get Lisa out of his head.

"I physically can't take it. I don't sleep anymore," Travis said. "I need to get to the bottom of it with Lisa."

Two days later Travis decided he was "going big or going home."

At 5:20 P.M. on May 21, Travis called Lisa and left a voice mail.

"The voice mail has been left," Travis wrote in a text message to Taylor. "With a pounding heart I sounded positive and slightly casual I think. I'm sure she is listening to it right now. Now time to wait."

He received no response.

On May 22, it was raining. As Travis peered out the window, the murky skies mirrored his melancholy mood. His thoughts were of Lisa. Travis was always proactive when it came to problem solving. But with this particular problem he had no control.

He wanted to sit down and talk with Lisa face-to-face and tell her everything.

"I am going to do whatever I can to get her back, no matter how bad it hurts, I'll take the risk," he said. "I don't know how but I need to sit down with her. It must happen."

"Keep your posture," Taylor said. "Just go to where she is."

But Travis no longer knew her schedule, and he was worried if he just showed up he would "creep her out." He wanted to arrange a time to meet with her.

"I made a mistake, but I've learned from it and I love her," he told Taylor. "Everyone should be as loved as I do her."

The last two weeks of his life, Travis continued to mope about Lisa. He loved her passionately and considered Lisa the "one that got away."

"Up until the day he died, he was completely heartbroken by Lisa," Taylor later recalled. "I always imagined that she was the last thing he thought about while he was dying."

* * *

On Saturday, May 24, Travis hosted his last UFC party. He sent out an invitation that referred to his house as Casa del T-Dogg.

He ordering several takeout pizzas, and more than a dozen of his friends gathered around his big-screen television to watch the battle in the Octagon between UFC Lightweight Champion BJ "the Prodigy" Penn and former champ Sean "the Muscle Shark" Sherk. UFC 84 was being broadcast live from the MGM Grand Garden Arena in Las Vegas.

The main fight that night went three rounds. Travis cheered loudly as BJ Penn landed a flying knee to win the fight in the last seconds of the round.

For the next week, Travis worked, went to church, and spent time with his friends. One night in late May he met Taylor Searle for sushi.

"He and I were talking about our lives, and our girl situations, and what we wanted to make of ourselves," Taylor recalled.

Travis also mentioned the Cancún trip he had been planning all summer. Taylor knew it was in a week or so but wasn't exactly sure of the dates.

Two days later, he met with Aaron Mortensen to watch the movie *The Sandlot,* which was one of Travis's favorites. Afterward they read each other's blogs and commented on them. That night Travis was his old self. He was jovial and seemed positive about the future.

"He was in a good place mentally and emotionally," Aaron recalled.

The last Friday in May, Travis also attended a session at the temple. He told several people he hoped to run into Lisa there.

Travis's friends would later reflect on his decision to attend the temple the last week of his life. If he had been permitted to go back to the temple, it would have meant that he had been working on repenting for his sexual indiscretions and was on the righteous path.

* * *

On May 26, Travis and Jodi got into a vicious argument.

It's unclear what exactly triggered the fight. Jodi would claim Travis became enraged when he saw a comment she had posted on another man's photo on Facebook. Travis would later tell friends he had caught Jodi hacking into his Facebook account.

Some would later speculate that Jodi had threatened to release the recording of the phone sex call. Others still believe that Travis had discovered something truly disturbing about Jodi—something she never wanted exposed.

Whatever the cause, Travis exploded with a flurry of angry text messages. The fight continued late into the night through short phone calls and instant message chats. He berated Jodi, his words cutting.

Repeatedly, he called her a "sociopath," "evil," and referenced all the "crazy things you have done."

"You are a sociopath. You only cry for yourself. You have never cared for me and you have betrayed me worse than any example I could conjure. You are sick and you have scammed me."

In reference to a conversation Jodi had with another man, he called her a "slut" and a "whore."

"If he knew what I knew about you, he'd spit in your face."

Travis referred to something Jodi had done to him, something so bad it destroyed him emotionally.

"I had never, never in my life been hurt so bad by someone," he wrote. "But why even say it because you don't care. It doesn't serve your evilness."

In one of the final messages, Travis told her that he wanted her out of his life.

"I want you to know how I feel about you. I want you to understand how evil I think you are," he wrote. "You are the worst thing that's ever happened to me."

Two days later, in Yreka, Jodi's grandfather came home and discovered the back door of his house had been kicked in, splintering the wooden doorframe.

Carlton Allen went room to room, checking the house. At first, it didn't appear as if anything was missing. Then in the living room he noticed the DVD player was gone. In the spare bedroom, which was cluttered with boxes, was a wood cabinet that had been transformed into a gun cabinet. Inside, Carlton discovered one of the guns was missing—a small .25 caliber pistol.

Carlton called the police to report the burglary. An officer arrived at the house around 3:30 P.M. on May 28.

Although there had been a rash of robberies in Yreka in the past few weeks, to the officer the incident seemed unusual. Hardly anything had been taken and many of the valuables had been passed over.

In the spare room inside the gun cabinet were two rifles that had been left. On top of a nearby dresser were stacks of quarters, untouched.

Half an hour after the officer arrived on the scene, Jodi returned to the house. At the time of the robbery, she explained, she had been at a Buddhist monastery near the Oregon border, where there was no cell phone reception. She told the officer that she had been at the house earlier, around 1:30 P.M.

The officer asked Jodi to check her bedroom.

On the dresser, Jodi claimed she had left cash—a $20 and a $10—that were now missing. Jodi searched through the green laundry basket next to her bed. Inside she found her laptop.

"I'm lucky," Jodi told the officer. "I had hidden my laptop under some dirty clothes."

Carlton also asked Jodi if she had seen the gun.

"I don't even know what a .25 caliber gun looks like," Jodi said.

"It's real small," Carlton said. "It looks like a toy."

Jodi shook her head. "I've never seen it."

On May 28, Travis called Lisa again. She didn't answer so he left a funny voice mail.

Seeing Travis's number on her cell phone screen, something got to Lisa that day. After ignoring several calls, she picked up her phone and called him back. Travis was thrilled she finally agreed to speak with him.

At first it was uncomfortable; neither knew exactly what to say. Travis told her he missed her. Lisa explained she had been keeping her distance because she needed time to heal.

"We talked for about forty minutes and ended on good terms," Lisa recalled. "I promised to try harder to make things less awkward."

After their conversation Travis was much less sullen.

"He felt at peace with the whole situation because he got to talk to her," Taylor recalled.

For the next few days Travis returned to his positive, upbeat self. He posted on his Facebook status: "Feels Freaking Fantastic!"

A few days later he posted a video of his alter ego, Eddie Snell, and a photo of him and Taylor riding their bikes.

His last post was a photograph he had taken of himself. On May 29, Travis was in his master bathroom when he caught his reflection in the mirror. He was wearing a brown baseball cap and button-down shirt with oversize black jeans. Staring at his profile, Travis thought his rear end looked flat.

He grabbed his camera and snapped a photo of the mirror, capturing his reflection. Travis posted the picture on Facebook, along with a caption.

"I was walking past my bathroom mirror and my worst fear was realized, I was literally running my butt off," he wrote. "I think I have a bad connection to the Heavens. I've been praying to lose my gut not my butt."

Underneath the caption he wrote the following.

"T-Dogg's Gluteus R.I.P. July 28, 1977 to May 29, 2008. We'll miss you big guy."

It was meant to be a joke. Later, it wouldn't seem so funny. The photo was taken in the same bathroom his body would be found days later.

In Yreka, meanwhile, Jodi was making plans for her road trip.

She told Ryan Burns that she was coming to Utah on Wednesday, June 4, the day of the Prepaid Legal briefing.

Jodi wasn't scheduled to be part of the meeting. She told Ryan she was just passing through and wanted to see him. She told others that she was going to Salt Lake just to see Ryan.

Then, she began making phone calls, searching for a rental car.

She also phoned her ex-boyfriend Darryl Brewer.

"I need a favor," she said.

During the last week of May, Travis spoke to Taylor Searle and told him about a fight he had with Jodi.

As Travis explained it, he had logged on his Facebook page and noticed some unusual activity on his account. Immediately, he knew Jodi had hacked into his page.

During the conversation, Travis told Taylor that he had finally confronted Jodi about his slashed tires and stolen journals. She was a fraud and an evil, horrible person, he said.

"You know, it's over," Travis said he told Jodi. "I never want to see you again. This is it."

As Travis related the conversation to him, Taylor was unnerved.

"They had a chat where he tore her apart," Taylor Searle recalled. "He called me and told me what he said to her. I said, 'Aren't you afraid she's going to hurt you?' "

Travis brushed it off.

"No. She's crazy," Travis said, "but she's harmless."

CHAPTER 18

T he car was candy apple red—metallic tinted, brightly colored. When Jodi made the car rental reservations she had requested something less flashy.

Before making the hundred-mile trek from Yreka to the Budget car rental office in Redding, California, she had called several times to confirm a specific vehicle would be available for her.

The red car simply wasn't suitable. She walked back into the rental car office and plopped the car keys on the desk.

"I'd rather have something lighter in color," she said.

The owner, Raphael Colombo Jr., a heavyset man with gray hair and a goatee, exchanged the vehicle for a 2008 white Ford Focus.

"Where are you headed?" he asked, as he filled out the paperwork.

"Just around town," Jodi said. "Nowhere big."

Jodi took the keys and transferred her luggage into the rental car. She got behind the wheel and headed south toward Santa Cruz.

It was about 8 A.M. on Monday, June 2, 2008, and Jodi was on a road trip to see Ryan Burns, as well as visit her ex-boyfriends: She planned to go to Santa Cruz to spend a night with Matt McCartney and then head to Monterey to meet up with Darryl Brewer. The next day she would stop by Los Angeles to photograph Darryl's sister's new baby for her portfolio, before proceeding to Utah.

The night before, Jodi had stayed up late talking to Travis. Between 1 and 4 A.M. Jodi called Travis four times, the longest conversation lasting just a few minutes. Around 3 A.M. Travis called Jodi twice, and they spoke for over an hour.

During one of their calls, Jodi mentioned her trip to Utah. She would later say Travis encouraged her to come to Mesa and see him as well, but she declined.

After renting the Ford, Jodi drove three hours to Lodi, a city in the northern portion of California's Central Valley. At 4:03 P.M. she called Travis. An hour and a half later, she called Travis again.

She drove to a nearby McDonald's, where she curled up in her backseat and slept for a few hours. When she awoke it was dark.

At 7:32 P.M. she ate dinner at McDonald's, and an hour later she filled her gas tank at a Valero station.

She then drove to Santa Cruz, a city near Monterey Bay, where she met Matt McCartney and his roommate. The three went to a restaurant, where they had appetizers and passed the hours singing tunes at a karaoke bar. She spent the night at Matt and his roommate's apartment, sleeping on the floor.

The following morning, Jodi woke up early and went to Monterey, a city located on the southern edge of Central California's Pacific coast.

Around 7 A.M. on June 3, she stopped by the apartment of Darryl Brewer and his son, in Pacific Grove. Over the last year they had kept in touch with occasional phone calls. This visit, however, was the first time they had seen each other in more than a year.

That morning Jodi joined Darryl and Jack for breakfast. Darryl made omelets; Jack then left for school. Using Darryl's computer, Jodi checked her e-mail and MySpace page.

Jodi reminded Darryl of her request: a few days earlier, she had called asking to borrow two gas cans.

"What do you need them for?" Darryl had asked.

At first, Jodi didn't say. Eventually, she told him she needed them for a long trip she was taking.

From the garage Darryl retrieved two red five-gallon gas cans and gave them to Jodi. While she didn't discuss many details of her plans with Darryl, Jodi mentioned something about a trip to Mesa.

Jodi took the gas cans, loaded them in her car, and drove off.

At 10 A.M. she stopped at a nearby Washington Mutual in Monterey and made three bank deposits, totaling $800—juggling money between her personal and work account. Then she got back in her car and headed twenty miles east to Salinas, where she stopped at a nail salon and got a manicure.

At 12:57 P.M. she called Travis. An hour later, at 1:51 P.M., she called him again.

At 3:22 P.M. Jodi went to a Monterey Walmart, where she bought face wash, sunscreen, and another gas can for a total of $45.

Late that afternoon, she got back on the road and drove another six hours toward Los Angeles. On the way, she called Darryl's sister, but there was no answer. Despite driving the long distance, Jodi would not end up seeing her former lover's sister, or her new baby.

As she drove toward Los Angeles, Jodi called Ryan Burns. She told him she was about twelve hours away and would be in Utah at around 11 A.M.

"Please be careful," Ryan told her. "I don't like the idea of you driving all night by yourself."

"If I get tired, I promise I'll pull over and sleep," she assured him.

At 8:16 P.M. Jodi again called Travis. The call was short, lasting just two minutes.

Jodi stopped just outside of Los Angeles in Pasadena. At 8:31 P.M. she made a purchase for $6.37 at a Pasadena CVS. A few minutes later, at 8:34 P.M., she called Travis once again.

She then stopped at a local Starbucks and bought a strawberry Frappuccino.

At 8:42 P.M. Jodi filled her gas tank. Minutes later she made two separate purchases of gas, filling the gas cans and loading them in the back of her truck.

Jodi got back behind the wheel of the car and turned off her cell phone.

CHAPTER 19

On the last day of his life, Travis awoke at dawn, still weary. The night prior he had worked in his downstairs office until the early-morning hours. At 4:30 A.M. he'd finally gone to bed, sleeping for less than an hour.

It was June 4, 2008, a Wednesday.

Travis rose and went downstairs to get a glass of water. Zachary and Enrique were in the kitchen, preparing to leave for work.

"Hey, how's it going?" Enrique asked.

"I'm tired." Travis yawned. "I only slept for like forty-five minutes last night."

In passing, Travis mentioned a conference call he was hosting later that day. When both roommates left the house a short time later, Travis crawled back into bed and drifted off to sleep. He woke up again at noon and grabbed his cell phone from the nightstand.

There was a text message from Chris Hughes, who was already in Cancún with his wife. The Hughes had arrived a few days early for the trip and were expecting Travis in six days. Travis replied to the text about a purchase Chris made in Mexico, "Did you buy me one?" Five minutes later, Travis checked his voice mail.

Turning on his side in the bed, Travis dozed back to sleep—awaking for the last time at 1 P.M.

As the afternoon crept by, Travis divided his time between the bedroom, his home office, and downstairs in the living room. He fed Napoleon and did some housework. To prepare to clean the floors, he moved the barstools off the tile and stacked them on the couch. But before he could finish the floors, something distracted Travis. He went into his home office, where he would remain for the next hour.

At 3 P.M. Enrique arrived home from work. As he was grabbing something to eat from the kitchen, he heard voices coming from the den. It sounded like Travis was talking to someone—Enrique assumed it was the conference call. An hour later, Enrique left the house for the night.

At 4:19 P.M. Travis checked his e-mail on his laptop in the den. An hour later he went back upstairs. At 5:22 P.M. he took a shower in his master bathroom.

Exactly what happened next would remain shrouded in mystery for years to come. Evidence would later be collected, examined, and dissected for clues, painting a horrifying picture of Travis's final moments on earth.

Eight minutes after stepping into the shower, Travis was slaughtered inside his master bathroom. He was shot in the face, his throat was slit, and he was stabbed more than two dozen times. At the edge of the bathroom hallway Travis gasped his last breath, collapsing on the carpet. His corpse was dragged along the tile floor and stuffed in the shower stall, where he was washed clean of blood.

His body was left to rot. Five days would pass before anyone would notice the smell.

For more than twenty-four hours Jodi Arias's cell phone had been turned off, her whereabouts unknown.

Then just before midnight on June 4, as she was driving her rented Ford Focus along Interstate 93, about twenty-seven miles south of the Nevada border, she switched back on her phone.

At around 11:45 P.M. she called Travis, but he didn't answer. A few minutes later she called again and left a message.

"Hey, what's going on? It's almost midnight, right about the time you're starting to gear up," she said. "Um, my phone died so I wasn't getting back to anybody, um, and what else? Oh, and I drove a hundred miles in the wrong direction, over a hundred miles—thank you very much. So yeah, remember New Mexico? It was a lot like that. . . . I'll tell you about that later. Also, we were talking about when your travels would be up my way. . . . We could do Shakespeare, Crater Lake, and the coast, if you can make it. If not, we'll just do the coast and Crater Lake. Anyway, let me know and we'll talk to you soon. Bye."

Late that night, Jodi had also phoned Ryan Burns.

Ryan was at a Cheesecake Factory with friends when he saw Jodi's name appear on his cell phone screen.

"Jodi?" Ryan asked, answering the phone.

"Hey," she replied.

"Are you okay?" he asked. "Where have you been?"

After Jodi failed to arrive in Salt Lake City that morning as expected, Ryan had grown concerned. He called several times but each call went straight to voice mail.

"I've been worried about you," Ryan said.

Jodi apologized. "I took the wrong freeway."

Jodi told Ryan that while en route to Salt Lake City, she had gotten lost and drove a hundred miles in the wrong direction. As she drove, her phone battery had died and she was unable to locate the charger. Exhausted, she said she had pulled over to the side of the road and slept for a while. When she awoke she had found the charger under the passenger seat.

"I can't believe I slept so long," she said.

"I'm just glad you're okay," Ryan said.

On the phone, Ryan helped Jodi navigate a course to Salt Lake City.

"I just passed a sign that said I'm a hundred miles from Vegas," she said.

After hanging up, Jodi stopped by an In-N-Out Burger in Reno, Nevada, and got dinner. Five minutes later she filled her gas tank at a Tesoro station and got back on the road, headed toward Utah.

She was still more than twelve hours away from Salt Lake City.

The next day, things seemed odd at the house on East Queensborough Avenue. It wasn't anything in particular Enrique Cortez could pinpoint. The place just seemed out of sorts.

That afternoon—Thursday, June 5—Enrique had arrived home from his job, approached the front door, and tried the handle. It was locked.

That's strange, he thought, furrowing his brow. Travis rarely locked the front door.

Enrique approached the garage and punched in the code on the keyless display. As the door rose, he noticed Travis's black Prius was parked inside. For a moment, he expected to see his roommate. But when he stepped inside, the house was empty.

In the living room Enrique noticed the stand-up floor cleaner on the tile. The furniture had been moved; the dining room chairs were resting on the couch. Last Enrique could remember Travis hadn't finished assembling the machine. It appeared he had been preparing to clean, but hadn't finished.

At the base of the steps Enrique discovered the dog fence was up, restricting Napoleon's access to the upstairs. Normally, the dog roamed the entire house. Enrique stepped over the gate and climbed the steps.

He passed by Travis's master bedroom—the double doors were shut. Making his way to his own room on the other side of the loft, Enrique spent the next three hours watching TV and playing a video game. At 6 P.M. his girlfriend, Kim, arrived. They grabbed a couple of bottles of water in the kitchen.

"What's Travis's ring doing out here?" Kim pointed to Travis's CTR ring and watch, which were lying on the kitchen counter.

"I don't know." Enrique shrugged. "I haven't seen Travis all day. He doesn't usually go anywhere without them."

Enrique mentioned that Travis had been talking about an upcoming business trip.

"He's probably out of town," he said. "He must have forgotten his ring."

In the kitchen, Napoleon's dog bowl was empty. Kim filled it and the couple left for church. Periodically throughout the week Kim would fill the dog's bowl with food.

For the next four days Enrique would split his time between work, his girlfriend, and the house on East Queensborough Avenue. He watched movies in Travis's loft, ate meals in the kitchen, and showered in the second-floor guest bathroom. Each night he slept in his room, just down the hall from Travis's master bedroom suite.

With no sign of Travis, Enrique convinced himself his roommate was out of town.

The truth was far more sinister. Enrique was living with a dead man.

Curled at the bottom of the shower stall, Travis's corpse had gone cold, its skin a dull gray hue. In full rigor mortis, the remains had become stiff and rigid. The blood, no longer pumping through the veins, had pooled in the lowest part of the body, bruising the backside.

The blood spatter slathering the bathroom had darkened. The pools of blood on the floor thickened to a sludge. The walls wept with dark red drips.

Downstairs in his home office, Travis's cell phone silently lit up as he missed dozens of calls from friends and business associates—including two from Jodi. After Travis had missed the conference call at 7 P.M., Chris Hughes phoned repeatedly and sent text messages.

Each message went unreturned.

At 11:00 A.M. on June 5, Jodi arrived at Ryan Burns's apartment in West Jordan, a suburb of Salt Lake City.

When Ryan saw Jodi, he complimented her on her new look. The last time he saw her she had been a blonde. Now her hair was dark.

He also noticed her hands—she had two small bandages on her fingers.

"What happened?" he asked.

"I work at Margaritaville," she told Ryan. "I broke a glass and cut my fingers."

Around noon, Jodi accompanied Ryan to a Prepaid Legal sales appointment a mile from his house. They drove separately, with Jodi following him in her car.

As she pulled onto the main road, Jodi saw red and blue lights flashing in her rearview mirror. Both she and Ryan pulled their cars to the side of the road.

The officer approached Jodi's car. "Do you know your license plate is upside down?"

"Oh, my friends must be playing a joke on me," she said with a laugh.

She provided the officer with her license and registration. Because everything else was in order, the officer let her go with a warning.

"Make sure to correct that license plate as soon as possible," he told her.

Ten minutes later, when Jodi and Ryan arrived at the appointment, Ryan asked about the incident.

"It's a funny story," Jodi said.

Earlier on her road trip, Jodi said, she'd noticed a couple of kids on skateboards messing with her front license plate. When she caught them, the children dropped the plate and ran off. Jodi picked up the front license and placed it in the backseat. She said she hadn't noticed the back plate, but the teenage troublemakers must have turned it upside down.

In the restaurant, Ryan borrowed a screwdriver and mounted the license plate correctly. After the appointment, they returned to his apartment to watch a movie. As they cuddled on the couch, they began to kiss.

"At some point we were talking and we kissed. Eventually, we kissed many times. Every time we started kissing, it got a little more escalated," Ryan testified. "She was kissing my neck, I was kissing hers. . . . At one point I had my hands on her thighs."

As a motivational speaker for Prepaid Legal, Travis used his own background to encourage others to achieve their ultimate potential. *Courtesy of Prepaid Legal*

After discovering the book, *1,000 Places to See Before You Die*, Travis and Jodi began traveling the country, crossing off destinations on the list. In 2007, they visited the Sacred Grove, a forested area near the border of western New York, across from the former home of Joseph Smith, the prophet founder of the Latter-day Saints movement. *Courtesy of the Alexander family*

In June 2007, Travis and Jodi traveled to New York to see Niagara Falls. By then Jodi had already discovered Travis had been cheating. *Courtesy of the Alexander family*

Even after their breakup, Travis and Jodi continued to travel together. In October 2007, they attended the Albuquerque International Balloon Fiesta, the largest hot air balloon festival in the world. *Courtesy of the Alexander family*

In 2004, Travis purchased a spacious, two-story home in East Mesa, Arizona. The far-flung community sat on the edge of the city along a vacant swath of desert. *Courtesy of the author*

LEFT: On June 9, 2008, after not hearing from Travis for five days, three of his friends entered his home and found the master bathroom covered in blood. *Courtesy of the Mesa Police Department*

ABOVE: Investigating the crime scene, detectives discovered dried blood on the walls, mirror, and sink of the master bathroom and in thick puddles on the floor. *Courtesy of the Mesa Police Department*

ABOVE RIGHT: Blood spanned the entire width of the bathroom. The pattern on the sink indicated it was caused by heavy arterial spurting—the intermittent gush of blood that occurs when an artery is cut. *Courtesy of the Mesa Police Department*

RIGHT: By the time he was discovered, Travis's body was severely decomposed. The corpse was grotesquely bloated, the skin marbled with discoloration. *Courtesy of the Mesa Police Department*

ABOVE LEFT: Photos recovered from a camera found in the downstairs washing machine showed Travis alive in the shower on the last day of his life. *Evidence*

LEFT: One of the last images of Travis alive showed him looking directly into the camera, seemingly stoic. *Evidence*

Among the images recovered from the camera were nude photos of Jodi sprawled out on Travis's bed. *Evidence*

One of the blurry images recovered from the camera showed Travis's body on the ground. The dark image in the foreground is the foot and pant leg of his killer. *Evidence*

When she was arrested on July 15, 2008, Jodi appeared flippant, even smiling in her mug shot. *Courtesy of the Siskiyou County Sheriff's Department*

Detective Esteban Flores never believed Jodi's strange stories of how Travis was killed. *In Session*

On the witness stand Travis's former girlfriend, Lisa Andrews, admitted she thought Travis had been a virgin throughout the time they had dated. *In Session*

Less than a day after the murder Jodi had a romantic rendezvous with Ryan Burns in Utah. *In Session*

Prosecutor Juan Martinez's dynamic courtroom performance earned him a cult following. His relationship with defense attorneys Kirk Nurmi and Jennifer Willmott was often contentious. *In Session*

In court Jodi often seemed to mimic the clothing and hairstyles of her attorney, Jennifer Willmott. *In Session*

Judge Sherry Stephens, a shrewd former prosecutor, presided over the high-profile trial. *In Session*

Travis Alexander was laid to rest in Olivewood Memorial Park in Riverside on June 21, 2008. *Courtesy of the author*

During their tryst they both remained clothed. From what Jodi had told him, Ryan believed she was deeply religious and he was cautious about going too far sexually.

"I don't think either one of us said stop; we just stopped," Ryan recalled. "I didn't want to go any further. I didn't want her to regret her trip."

At around 7 P.M. Jodi and Ryan attended a Prepaid Legal business briefing. At the event Jodi encountered several people she knew, including her friend Leslie Udy. Leslie asked Jodi how long she was staying.

"I have to go back tonight," Jodi said. "I have to get back to work."

The business briefing lasted an hour. Afterward, Ryan, Jodi, Leslie, and a few friends from Prepaid Legal went to a nearby Chili's for dinner. Leslie rode in the car with Jodi.

During the drive, Jodi spoke about her breakup with Travis. Leslie had been aware of the breakup and had been worried about how Jodi was coping. But speaking with her, Jodi seemed fine.

"Travis and I will always be friends," Jodi said. "We joke that one day, in the future, we'll run into each other at Prepaid Legal events and our children will play together."

Jodi added that she had recently moved back to California to create some much needed distance. When she last spoke to Travis a few days earlier, Jodi said, he had actually pressured her to come to Mesa.

"I told him no," Jodi said. "I'm trying to create some separation there."

Following dinner that night, at around 10:30 P.M., Jodi and Ryan returned to his apartment and took a nap in his bed. They both awoke after an hour.

"The second we woke up we were kissing. She got on top of me pretty aggressively and we were kissing," Ryan later said. "She was right on top of me."

Ryan reminded her of her plans to leave earlier.

"Don't you have to go to work?" he teased.

"I just want to stay a little bit longer," Jodi said. "Maybe just a few more minutes?"

At around 1 A.M. Ryan walked Jodi to her car and kissed her good-bye. Jodi headed back to Yreka.

The alarm rang at 7 A.M. on Friday morning, June 6, rousing Zachary Billings. Groggily, he rolled out of bed, rubbing the sleep from his eyes.

The previous evening, Zachary hadn't returned home until after midnight. It had been his day off work, and he had spent it with Amanda at the Tempe Marketplace, an outdoor mall. They had lunch, saw a movie, and shopped.

Today, he was working the early shift at McGrath's Fish House.

In the upstairs guest bathroom, Zachary showered and dressed, after which he headed downstairs. As he grasped the banister, he noticed it felt slick. In the living room he saw the furniture in disarray and the floor cleaner in the middle of the tile. He didn't think much of it, assuming Travis had cleaned.

Zachary worked until 2 P.M., and then visited his girlfriend at her house. It was Amanda's mother's birthday and they celebrated with a homemade meal and cake. After dinner, Zachary brought Amanda to his place, and they watched movies in his room. At midnight he dropped her off at her parents', returned home, and went to bed.

The next morning—Saturday, June 7—Zachary's car wouldn't start. He knocked on Enrique's bedroom door.

"Do you have any jumper cables?" he asked.

"No. Sorry, man," Enrique said.

"Hey, have you seen Travis?"

"No. I think he's out of town or something. He hasn't been here all week."

Zachary was expecting mail and asked about the mailbox key. Neither roommate was sure where it was located. Zachary sent Travis a text message, but received no response.

After borrowing jumper cables from a neighbor, Zachary left the house to run errands. He spent the evening at Amanda's parents' house.

That night Enrique arrived home late. He noticed a glow from the second-story window. He assumed Travis had accidentally left the light on in his bathroom before leaving for his trip.

Upstairs in the house, the master bathroom light gleamed off Travis's corpse.

After thirty-six hours of being entombed in the bathroom, the face had turned dark purple, the rest of the body pale and limp—rigor had come and gone.

Gases had accumulated in the cadaver, causing the abdomen to become bloated and the intestines distended. The pressure of gases forced greenish-black body fluid to seep from the wounds.

As the bacteria inside the intestines grew, the body's skin began to slip away from the muscle. Pancreatic enzymes digested the organs.

A rancid stench emanated from the corpse. For a while it would be contained behind the master bedroom double doors.

Soon, it would infiltrate the entire house.

At about 1 P.M. on June 7, Jodi returned her white Ford Focus to Budget, six days after she picked it up. When Raphael Colombo Jr. saw the mileage on the car, he expressed surprise. Jodi had put 2,834 miles on the new vehicle. Colombo asked about her apparent change of plans.

"I decided to take a longer trip," Jodi said.

Inspecting the car, Colombo noticed the floor mats were missing. On the front and back seats were red stains that looked like Kool-Aid or juice. Using some cleaner, he dabbed the seats with a damp cloth until they were wiped clean.

Jodi left Redding and went back to her grandparents' house. That evening she worked her shift at Casa Ramos.

At 4:58 P.M. she sent Travis a text message about a $200 BMW payment. "Hey, I need to know when you're going to deposit that check."

At 10:21 P.M. that night, Jodi sent Travis an e-mail.

Hey You . . .
I haven't heard back from you. I hope you're not still
upset that I didn't come to see you. I just didn't have
enough time off. It's okay, sweetie, you're going to
be here in less than two weeks—we're going to see the
sights, check things off "the list," and all kinds of fun
things. Oregon is beautiful this time of year.

Jodi went on to discuss a possible visit to Mesa. She wanted
to stay at Travis's house while he was gone, if her budget allowed.

I know you'll be in Cancun, but I'll probably crash at
your house in your cozy bed anyway. . . . I know you
said the door is always open, but I wanted to give you
a heads up. If for any reason that won't work, let me
know and I'll make other arrangements. Your house
has always been my second home.

Jodi ended the e-mail telling Travis to get ahold of her before he left for Mexico.

That Sunday, Travis missed church—something he never did
when he was in town. At 9 A.M. both Zachary and Enrique
attended services, commenting on their roommate's absence.

"You haven't heard from Travis, have you?" Zachary asked.
"He never responded to my text."

By then, both Enrique and Zachary were convinced he was
out of town. They knew about his upcoming trip to Mexico;
it wasn't uncommon for him to leave without telling them.
Neither Enrique nor Zachary was concerned that something
could have happened to Travis.

That afternoon, Zachary sent Travis another text about the
mailbox key but received no response.

When Mimi Hall didn't see Travis at church, she was filled
with a sinking sense of dread. All week she had called,
e-mailed, and sent text messages. Each message went unanswered.

At first she was irritated. She thought he might be angry about the breakup or trying to prove a point. Eventually, she convinced herself that he must just be busy. He would call soon, she reasoned. By the weekend, her frustration had turned to worry.

Meanwhile, in Cancún, Chris and Sky Hughes had begun to panic. For days Chris had been calling. They had found an LDS Tour of Chichen Itza and Tulum, as well as an opportunity to swim with whale sharks. They wanted to know if Travis wanted to join them on the tour.

Chris left a voice mail and sent several text messages but received no response. Chris called again, only now Travis's voice mail was full. His stomach sank. Hanging up his cell phone, Chris turned to his wife. "Something's wrong."

By Monday a foul odor had consumed the house on East Queensborough Avenue. Enrique was the first to notice. It was like nothing he had ever smelled before—a noxious scent, tinged with sickly sweetness.

What is that? he wondered.

Enrique didn't see Zachary that morning and didn't have a chance to mention the smell. Later, it would seem strange that no one had noticed it earlier.

Both Enrique and Zachary worked that day. After dinner Zachary picked up Amanda and they returned to Travis's house. Zachary brought Amanda upstairs and they stayed closed off in his room watching the 2002 romantic comedy *Sweet Home Alabama*.

At 9:30 P.M. Enrique arrived home from a church activity. He showered in the guest bathroom, got dressed, and went to his room.

An hour later the doorbell rang.

Outside the house on East Queensborough Avenue, Mimi peered through the glass cutouts in the front door. Inside she could see the dog in the foyer. She rang the doorbell again. No answer.

Earlier that night Mimi went to Family Home Evening,

expecting to see Travis. When he wasn't there, she tried to call him—no answer. Their flight was in less than twelve hours and she still had not heard from Travis in a week.

Finally, at 10 P.M., she drove to his house. When no one came to the door after her repeated rings she got back into her car and returned home.

"I tried calling and texting him. He didn't respond," Mimi later recalled. "At home I sent him a Facebook message because I was getting scared."

A few minutes later, she scrolled through her cell phone, searching for numbers of mutual friends that may have heard from Travis. She called Michelle Lowery.

When Michelle heard the concern in Mimi's voice, she knew something was wrong. Michelle was with her boyfriend Dallin Forrest. They had just returned to Dallin's house following an errand.

Michelle told Mimi that she would call Taylor Searle.

After work Taylor had decided to go for a bike ride. He had ridden to a friend's apartment where he spent a few hours and had just left when he got the call.

"Have you heard from Travis lately?" Michelle asked.

Taylor thought about it. He hadn't actually seen Travis since they went out for sushi a week prior. Normally they talked and exchanged texts or online chats every other day. When he didn't hear from Travis, he assumed he was in Cancún.

"I thought he was out of town," he said.

Michelle explained that his trip with Mimi was the next day.

"I'm concerned," Michelle said. "Do you think we should go over there?"

Michelle turned to her boyfriend. "Do you mind if we drive over to Travis's and see what's going on?"

A few moments later Dallin and Michelle were parked outside the house on East Queensborough Avenue, waiting for Mimi to arrive.

From his car, Dallin noticed a single light shining from the second-story window. It was the only light on in the entire house.

CHAPTER 20

"Oh my God," Mimi Hall cried as she dialed 911 on her cell phone.

"Okay, what's going on?" the operator asked.

"A friend of ours is dead in his bedroom," Mimi said, her voice shaking. "We haven't heard from him in a while. We think he's dead. His roommate just went in there and said there's a lot of blood."

After stumbling away from the grisly scene, Dallin Forrest had whisked Mimi and Michelle down the stairs and out the front door. Travis's dog had followed. Michelle hunched in the driveway, holding the pug's collar, while Mimi phoned for emergency assistance on her cell phone.

On the front lawn, Dallin observed Zachary standing close to his girlfriend. After fleeing Travis's room, Zachary had retrieved Amanda from his bedroom and exited the house. Zachary appeared somber and shaken—an expression Dallin imagined mirrored his own.

Dallin approached Zachary. "Is everybody out of the house?"

It was then that Zachary realized Enrique was likely still inside.

"Stay here," he told Amanda. He went back inside the

house, up the stairs, and toward his roommate's bedroom. Zachary pounded on the door.

"Something happened to Travis," he said. "The police are on their way."

Meanwhile, Mimi had passed her cell phone to Dallin. The 911 operator had dispatched police and paramedics, but requested to speak with someone who had seen the body.

"What's going on?" the operator asked.

"He's dead. He's in his bedroom, in the shower," Dallin blurted out.

His mind reeling, Dallin tried to compose himself.

"I freaked out on the inside but I tried to steady myself, you know, cause you're trying to talk on the phone with 911," Dallin later recalled. "I didn't want the girls to go nuts."

"Okay, how did this happen?" the operator asked. "Do you have any idea?"

"No, we have no idea, everyone has been wondering about him for a few days."

"Okay, she said that there is blood. Is it coming from his head? Or . . ."

"It's all over the place."

The operator asked if Travis had been displaying signs of depression.

"I don't know Travis," Dallin told the operator. "I'm the wrong person to be asking."

"Okay, please put someone on the phone who knows Travis," the operator requested.

As Dallin passed the phone to Michelle, he noticed that Zachary had reappeared on the lawn with another man—Enrique Cortez. The roommates and Amanda stayed huddled together, a few yards away from where Dallin, Mimi, and Michelle were standing.

Haltingly, Zachary explained the situation to Enrique. Dallin overheard him mutter something about the master bathroom.

"That's why the light has been on for so long," Enrique exclaimed.

Mimi called out to the roommates, "When was the last time you saw Travis?"

"It was either Wednesday or Thursday," Enrique said.

Zachary nodded in agreement. "Wednesday. Maybe Thursday."

"Had you checked his room since the last time you saw him?" Dallin asked.

Zachary shook his head, mumbling about "Cancún" and a "business trip."

"His car was in the garage," Enrique said. "I thought someone drove him to the airport."

Dallin explained that the 911 operator had asked if Travis was suicidal.

"I didn't know Travis well enough to know if he was self-destructive," Dallin told the roommates.

They discussed Travis and his recent relationships with Lisa and Mimi. Neither roommate thought he appeared depressed.

"Who could want to hurt him?" Dallin asked.

Only one name came to mind: Jodi Arias.

Travis hadn't been scared of her, but those close to him found her behavior unsettling. Standing outside Travis's house that night, talk turned to Jodi. They each shared stories about stalking, stolen journals, and slashed tires. Many close to Travis believed Jodi was fixated on him. But had her obsession turned deadly?

Before Travis's death could even be declared a homicide, his friends would identify Jodi as a strong potential suspect. Tales of her obsession would fill the pages of the police report.

A few blocks away, Taylor Searle was racing toward Travis's house. He had been on the phone with Michelle during the search and was the first person, outside the house, to learn Travis's fate.

Taylor had just arrived back at his house on his bike when Zachary had retrieved the key to Travis's bedroom. As

Dallin and Zachary searched the room, Taylor spoke with Michelle.

Suddenly, Michelle had begun to scream. "There's blood on the carpet. A lot of blood!"

Seconds later Zachary had come out of the bathroom, telling Michelle what he had found. "He's not alive!" she cried into the phone.

Taylor went numb.

She killed him, he thought. *Jodi killed him. She did it.*

Grabbing his laptop, Taylor jumped in his car.

He raced toward Travis's house, going nearly a hundred miles an hour. On the way, he ran every stop sign and red light.

Taylor had something urgent police needed to see. He believed Travis had known his killer. Taylor had warned Travis about her just a week prior to his death.

Through a fog of tears, Michelle spoke with the 911 operator.

"You're a good friend of Travis's, correct?" the operator asked.

"Yes, I am," she said. "Yeah."

"Has he been depressed at all? Thinking about committing suicide? Anything like that?"

"I don't think he's been thinking about committing suicide. He's been really depressed because he broke up with this girl. And he was all upset about that. But I don't think he would actually kill himself over that."

"Has he been threatened by anyone recently?"

"Yes, he has. He has an ex-girlfriend that's been bothering him. And following him and slashing tires and things like that," Michelle said.

"Do you know the ex-girlfriend's name?" the operator asked.

"Her name is Jodi."

"Do you know if he's ever reported it to police?"

"No, he hasn't reported anything about Jodi's behavior," Michelle said.

Michelle handed the phone back to Mimi.

"There's a girl who has been stalking him and she might have some information," Mimi told the operator.

"Okay. I'm just going to keep you on the phone until officers or paramedics arrive," the operator said.

"Okay, I think I can hear the sirens now."

Sirens wailed in the distance, growing louder with each passing second. As police cruisers and paramedics surrounded the house, Dallin's gaze drifted to the light shining in the upstairs window. He closed his eyes, yearning to erase the image of Travis's naked corpse from his memory.

Detective Scott Molander, a seven-year veteran of the Mesa Police Department with dark hair and a strong build, approached Dallin and requested to take a statement. Other detectives isolated Michelle, Mimi, Zachary, and Enrique for interviews. Later, they would all be taken to the Mesa Police Department to give official statements.

Still in shock, Dallin explained to Detective Molander his relationship to Travis—that he had only met him a few times and knew him mostly through Michelle. He couldn't provide much information about Travis's relationships, aside from what he had heard about Jodi.

"I heard random talk tonight about some crazy girl that I don't know, I've never heard of," he said. "I just picked up some random talk tonight about her slashing his tires and breaking into his house."

"But this is what other people were telling you?" Molander asked.

"This is just things I heard tonight about, you know, some crazy stalker girl," he said.

Dallin filled the detective in on the events of the evening, carefully walking through the details about how the three friends met outside the house, encountered Zachary upstairs, and made entry into the master bedroom.

"I looked down and could see blood on the carpet," he recalled. "It wasn't like blood when you get cut. It looked really dark, it looked chunky. It looked like mud, almost like an odd color of mud."

It was then that Dallin said he began to panic.

"I'm kind of hesitant," he recalled. "I'm freaking out and, you know, I turn the corner and see the bloody footsteps. Huge blood puddles like footsteps."

"Take your time. This isn't something that people run across every day, okay?" said Detective Molander.

The glass door to the shower stall was open, Dallin said. The smell and sight were sickening.

"It looked like his body was halfway sitting," Dallin recalled. "It looked, from what I saw, that the neck and face was really blue, or purple, even."

Meanwhile, Zachary Billings explained to another detective how Travis's disappearance went unnoticed. Zachary said he hadn't been in the house that much, having spent most of the week at his girlfriend's place. Wednesday or Thursday was the last time he saw Travis. Both he and Enrique assumed he was out of town.

Earlier in the evening the doorbell had rung repeatedly, but neither he nor Enrique answered. This was not unusual because neither roommate answered the door unless they were expecting company, Zachary said. For the most part, the three men kept to themselves.

"Can you think of anyone who would want to harm Travis?" the detective asked.

Zachary immediately mentioned Jodi. When he first moved into the house in January, Jodi had been around constantly. She often showed up at odd hours. This was something that had fueled many arguments between Travis and Jodi, Zachary said.

"How would she get into the house?" the detective asked.

"She would just walk in," Zachary said. "Travis never locked his doors. She would just let herself in and make herself at home."

"What was security like in the house?"

"There really wasn't any," Zachary said. "When Travis is home the front door is almost always unlocked. I don't even have a key."

Zachary explained Jodi had moved to Arizona only after her breakup with Travis. He felt Travis was helping her out since she didn't have any friends in town. Over time, however, Travis became upset by her behavior.

Zachary also told police about Travis's relationship with Lisa. To Zachary, it seemed Jodi's interference had doomed the relationship. Lisa didn't like the fact that Jodi was always hanging around. Finally, in April, Jodi moved back to Yreka.

It was the last time Zachary could remember seeing Jodi. As far as Zachary knew, Jodi was still in California.

Detectives also interviewed Enrique, although he didn't have much to add. Enrique had only lived there a few weeks and knew little about Travis. During the two weeks he rented his room, Enrique said he had never even had a meal with Travis.

Neither he nor Zachary remembered any strangers at the house or unusual cars parked in the neighborhood.

In separate interviews, Mimi and Michelle also spoke with the police. Mimi explained her relationship with Travis, their breakup, and the Cancún trip. Michelle told the police about Travis's previous romantic relationships.

Both women also told stories of Jodi. Neither had met her personally, but had heard much about Travis's "stalker" ex-girlfriend. They reiterated stories of her obsessive behavior to the investigators.

"I was worried because he had told me about an ex-girlfriend who had done some pretty serious, psychotic, obsessive things to him and his friends," Mimi said in a statement. "I was actually afraid that girl would be at his house."

As the witnesses were being questioned, Taylor Searle arrived at the house. He approached the nearest detective and opened his laptop. The image on the screen was a picture of Jodi from her Facebook page.

"This is the girl who did it," Taylor told the detective.

"When he showed up dead, I knew it was her right away," Taylor later recalled.

Since his breakup with Jodi, Taylor said that Travis had

caught her stealing his journals, taking pages of the new book he was writing, and hacking into his Facebook page, he told detectives. On one occasion, Travis caught her breaking into his house. Travis had also been convinced that it was Jodi who slashed his tires and sent harassing e-mails to a girl he was dating, Taylor said.

Travis had spoken to Jodi last week. He confronted her for hacking into his Facebook account. In the conversation, Travis had scolded Jodi.

"Aren't you afraid she's going to hurt you?" Taylor had asked Travis.

"That was a week before his death," Taylor now told the detective.

Word of Travis's death spread quickly. Within moments of the discovery, many of his friends and family had learned of his death through a series of macabre phone calls and text messages.

A revolving group of friends gathered outside Travis's house that night, some staying until the early-morning hours. At any one time nearly a dozen stunned, teary-eyed people sat on the curb desperately seeking answers.

Among those gathered near the house was Aaron Mortensen, who had watched movies with Travis just about a week prior. At first he had only heard that a body was found at Travis's residence and that it looked as if it was a possible suicide. When he arrived on the scene he began to learn more details.

"I went over to his house and saw the police there," Aaron later said. "I just kind of sat there on the curb, across the street from his house, with everyone else, till probably five thirty in the morning, just sitting there. We were all just in shock. I was a wreck."

One thousand miles away in Yreka, Jodi got a phone call from her and Travis's friend and former travel companion, Dan Freeman. She was at her grandparents' house in the living room when her phone rang.

"Something is wrong. There are some police at Travis's

house. He . . . he is . . . . ," Dan stuttered. "They're saying he's dead."

Doubling over, Jodi began to sob uncontrollably. Jodi began making phone calls to anyone she knew who knew Travis. Several of the friends outside of Travis's house saw her number on their phone.

As one of those friends was telling an officer about Travis's slashed tires, his phone rang. It was Jodi. He showed his phone to detectives.

"Don't answer it right now," the detective said.

After midnight Jodi called Travis's bishop, confirming the news that Travis was dead.

Jodi appeared desperate to know what was happening, what police had discovered. That night Jodi also called the Mesa Police Station. She wanted to speak with a detective.

In Cancún, Chris and Sky Hughes were asleep in their hotel room when the phone rang. Sky answered groggily.

"Hello," Sky said. "He's asleep. Okay."

She passed the phone to her husband. "It's Dave Hall."

As he reached for the phone, Chris knew the news would be bad.

"I hate to tell you this, Chris," he said. "Chris, Travis is dead."

The color drained from Chris' face. *It can't be true. Travis can't be dead. How can this be?*

"I went numb," Chris later said. "I can't believe it. I just can't believe it. My friend, my brother, my business partner is gone."

Late that night, after being briefed on the situation, Detective Esteban Flores got his first glimpse at the victim. Immediately, it was clear: this was a homicide.

"Let's get out of here," Flores told the other detectives, "and come back with a warrant."

CHAPTER 21

Sunlight cut through the slats of the blinds, spilling onto the tile floor. The blood drops slathering the master bathroom on East Queensborough Avenue glistened in the light of day—slick and shiny.

From the doorway of the bathroom, Detective Esteban Flores observed the scene as one of the forensic investigators photographed the body. Squatting at the end of the shower stall, the investigator framed a photo with his digital camera. The flash brightened the room.

"How long do you think he's been there?" Flores asked.

The investigator leaned in to frame a close-up of the hacking wound across the victim's throat.

"Three or four days, at least," said the investigator. "He's well into decomp."

Detective Flores had spent the morning of June 10—the day after the body was discovered—obtaining a warrant and assembling a team of detectives and forensic investigators to execute a search of the house. They arrived at 9:53 A.M. and relieved the officer on guard by the front door. Throughout the night police had been stationed at the house for security purposes.

The initial focus of the investigation that morning was on

Travis's body and the surrounding areas, including the master bedroom and bathroom. After preliminary photos were complete, the team entered the house, wearing protective footwear and gloves to minimize contamination.

Flores and a fellow detective documented the scene and searched for evidence. Meanwhile, two forensic chemists collected and photographed biological evidence. In addition, two latent print examiners looked for fingerprints. Bright yellow numbered placards were placed around the bathroom as evidence was photographed and collected.

The shower stall where Travis's body was discovered sat alongside a stand-alone tub. Hanging on the wall above it was a framed painting of a tropical paradise—palm trees swaying in the wind at sunset. Three candles sat on the corner edge of the tub.

A long mirror was affixed to the adjacent wall, above a white countertop with double sinks. On the opposite wall was a linen closet and enclosed toilet room.

Blood and castoff spanned the entire width of the bathroom. Such a large amount indicated a savage attack—one where the victim had fought back.

In many knife attacks, Flores knew it was not uncommon for the assailant to accidentally cut themselves. It was possible that not all the blood in the room was Travis's; some may very well have come from the killer.

Standing in the doorframe, Detective Flores examined the blood pattern. Each stain—every drop—told a story. Each time the knife was plunged into Travis's body—every droplet that flung from its blade—created a coded missive. It was Detective Flores's job to decipher it.

Carefully stepping over the puddles on the floor, Flores approached the bathroom counter. Dried blood coated the mirror and sink. The spatter was heaviest near the sink closest to the shower. Some of the blood appeared diluted, as though water had been spilled on it for a period of time. On top of the diluted areas were fat, chunky blood drops.

Flores recognized the pattern as heavy arterial spurting—

the intermittent gush of blood that occurred when an artery is cut. In this case, it may have come from any number of the wounds.

The sink had a combination of both diluted blood and heavy spatter on top of it. When the attack began, the faucet in the sink may have been running. The water was possibly turned off as Travis continued to bleed for a few seconds.

Glancing around the countertop, something caught Flores's eye—a glint in the sunlight. Flores's stare shifted from the counter to the floor, where a small brass object was resting in a tacky gob of blood. It was a spent bullet casing.

"Was he shot?" Flores asked the investigator photographing the body.

"It's hard to tell, there's so many wounds. It's possible." The camera lit up the bathroom as the investigator snapped another photo. "Why?"

"There's a shell casing over here," Flores said. "It looks small caliber. A .22, possibly .32."

The casing was photographed and marked for collection. With a gloved hand, Flores then picked it up. A closer examination revealed it was a Winchester .25 caliber shell casing.

But there was no weapon near the body. A thorough search of the house would reveal no gun, bullets, or holster.

Flores followed the blood path toward the adjacent wall where two windows faced the street. The white wood blinds were speckled with crimson drops. Some of these droplets were below waist level; others were as high as the very top slat of the blind—over six feet.

The blood spatter continued low on the adjoining walls, trailing toward the doorjamb of the enclosed toilet room. Flores entered the cramped room, crouched down, and cocked his head, discovering blood speckled even on the underside of the toilet bowl.

Stepping out of the toilet room, Flores followed the blood trail out of the bathroom and into the long tiled hallway toward the bedroom. On the carpet, near the entryway was the largest blood pool—several days old.

At some point during the struggle Travis broke away from

the killer and headed toward the bedroom. The blood had pooled in large puddles as he fled. The killer had likely continued to stab Travis as he attempted to escape, preventing him from breaking through the double doors and running for help. The large blood pool at the edge of the carpet may very well have been where the killer dealt the fatal blow and possibly where his neck was slit.

Glancing back down the hallway, Flores noted blood on the tile floor and smeared down the entire length of both walls. Narrowing his eyes, Flores looked closer at the tile—down the center of the path was a section void of blood. For a moment, Flores was puzzled. *What could have caused that sort of pattern,* he wondered.

Flores examined the varied blood trail. Large, thick puddles of dried blood textured parts of the tile floor; other areas were diluted.

Flores opened the linen closet, next to the sink. The shelves were filled with towels, toilet paper, and soap. On the floor in the closet sat a large box of copy paper. On the outside of the box were reddish watermarks about three inches high.

At some point, likely after the attack, there had been a large amount of water on the floor, diluting some of the blood. It appeared as though the murderer had flooded the bathroom in an attempt to destroy evidence.

The absence of blood in the path was likely caused as the body was dragged back into the shower. Perhaps the water on the tile floor had helped the killer slide the dead weight toward the stall.

Flores approached the shower stall, crouched down, and examined the corpse. There were several visible wounds—the most prominent the deep laceration to the throat, spanning from ear to ear.

Blackish body fluid trickled from a puncture wound in the center of the chest. The flow pattern was consistent with the position the body was sitting.

The rest of the chest was clear of blood and body fluid. The other wounds on the torso and hands were clean. It appeared as if Travis's body had been washed postmortem. On the shower floor, next to the body, was a clear plastic cup, which had very little blood on it. The cup may have been used to clean blood from the body.

Travis's corpse was photographed where it lay—each visible wound on his torso, neck, and head documented.

In addition to the blood and bullet casing, the forensic investigators located several items of interest. On the floor and baseboards near the shower were multiple hair fibers. One of the strands was long and could not have come from the victim. The hair would be tested for DNA comparison, which could later possibly be linked to a suspect.

During the search by the latent print examiner, a bloody palm print was found near the entrance of the bathroom hall. The print was at waist level alongside several bloody smudges on the wall. The print may have come from Travis as he was attempting to break free. It could also have come from the killer.

The forensics team cut out and removed the section of the wall containing the latent print. The rectangular piece of drywall was seized so that it could later be analyzed at the crime lab.

At about 11 A.M. investigators from the Maricopa County Office of the Medical Examiner arrived to remove the body. The coroner noted the numerous injuries on torso, hands, head, and throat—all of which appeared to be stab wounds. Shifting the remains forward revealed several additional gashes on Travis's upper back. As the corpse was lifted, body fluid dripped thickly from the wounds.

All his injuries could not be accurately documented at the scene because of the amount of trauma, dried blood, and decomposition. The coroner carefully scooped up the body and zipped it inside a black body bag. Travis's remains were wheeled out of the house on a gurney and secured in the back of the coroner's van.

While still at the crime scene, executing the search warrant, Detective Flores got a message from a dispatcher at the Mesa Police Station. A woman had called several times wanting to speak to the investigator in charge of Travis Alexander's homicide. It was Jodi Arias.

By then Flores had been briefed on the witness statements and the name Jodi Arias had become familiar. Jodi was described by Travis's friends as being completely obsessed with her ex-boyfriend. If these allegations were true she had a strong motive for murder.

Flores was anxious to nail down her statement. She wasn't yet considered a suspect, but she was a strong investigative lead. Breaking temporarily from the scene, Flores stepped outside the house and returned her call early that afternoon.

"I got a message from one of my patrol officers that you needed to talk to me about something?" Flores began the conversation.

"Well, I just wanted to offer any assistance. I was a really good friend of Travis's. And I don't know a lot of anything," Jodi said.

"What have you heard so far?" asked Flores.

"I heard that he was—that he passed away," she said. "I heard all kinds of rumors that there was a lot of blood. I heard that his roommate found him, people were . . . I'm sorry. I'm upset. I heard nobody has been able to get ahold of him for a week."

Jodi told the detective that she had dated Travis, explaining the relationship and eventual breakup. The cause for the breakup, she said, was jealousy.

"Even though we broke up, we're no longer boyfriend and girlfriend, we decided to remain friends," Jodi said.

"Okay, so you guys were not, like, romantically together?" Flores asked.

"We were intimate, but I wouldn't say romantic as far as the relationship goes," Jodi said.

The last time she spoke to Travis was on Tuesday, June 3, at 11 P.M., or 11:30 P.M., she said. The week of the murder Jodi said she was in Utah visiting friends. Jodi said she knew of Travis's business trip to Cancún and had wanted to stay at his place while he was away.

"That was around April that you last saw him, right?" Flores asked.

"Early April."

"You haven't been back in town since then?"

"No, I haven't at all."

Jodi explained that she had heard about his death through mutual friends.

"I heard a lot of rumors, and that there was a lot of blood," she said.

"I can tell you that we're investigating it as a homicide," Flores said. "It's important for us to find out who would want to harm him."

Flores asked if she could think of anyone who might want Travis dead.

"He got his tires slashed. It was last year," she said calmly. "I was worried about that. He never locked his doors. And I told him—I would tell him, 'Lock your doors.' And he'd be, like, 'You're not my mom,' you know?"

In preparation for his trip to Cancún, Travis had been working out to be able to look slim in his "boxer shorts or swim trunks," Jodi said.

"He's so strong. I don't see how anyone could overpower him," she said.

"Well, yeah. It would take two people, maybe more to overpower him," Flores said. "So no ideas come to mind on who might want to hurt him?"

She brought up one of Travis's former roommates, explaining that he had been kicked out of the house after it was discovered he had been preying on women in the ward. Other than that Jodi said she had no idea who would want Travis dead.

Flores then confronted her with what he had heard from Travis's friends.

"We did talk to certain people," he said. "And they didn't have the best of things to say about you."

He explained stories of her stalking, breaking into his house, and hacking his Facebook and MySpace accounts.

"He gave me his Facebook password and MySpace password," Jodi interrupted, explaining that it had been done to reestablish trust in their relationship.

It hadn't worked and he had changed his password, she said.

"We had a conversation where he made it clear he was not comfortable with that anymore," Jodi said. "We're both trying to move on."

"Why would they start pointing fingers in your direction right away?" Flores asked.

"Oh gosh," Jodi said. "I don't know. Maybe because I'm the ex-girlfriend, we've had lots of fights."

"Well," Flores said. "I'm glad you called because there were a lot of concerns."

At the end of the conversation, Flores reiterated how important it was to know who had such hatred toward Travis.

"It was an angry situation. Somebody went in there to hurt him and they did—hurt him really bad," Flores said. "When we see things like this we know people hate each other."

Throughout the conversation, Jodi seemed cool and collected. She asked questions about Travis's death and seemed genuinely upset.

Is she a distraught former girlfriend? Or an obsessed, jilted lover?

As Flores ended the conversation with Jodi, he wondered: *Have I just spoken to Travis's killer?*

While Flores was on the phone with Jodi, the forensics' team had completed the initial search of the second floor. Flores stepped back inside the house and began to investigate the downstairs.

In the den, Flores located Travis's cell phone, which was plugged into the charger. He switched it on and reviewed the activity.

The last outgoing text was made at 12:13 P.M., on June 4, the last day Travis had been seen alive. The message was sent to Chris Hughes. Five minutes later, at 12:18 P.M., someone called the phone and checked the voice mail.

There had been other incoming calls and text messages, but none had been answered.

Also in the den, detectives found Travis's Dell laptop computer, which they impounded. Computer forensic detectives with the Mesa Police Department would later examine the computer, determining the last activity was at 4:19 P.M. on June 4. Someone had checked Travis's e-mail.

Based on the computer and phone information, Flores would later roughly estimate the day of death as June 4. Evidence and witness statements would further narrow that time frame to between 5:30 and 5:35 P.M.

As he glanced around the office, Flores noticed an empty box for a black digital SLR Sony camera. He remembered the camera bag he had discovered in the loft. So far the camera hadn't been located.

After combing the remainder of the ground floor, Flores moved the search to the laundry room. As he was exiting the house the night prior, he had spotted a reddish brown stain on the washing machine, which appeared to be blood.

Earlier this day a forensic chemist had swabbed the machine, confirming it was indeed blood. A sample was taken for testing.

Flores opened the door of the dryer while another investigator photographed the rumpled knot of brown and beige sheets, blankets, and pillow cases—the missing bedding from Travis's room. The evidence was photographed, marked, and bagged for collection.

Next, Flores turned his attention to the washer. Tangled inside were towels, sweat pants, shorts, T-shirts, and underwear—Travis's Mormon undergarments. Sitting on top of the clothing was a digital camera.

"This is interesting," Flores said. It was a black digital SLR Sony—the same make and model camera as the box he found in the den. It appeared water damaged, as if it had been run through a wash cycle with the clothes.

What is a camera doing in the washing machine? he thought.

Once it was photographed, Flores picked it up and opened

the slat on the side of the camera's body. The memory card was still inside, although it also likely had severe water damage.

Both the camera and digital card were seized as evidence and sent to the Mesa Police Department crime lab to see if any information could be recovered. It was a curious discovery. There was no innocent reason for a new digital camera to wind up in the washing machine.

Whatever images this camera had captured, someone had wanted them destroyed.

Detectives would ultimately spend three full days in the house searching for evidence. Fingerprints would be processed from the master bathroom, bedroom, and laundry room, as well as the front and back doors. A bloody shoe print near the bathroom was also photographed as evidence. Additionally, the faucets and drain traps were removed from the master bathroom to be tested for DNA.

Detectives would also confiscate various electronics from the house, including multiple USB drives, two Toshiba laptops, hard drives, and a black laptop bag containing a Dell Inspiron1200 laptop. In Travis's home office, a Compaq Presario V2000 laptop, CDs, DVDs, and a Verizon Pocket PC phone were also seized.

Detective Michael Melendez, a computer forensic detective, would be placed in charge of recovering data from the electronics.

Melendez would spend weeks poring through Travis's e-mail, Facebook, and MySpace accounts.

By examining the dead man's final correspondence he would piece together the disturbing final hours of Travis Alexander's life.

CHAPTER 22

ravis is dead," Jodi scribbled in her diary on June 10, 2008. "What happened?!? Travis, what is this?"

In Yreka, Jodi seemed to be in deep mourning. She took to her diary to express her grief.

"I've been numb, mostly. But last night was extremely hard," she wrote on June 11. "I broke down as I finally brought myself around to going to bed. It was 2:30 A.M. I wanted so badly to call Travis, but knowing he wouldn't answer was too much to bear. And knowing he wasn't calling me anytime soon was just killing me. I broke down as I climbed into my bed and cried and cried until I fell asleep."

Jodi spent the next few days walking around in a trance.

"It feels like he hasn't called me in too long. I hear him singing, I hear him laugh," she wrote.

Jodi didn't have many friends, and even fewer close friends. But over the next few days she reached out to some of the people in her life, including Leslie Udy.

"I can't imagine why anyone would do that to Travis," Jodi cried to Leslie. "How could anyone do that? He was such a wonderful person!"

To Leslie, Jodi seemed distraught, crying and sobbing. They spoke for several hours. Leslie told Jodi that she would be there for her if she wanted to speak.

"If you need someone to talk to I keep my phone by my bed," Leslie said.

At 2 A.M. the following morning Jodi called Leslie. Through tears Jodi told Leslie that this was the time at night that she and Travis would always talk.

"I've lost my best friend," Jodi cried. "I don't know what to do."

Over the next few days she wrote poems to Travis. She posted a letter directed at Travis on her MySpace page. Later, she took it down.

Just days after the murder she transformed her MySpace page into a digital shrine to Travis. Creating an online photo album, she posted twenty-five photographs that seemed to tell the story of their relationship.

In it were photos of Travis at Prepaid Legal conferences and various images from their trips. The cover was an over-exposed black-and-white photograph of Travis and Jodi. In the picture they were sitting close together, their heads touching. Both were softly smiling. Jodi titled the photo "Friends Forever."

Jodi also changed her MySpace status, listing her mood as "melancholy," represented by a frowning face. On her status she wrote she "misses Travis."

"See you soon, my friend, but not soon enough," she wrote.

The following day she signed his online obituary guest book.

"Travis, what can I say to you that I haven't already said? I am so grateful for the endless hours of conversation and amazing experiences we've shared. Thank you for having the courage to share the Gospel with me. You've had one of the greatest impacts on my life, and have forever altered its course for the better. I love you, my friend, and always will."

As she appeared to grieve, Jodi reached out to Travis's family, sending his sister, Tanisha Sorenson, a direct message through MySpace to express her condolences. Tall and thin, with long reddish-brown hair, Tanisha was a mother of four who lived in Southern California.

On June 13, Jodi also sent twenty white irises to Travis's

grandmother Norma. The flowers held special significance to Jodi.

"Travis always told me he liked the name Iris for a girl," Jodi wrote in her journal. "If I ever have a son I'll name him Alexander."

Travis's family had suffered many tragedies. The Alexander children had lost both their mother and father. Now, they had the agonizing task of burying their thirty-year-old brother.

Late on the night of June 9, a church friend had called Travis's grandmother Norma Sarvey, in Riverside.

"I hate to have to tell you this," he said, "but Travis has been killed."

In despair, Norma phoned Travis's sister Samantha Turbeville. Thin, with deep-set eyes and dark hair, Samantha worked for the police department in Carlsbad, California. When Samantha later spoke with Detective Flores, he confirmed the worst.

"We're investigating it as a homicide," Flores told Samantha.

The rest of the family learned of the murder through a series of agonizing phone calls. All the siblings were in a state of shock and disbelief.

"Everyone loved Travis," said Samantha, the week Travis's body was discovered. "His life was about helping other people and making the world a better place. He was a great person and very religious. This doesn't usually happen to people like him."

Over the next few days several of Travis's siblings traveled to Mesa to search for answers and to make his final arrangements.

Travis's older brothers, Greg and Gary, were the first to arrive and to speak directly with detectives. Although they asked many questions, they were given few answers. To avoid compromising the investigation, detectives kept many of the details quiet.

Both Greg and Gary told investigators they hadn't been

close with Travis since he moved to Mesa and had no idea who could have done this to him.

The day following the discovery of the body, Hillary and Samantha also arrived in Mesa, along with Travis's best friend, Deanna Reid. They, too, were told little. With no clues and scant information, all they could do was pray.

Over the next few days, Greg expressed his disbelief at the loss on a memorial Web page established for Travis.

"Travis, little brother this is so hard to accept," Greg wrote on June 12. "Who would ever hurt you? I love you, and I promise I will never rest until I see justice. I love you."

Stepping inside the house on East Queensborough Avenue was eerie for Travis's family.

By June 13, police tape no longer cordoned off the house. Homicide detectives had completed the search, confiscating much of the personal property deemed evidence. Still, to the family it was impossible to forget that this had once been a crime scene—that it was where their brother had died.

It was strange how much of it appeared normal, just as Travis had left it. Food in the refrigerator had only just begun to spoil. It felt like Travis had gone on vacation, as if he would come through the front door at any moment.

As the siblings traveled deeper inside the house, however, they discovered the remnants of the investigation. In the den, the computer cords sat at the edge of the desk next to a faint outline in dust where Travis's laptop had been. Upstairs in the hallway was a large rectangular hole in the wall, where a piece of the drywall had been removed.

A section of blood-stained carpet had been cut from the master bedroom. In the bathroom, light pink streaks marred the white floor trim where areas were tested for blood. Black fingerprint dust smeared the doors.

Although a crime-scene clean-up team had been brought in to scrub the blood from the bedroom and bathroom, no amount of cleanser could erase all traces of the murder.

For the next few days the family inventoried their brother's belongings. Sorting through his possessions was emotionally draining. The house was filled with memories of Travis—his journals, his books, his furniture, his clothes.

In the den, they discovered a quote printed out and pinned to the wall. It read: "The difference between a stumbling block and a stepping stone is the character of the individual walking the path."

It was so like Travis to keep inspirational reminders to battle through life's difficulties. At a time like this it helped to remember Travis's character.

While in town making arrangements for the funeral, Travis's sister Hillary Wilcox visited the Mesa Arizona Temple. She sat in the Celestial Room, a space in the temple where individuals pray, meditate, and converse with God. In most temples, celestial rooms were elegant, beautiful, and brighter in decor than other rooms.

After an hour sitting in the room, Hillary became lost in thought. Suddenly, she was struck with an overwhelming sense of peace. She felt Travis's presence—in her mind she could see him in heaven. She knew he was where he needed to be.

"I was gazing and I totally saw my brother with that big cheesy smile just as happy as can be," Hillary said. "I know that he's there and I know he's so happy. I know this is true and we will see him again one day."

In the days following the discovery of Travis's body, Jodi contacted several of their mutual friends, inquiring about the details of the homicide. Among the people she spoke with was Travis's bishop.

Jodi had been convinced that Travis had found the woman he wanted to marry, but the bishop said it hadn't worked out with Mimi.

"Mimi wasn't interested in Travis," the bishop told her.

Jodi seemed surprised. In her mind Travis was moving toward marriage.

"It was the bishop who told me that she essentially turned

him down," Jodi later told detectives. "I didn't know that Mimi didn't feel that way."

Jodi confessed to the bishop her ongoing sexual relationship with Travis. As he explained the process of repentance, Jodi asked an unusual question.

"Should I tell Mimi that Travis and I were sleeping together?" she asked.

"No." The bishop shook his head. "Nothing good would come of that."

To several of Travis's closest friends, Jodi confessed the true nature of their sexual relationship. Following his death, it seemed as if she wanted people to know that Travis wasn't the devout Mormon he presented himself to be.

While seemingly in the throes of grief, life generally went on as normal for Jodi. She worked her job, spent time with her friends and siblings, and made plans for future trips.

And she continued to develop her budding relationship with Ryan Burns. Over the next few weeks they continued to speak nearly every day and exchange e-mails. During many of their conversations Jodi talked about Travis and the investigation into his murder. Mostly, however, they discussed their new relationship.

In one conversation, Jodi brought up their sexual encounter in Utah and why it hadn't progressed further.

"I didn't want you to regret anything that happened," Ryan told her.

Jodi complimented him on his restraint.

"I'm a big girl," Jodi said. "You don't have to protect my feelings."

In the days following the discovery of Travis's body, suspicions about Jodi swelled. Those closest to Travis, who had witnessed some of the more bizarre encounters between the couple, were all but certain that Jodi was the killer.

Others who had befriended Jodi throughout the time she lived in Mesa believed it was impossible. A tension formed between Travis's groups of friends.

As the whispers grew louder, several people mentioned to Jodi what people were saying. She became increasingly aware she was being identified as a murder suspect. Later, she told her mom and dad she was worried—but not because she had anything to do with the crime. Jodi was bothered her name was being sullied.

"I told them that a lot of people were dropping my name. And I said I'm not worried about it because I didn't do it but it's hurting my reputation," Jodi later told detectives. "It's casting me in a bad light."

When Sandra Arias heard her daughter's name was being tied to a murder investigation, she grew concerned. Jodi had been desperately in love with her ex-boyfriend and, on the day of the murder, she had been out of town. Sandra knew her daughter had mental issues, but it seemed unfathomable she would resort to murder.

"Did you go to Arizona?" Sandra asked Jodi.

"No. I was nowhere near Arizona," Jodi insisted. "I have gas receipts and everything to prove it."

Intertwined with questions about who had taken Travis's life, his friends endured a wide range of emotions. Each of his loved ones seemed to handle the loss differently.

Some delved further into their faith, believing Travis was with God. Others found it difficult to see how this could be part of God's plan.

For Taylor Searle, it was a struggle to find meaning in something so heinous. If everything happens for a reason, what could the reason be for this?

Travis had given so much of himself to others, impacted so many lives. But he hadn't been done with his mission—there was so much more he wanted to accomplish. It was heart-wrenching to know he wouldn't have the opportunity to fulfill many of his life goals.

"He really wanted to be a force in the world for good. He had that dream, he believed it, and I thought he really could have accomplished it," Taylor said years later. "Now he's gone. When I think of things from a divine perspective, like if he was put on this earth for a reason, then that totally sucks that the world just got robbed of such a great person."

Taylor didn't want his friend to be forgotten, his memory to be tarnished. He wanted to find some way to keep Travis's memory alive. Shortly after the murder Taylor began moderating a Facebook group called In Memory of Travis Alexander.

It started as a way for his friends and family to share memories and photographs and keep up-to-date about funeral arrangements. It would grow to become much more.

Initially, Sky Hughes felt a sense of regret about Travis's death. In the days and weeks before the murder, she knew he had been upset about things going on in his life—especially with his breakups with Lisa and Mimi. Sky lamented the fact that she hadn't done more.

"He had been really down and stuff had been really bothering him," Sky recalled. "I didn't know the extent of it, but I felt like I should have just gone and picked him up and brought him to my house, where he would have been safe."

Later, the regret would be replaced with a hole in her heart that could never be filled.

"There was just such a huge void when Travis died," Sky said. "Travis was one-of-a-kind. There's no one like him. With everyone in his life that he left there was such a big void because he was such a big personality and impossible to replace."

CHAPTER 23

What remained of Travis Alexander was deposited on a cold aluminum table in the Maricopa County Medical Examiner's Office. A high beam of light above him, the body was prone, chest protruding forward, propped on a body block.

It was 9:30 A.M. on June 12, 2008, and Travis had been dead for more than a week. For the past day and a half, his remains had been sealed in a body bag and stored inside a morgue refrigerator awaiting the autopsy, which is required after any suspicious death.

From the observation bay, separated by glass, Detective Flores, along with another detective, observed as forensic technicians swabbed Travis's flesh, clipped his fingernails, plucked his hair, and drew blood. The samples were collected and bagged for DNA testing.

Another forensic technician photographed the body, while the medical examiner, Dr. Kevin Horn, began the autopsy. Tall and powerfully built, with blue eyes, carefully coifed brown hair, and a neatly trimmed beard, Horn was a graduate of the University of Maryland. Since 2001, he had been working with the Maricopa County Medical Examiner's Office, during which time he had performed more than six thousand autopsies.

Wearing blue latex gloves and a long white coat, Dr. Horn began by inspecting the condition of the body. The cadaver was veined by a motley of pink and purple discoloration. Flesh appeared waxy as the skin had begun to slip away from the muscle. The stomach was severely distended—the result of gas formation following death.

Travis's face looked emaciated, the withered lips pulled back, exposing the upper teeth. The eyelids were black and swollen.

Passing the ultraviolet light over the torso, Dr. Horn counted each gash. There were four lacerations to the upper torso—including one in the center of the chest and three to the belly. Studying the depth of each puncture wound, Horn determined the murder weapon was a single-edge blade, at least five inches in length.

One of the cuts had pierced Travis's pectoral muscle below his right nipple; another on his abdomen was six inches in length. The wound to the center of Travis's chest penetrated at a straight angle, plunging more than three inches through the rib cage. It would have bled considerably, and without immediate medical attention would have been fatal.

Near the top of Travis's head was a small cut. To the back, left side of the neck was another gash about an inch in length.

There were two large slices—each about two inches long—across the top and back of Travis's head. Horn would later shave portions of the scalp to get a better look. The cuts were so deep they had chipped away at the bone of his skull, leaving two small divots. Because the scalp wounds had bleeding associated with them, Horn determined they likely occurred before death.

To further document the internal injuries, Horn X-rayed the body, revealing a small bullet lodged in Travis's cheek. Horn leaned close to the body to inspect the wound. On Travis's forehead, directly above the right brow, was a small, round puncture, previously masked by discoloration.

On the X-ray, Horn traced the trajectory of the bullet. It had entered above the brow, ripping downward through Travis's face, coming to rest in his cheekbone. Examining the wound, Horn found no soot or gunshot residue, which would be present if the gun had been fired in close proximity to the victim. Because of the lack of stippling it was determined to have been fired at least three feet away.

Horn cut away the flesh of the left cheek and, using a metal protractor, fished inside the gash to retrieve the bullet. He dropped it in a metal tray, where it fell with a dull thud.

The bullet was small caliber. Based on the location of the wound, Horn would later determine the bullet had passed through the right frontal lobe of the brain. A potentially fatal wound, it would have caused rapid incapacitation and eventual death, according to Horn.

Later, Horn would examine the brain. Due to decomposition, however, the brain had softened and begun to liquefy. Because no hemorrhaging was visible, it was impossible to determine if the bullet had been fired when Travis was alive, or after he had died.

The most significant injury was the gash to the throat. The tissue around the wound had dried and retracted. Horn lifted Travis's head and measured the wound, which was six inches across. Slashing three to four inches deep, to the back of the spine, the knife had severed the airway and windpipe below the larynx and voice box.

"The jugular vein and carotid artery were both cut," Horn later said. "It goes all the way back to the soft tissue at the front of the neck and stops at the bone."

It was a deadly wound, causing almost immediate death by exsanguination.

Next, Horn examined Travis's hands. The palms were purple and red, the fingernails black. The ridges of the hands were stained with blood. The left hand was the darkest in color, where the blood had pooled in the palm. Both hands appeared skeletal, the fingertips moss green from decay.

Five wounds marred Travis's hands. Horn recognized the injuries immediately as defensive wounds—those that occur when a victim attempts to protect themselves during an attack. Most were on Travis's left hand, which is typical if the attacker is holding the weapon in the right hand.

During the attack, a chunk of Travis's right thumbnail had been lopped off. The knife split the webbing between his thumb and index finger. The deepest wound was nearly two inches on the palm of his left hand. Because of the hemorrhaging associated with the injury, it was clear the cuts occurred before death.

Horn then turned his attention toward the lower part of Travis's body. The legs had begun to dry and shrivel, showing early signs of mummification. The shins were bruised and the legs were scraped. There was tearing of the skin on the back of the ankles, consistent with being dragged.

Propping the body on its front, Horn inspected Travis's backside, which was magenta and purple, due to lividity when the blood settled to the lowest part of the body.

Clustered together on the upper back between the shoulder blades were nine puncture wounds, which were shallower than those on the front of the torso. Whatever force was applied had not been significant enough to cut through the bones.

Starting at the top of each shoulder and meeting at the breast bone, Horn made a Y-shaped incision across Travis's chest with his scalpel. Cutting away the soft tissue with the blade, he pulled back the skin and muscle, exposing the rib cage. Using cutters, Horn sheared through each side of Travis's rib cage and set the chest plate aside, exposing the organs.

Horn removed each organ—weighing and measuring the stomach, liver, and lungs. Next, he carefully made an incision to the pericardial sac to examine the heart. There was a small cut to the superior vena cava, the large vein that receives blood from the head, arms, and chest, and empties into the right atrium of the heart. The puncture in the center of Travis's chest had also pierced his heart.

Horn would later determine that three of Travis's injuries would have been fatal—the slashing of the throat, stab to the chest, and bullet to the brain.

"The one to the chest had not caused immediate death," Horn said. "The throat and the head would have been immediately incapacitating."

Travis had died primarily from rapid blood loss. His death would have been excruciating.

Around 11:30 A.M. Dr. Horn completed the autopsy. He filled out the death certificate: Travis Victor Alexander, white male, 5′9″, 190 pounds. Dead at the age of thirty. The manner of death: homicide.

In life, Travis's Mormon faith had been unwavering. If his beliefs were indeed true, Travis's spirit was far away from this grim pathology office. When his heart stopped beating he would have sloughed off his physical body and returned to the spiritual state.

His friends and family would take comfort in the knowledge that he was in a better place.

If Travis was anywhere but here, he was in a better place.

CHAPTER 24

The caller was anonymous, the message was short. It was a female voice and she claimed to have information about the death of Travis Alexander.

"Police need to investigate a person named Dustin Thompson," the woman said. "He may have information regarding Travis Alexander's murder."

The tip came into the Apache Junction Police Department from a local cell phone number two days after Travis's body was discovered. That same day Flores got the tip. Tracing the cellular phone number, he determined it belonged to a man named Dustin Thompson, a friend of Travis's.

Flores reviewed the records on Dustin. They showed he was married to a woman named Ashley Thompson, who was employed at a Dillard's Department Store distribution center in Gilbert.

At 3:30 P.M. the next day—June 12—following observation of the autopsy, Flores and Detective Domenick Kaufman met with Ashley at the department store.

Flores began the interview by asking her her cell phone number—confirming it was the same number that had phoned in the anonymous call. Still in the process of gathering intelligence on Dustin, the detectives did not confront Ashley about the tip. During the interview, she too never mentioned that she had called the police concerning her husband.

Ashley told detectives that she and Travis were close friends for the past three years and that her husband also knew Travis.

"Were you and Travis more than friends?" Flores asked.

"No, we were just friends," she said, "nothing else."

As she spoke about her husband, Flores noticed that she referred to Dustin as her ex. Records showed the couple was still married. Flores asked Ashley about this discrepancy.

"We're divorcing," Ashley said. "We live apart."

Ashley said the reason for the divorce was financial issues that had added stress in the marriage. Their house was facing possible foreclosure, and a few weeks prior Ashley had moved out.

She had last seen Travis three weeks ago at one of his UFC parties, which she regularly attended, she said.

On the day his body was discovered Ashley said she had tried to call, but didn't get an answer. Later that same day a friend called and told Ashley that Travis was dead. Dustin also learned of the discovery that night and had driven over to Travis's house. Dustin had actually been standing outside the house, among a group of Travis's friends, as police were investigating the homicide.

Ashley provided Dustin's work address and schedule to detectives. Interviewing Dustin, detectives quickly determined he had an alibi and was not a viable suspect in the killing.

Days later Detective Kaufman re-interviewed Ashley. During this interview Ashley confessed that she was the one who left the anonymous tip about Dustin with the Apache Junction Police Department.

"We were having a lot of difficulties at the time," Ashley said. "And he had been acting real strange."

It was during the few weeks leading up to Travis's death that she had left Dustin. During that time Travis and Ashley had become very close. Ashley had even discussed possibly renting a room in Travis's house.

Ultimately both she and Travis agreed it was not a good

idea. They were just good friends and didn't want people to think there was something inappropriate going on between them.

When Travis was found dead, she kept thinking about how strange Dustin had been acting. Since the day she had made the anonymous phone call, her suspicions about Dustin had vanished.

"I regret calling the police," she said. "I don't think there is any way he could have done anything to Travis."

Besides Dustin, in the early days of the investigation, one other potential suspect emerged. As Aaron Mortensen was being questioned, he brought up Travis's former roommate, a man whom Travis had met through church. After it was rumored that he was manipulating women from the ward, Travis had asked him to move out.

"The guy who lived with Travis was a bit of a shady character," Aaron recalled. "I was concerned about him because they had had a heated argument when Travis kicked him out of the house."

Still, Aaron couldn't imagine that months later Travis's roommate would resort to murder. He told detectives he didn't think it had ever become personal.

As the investigation continued, however, the rest of Travis's friends only identified one viable potential suspect: Jodi Arias.

Over the course of the investigation, Travis's friends continued to call detectives, relaying troubling stories of Jodi's behavior. Jodi was described as "completely obsessed," "crazy," and "a stalker."

But suspicions were one thing. Hard evidence was what would ultimately solve the murder.

For the next few weeks the forensic lab would be busy at work examining the hair, blood, and fingerprint samples taken from inside the house.

Meanwhile, Detective Michael Melendez, a stout, dark-haired, seasoned computer forensic detective continued the task of examining the electronic equipment recovered from

Travis's house. Several of the computers and drives belonged to Travis's roommates, and would ultimately provide no evidentiary value to the case.

Travis's computer and hard drive, however, would be valuable in uncovering potential suspects.

The most unusual evidence uncovered by far was the Sony digital camera discovered in the washing machine with the SanDisk 2GB memory card inside.

The camera had no power, so Melendez purchased a power cord. Once it was charged and turned on, he discovered the camera was blinking and the date on the internal memory had been reset to January 1, 2007. It appeared the camera reset itself due to lack of power supply. The camera was not functioning and would no longer take pictures. No images appeared on the camera's internal memory.

Next, Melendez turned his attention toward the camera's memory card. The shocking images he would discover would ultimately expose a killer.

CHAPTER 25

"Our Dear Heavenly Father, it is with great humility and gratitude that we come before you this day as friends, family, and those who knew Travis to celebrate the impact that he had in our lives," Dan Freeman prayed before the Mesa congregation of the Church of Jesus Christ of Latter-day Saints.

It was Monday, June 16, just after 7:30 P.M., and Dan was at the center of the room, in front of the podium, speaking at the first of two memorial services for Travis. The second would be held a week later in Riverside, California.

Nearly a thousand people packed the pews of the church that evening, including Travis's friends, family, business associates, and fellow congregants. Amid the sea of heartbroken faces, one person seemed to stand out. Near the front of the church sat a woman—at times she appeared to dab a tear from her cheek. At others, a mischievous grin crept across her face. The woman was Jodi Arias.

It had been just one week since Travis's body was discovered and all anyone knew was that Travis had been murdered. His loved ones had been informed that it was not a suicide and that the crime scene showed signs of a struggle. Because it was an ongoing investigation, the police were not releasing many details.

Meanwhile, rumors had been swirling about Jodi's obsession with Travis. While a few friends embraced her, most kept their distance.

As distasteful as many found her attendance, no one spoke a word of disrespect. This day wasn't about Jodi. It was a day to celebrate Travis—to remember the man he was in life.

Dan continued his invocation: "We ask you to bless all those who are struggling with his passing and the questions they ask themselves," he said. "And we ask the Lord to help us, each and every one of us, to take the good, the example that he was to us, to take it with us and apply those lessons in our lives."

Following the opening prayer, the atmosphere in the church appeared to lighten. While Travis's loved ones were in mourning, they found solace in the belief that he was looking down on them from heaven.

For Mormons, death is not an end, but a step forward in God's plan. Travis's fellow Mormons believed he was continuing his eternal journey—learning, growing, and progressing. His spirit would retain the memories and knowledge he had gained on earth. Because of their belief in a life after death, a Mormon funeral is generally not dark and depressing. Instead, it's a celebration of the deceased's next phase of existence.

The highest degree of Mormon heaven is known as the celestial kingdom, which is the permanent residence of God and Jesus Christ. Only those individuals who are sealed in a celestial marriage are permitted into the highest level of the celestial kingdom.

Although Travis did not have a chance to marry his eternal companion, and therefore did not complete the required ordinances and covenants during his mortal life, he would still have a chance to ascend to the celestial kingdom. Because he accepted the teachings of Jesus Christ, in the afterlife he may still have a chance to meet and marry his eternal companion.

"I know I will see Travis one day," Travis's sister Hillary

Wilcox told the congregation. "I know that he will have an eternal companion and a family."

Hillary began her eulogy with tears in her eyes, her voice trembling.

"Many of you know him as a neighbor, a colleague, or a friend," she said. "But whatever the relationship to him, we all know him as a man who in his life played many roles."

Hillary spoke about Travis's life growing up in Riverside with his seven siblings. She told stories about Travis's passions—his love of writing, travel, genealogy, and the UFC. More than anything, Travis loved the Lord, she said. He used his faith to help guide others toward the righteous path.

"I admire Travis so much for his drive and everything he did. He always put his heart into it and everything he did he did it well," she said. "I'm especially grateful that he was such a good example to me. That I was able to continue and be active in the church and the blessings I do have because of his great example."

The void left by Travis's death would never be filled, she said. His family would have to live each day without Travis in their lives. All they had now were memories.

"What I'll miss most about my brother is his smile. I loved his big smile, it was so cheesy. I just loved it," Hillary said. "What I think I will most remember about him was his testimony and his love for the gospel. He wanted everyone to know it and he did his best to share it. He was such a spiritual giant and a great person."

Hillary ended her eulogy by sharing the quote she had found in Travis's house. "The difference between a stumbling block and a stepping stone is the character of the individual walking the path."

Travis's path on earth was finished, but his journey would continue, she said.

"If we all remember what the Lord has done for us and that he will always be there for us, the stumbling blocks in our lives will become stepping stones," Hillary said.

In between speakers, the Desert Ridge ward choir sang

songs and hymns. Following one of Travis's favorite songs, Michelle Lowery approached the podium, clutching a tissue.

"When you talk with Travis, the conversations are usually really long and very deep. He could talk about anything—politics, goals, education, dreams, the gospel," Michelle said. "But recently between me and him, most of our conversations turned towards relationships."

Travis had appointed Michelle his "wingman," as she assisted him through his relationships, talking him up to girls he was interested in. There was rarely a day when Michelle didn't get a call or text message from Travis about the girls he was dating, she said.

"Travis may not need me to be his 'wingman' anymore, but I'm extremely glad to have another opportunity to talk about him," she said.

Travis had so many great qualities, Michelle said. He was always genuine with his emotions—expressing his excitement for life.

"It hurts that I only knew him for a short while," she said, her voice cracking. "And it breaks my heart that he was taken away from us so abruptly. But he had a lasting impression so deep and so strong that no one can ever replace it. I know he's where he needs to be right now and that he's being taken care of. I know how strong our friendship was when he was here. And I know that we will be friends for the eternities. I know one day I will meet him there and he'll be standing there with just a big smile, his arms outstretched, and give me a hug. We're going to miss Travis, but he was definitely loved."

Next, Deanna Reid approached the podium. As she spoke, Jodi glared at her with a disturbing smirk. Deanna tried to look past Jodi as she shared memories of Travis.

"I think probably my favorite memory of Travis was while we were dating. Every year we would compete to see who could give each other the coolest and most thoughtful gifts. And most of the time he won," she said with an emotional chuckle. "We have a lot of special memories together."

Even when they lived a state apart, Travis and Deanna rarely went a week without speaking.

"Recently, I was on the phone with him. He had given me a call when he started writing his book," she said. "And he wanted to read to me some of what he had written."

When he was done reading, Travis anxiously asked Deanna what she thought.

"It's so amazing!" Deanna had declared. "I can't believe how well-written it is."

Deanna had heard the story of Travis's upbringing before, but the way he wrote it was so elegant. They began reminiscing about old times, telling stories and laughing.

There was a pause in the conversation. Deanna broke the silence, "I love you, Travie. And I'm so proud of you."

"I love you too," Travis replied. "More than you know."

"Travis changed my life. He made me a better person," Deanna told the congregation. "And I'm not the only one. He did that for almost everyone that he was associated with. He made people want to be better when he was around them. And even still he inspires us to make every moment count. To live the lives we know we should be living, so that we will be obedient so that we can see him again along with our Heavenly Father and Jesus Christ. And feel the happiness that he feels now."

The concluding eulogist for the evening was Aaron Mortensen.

"I stand before you neither as an eloquent eulogist, nor as someone with touching musical abilities. I am but a friend whom Travis referred to as 'brother,'" he said. "Indeed I am just like you. We cared about Travis, we admired him, and we probably took his greatest qualities for granted at times because he was such a constant in our lives. I hope that my thoughts relay a feeling of warm memories and calming peace as we are now one week from the news which shocked us all."

The seven days since Travis's body was found had been traumatic for everyone who knew him. Tonight, Aaron chose to remember fonder memories. As a tribute, he told a story of when Travis had shared his three life goals.

A few months before his death, Travis spent an evening with Aaron, and the discussion turned toward ambitions.

Travis showed Aaron a photo of himself at the International Balloon Fiesta in New Mexico—a goal he'd always wanted to accomplish and recently achieved.

"Travis, what's next?" Aaron asked, knowing it was one of Travis's favorite questions.

Travis told him he had three goals on his life's list. First, he said he wanted to ride a bull, rodeo style—the one thing left in the song "Live Like You Were Dying" that Travis had yet to complete at the time. Aaron, who was from Colorado and had witnessed many bull-riding injuries, couldn't understand why he would want to do such a dangerous thing.

"It is something that frightened me," Travis said. "If I could do it, I wouldn't have to be afraid anymore."

Travis didn't want to fear anything in life, he told Aaron. Next, Travis showed Aaron a picture of a lighthouse.

"I want to buy one someday," Travis said.

Travis explained he wanted to renovate the interior, with an elevator up the middle and a spiral slide that went all the way down the inner walls. Aaron gave him an inquiring look.

"It would be cool to have," Travis declared.

Aaron shrugged. It was a good point.

"Even my overactive pragmatic side couldn't argue with that," Aaron recalled in his eulogy. "It's definitely the best idea I've ever heard concerning lighthouse renovation."

Lastly, Travis told Aaron, "I want to someday have my picture on the cover of *Time* magazine with the headline 'Alexander the Great,'" Travis said. As Aaron pointed out in his eulogy, "This would help him to influence hundreds of thousands of people.

"At first, I thought this was such a different desire than I've ever had for myself," Aaron recalled. "But then, I reflected. Travis simply wanted to show other people that he could become great even from a difficult upbringing. And if he could, others could."

At the end of the service, Aaron held up a Photoshopped image of *Time* magazine with a photo of Travis. The headline read, "Alexander the Great."

"Travis, I can't get you a bull to ride, because I'm too afraid of them, too, and I can't afford a lighthouse to buy and dedicate to you, but—" He paused, displaying the photo. "I can put you on a cover of *Time* magazine. Your efforts to influence scores of people around you have been a success. You've been great to me, and you've achieved greatness in my eyes. I'll channel your wisdom and attitude now and in my future. Thank you."

Finally, Taylor Searle gave the benediction, a short blessing at the end of the service.

"Our dear Heavenly Father. We come before thee this day. And offer thanks for our opportunity to be here, and our thanks for the opportunity to know Travis. Please bless us all that we may remember the love that we have felt and the blessed time that we had to spend with thy son Travis," Taylor said. "Help us all to remember the influence that we each individually have had from Travis so he may live on in the ways that we respond to that influence."

Following the service, the congregants gathered for refreshments and to quietly and privately share memories. Mingling among Travis's friends and family was Jodi. Dressed in a form-fitting black dress, her long hair hanging loose, Jodi hugged tearful loved ones.

"Jodi wrapped her arms around me and thanked me for coming to the service," recalled Larry Smith, a friend of Travis's. "She had a smile on her face."

Shortly after a good friend and business partner pulled Larry aside.

"Larry, I know she did it," his friend told him.

Larry glanced back at Jodi. *Was hers the last face Travis saw on this earth?* he wondered.

As Taylor gave his condolences to Travis's siblings, Jodi approached him. At that point he was unable to summon even one ounce of tolerance. He exchanged short formalities, then brushed her away and kept walking.

"At the memorial service, I thought it was her the whole time so I was kind of thrown off by her showing up," Taylor said. "I shunned her. She kept coming up to talk to me and I was like, 'Get away.'"

Before she left, Jodi wrote a message in Travis's memorial book.

"Travis you are beautiful on the inside and out. You always told me that. I never stopped believing in you. I know you always believed in me. Thank you for sharing so much," she wrote. "This world has been blessed because you have been here. I love you."

Following a second service in California, Travis Alexander would be laid to rest at Olivewood Memorial Park in Riverside on June 21, 2008.

His gravestone was a simple slab with a white silhouette of a Mormon church. Engraved on the stone were the words IN LOVING MEMORY TRAVIS V. ALEXANDER. Below his name were the dates: 1977–2008.

In the bottom right corner was an oval black-and-white portrait of Travis—a peaceful smile across his face.

CHAPTER 26

The day of the memorial service in Mesa, Jodi received a phone call from Detective Esteban Flores. He wanted to know if she would be willing to come voluntarily to the station for an interview and to provide fingerprints and DNA samples.

"We need to be able to exclude you from anything we find in the house," the detective told Jodi.

Jodi said she was leaving the following day but would make every attempt to come in for an interview.

Flores also contacted Mimi Hall, Dallin Forest, and Michelle Lowery. The next day at 3 P.M., Jodi arrived with Dallin, Michelle, and Mimi at Mesa police headquarters.

They each gave voluntary buccal swabs, providing DNA samples from the inside of their cheeks, and were fingerprinted.

Dallin, Michelle, and Mimi all volunteered for follow-up interviews. Jodi, however, said she was no longer willing to talk. She said she had discussed the situation with a friend who convinced her that many people had been talking about her involvement in Travis's death. She now felt uncomfortable about talking without consulting an attorney.

"I'm sorry to hear that," Flores said.

Later, Zachary Billings and his girlfriend, Amanda

McBrien, came back for follow-up interviews and to provide fingerprints and saliva samples.

In the interview with Zachary, Flores asked about the digital camera. A few months prior Zachary said he had consulted with Travis on the purchase of a camera. Flores told Zachary the box and bag were located inside the home.

Zachary told Flores the make and model of the camera that Travis purchased. It was the same camera found in the washing machine.

Flores also conducted a follow-up interview with Enrique Cortez. Regarding the washing machine, Enrique said he had not done any laundry that week. Flores explained that he had found religious undergarments in the washer, which Enrique identified as belonging to Travis.

"I'm the only person in the house besides Travis who wears that underwear," Enrique said.

Detectives asked if he had detected an unusual odor in the house. Enrique said he first noticed the stench on Monday at around 9 P.M., after returning to the house following a church activity. He never asked anyone about it.

Continuing his investigation, Detective Flores interviewed several of Travis's friends.

Among the first people Flores spoke with were those who last communicated directly with Travis—Chris and Sky Hughes. According to Travis's phone, the last outgoing text from Travis to Chris was the last known contact he had had with anyone.

When they heard about what happened, both Chris and Sky immediately thought of Jodi. They knew she had been obsessed with him. In fact they had witnessed many of the encounters firsthand. They relayed these stories directly to the detective.

"Besides Jodi, does Travis have any enemies?" the detective asked.

"No. No one," Chris said. "Everyone liked Travis. I could not think of anyone who would ever want to harm him."

On June 16, Flores also called Travis's former girlfriend

Lisa Andrews, to follow up on an alleged car vandalism that had occurred outside her property.

Lisa explained that in December 2007, Travis had been at her house when there was a knock at her door. When they looked outside no one was there. The next day Travis discovered his tires had been slashed.

"We thought it was a random act until the next night," Lisa said. "The same thing happened again."

On the morning of December 8, Lisa received the hostile e-mail, addressed from a John Doe.

"You are a shameful whore. Your Heavenly Father must be deeply ashamed of the whoredoms you've committed with that insidious man," the e-mail began.

Lisa strongly suspected Jodi had sent the e-mail, although she had been unable to prove it. Lisa provided a copy of the e-mail to detectives. She also mentioned one other incident. Weeks later when she was at Travis's house, the tires on her car were slashed as well.

After the interview with Lisa, Flores returned a call from Clancy Talbot, who had left a message for the detective. Travis's friend Clancy had been in Utah and was at the Prepaid Legal seminar on the week of June 2, when Jodi didn't arrive as expected.

"That day several people tried calling Jodi but her phone was off," Clancy recalled.

When Jodi arrived on June 5, she seemed to be acting odd and her hair had been dyed brown. Although it was over 100 degrees outside, Jodi wore a long-sleeved shirt and had bandages on her fingers.

When Clancy learned that Travis had been murdered, her mind was reeling. She thought of Jodi and her strange story of being lost and sleeping in her car.

"What do you know about Travis and Jodi's relationship?" Flores asked.

"Ever since Travis told Jodi that he no longer wanted to see her, Jodi had been very clingy," Clancy said. "She had been acting very *Fatal Attraction*."

* * *

Over the next few days detectives combed Travis's block, interviewing several of his neighbors.

Few of the neighbors knew much about Travis. Most were aware he worked from home and traveled frequently. They were used to seeing people come by—especially on Wednesdays when Travis threw his UFC parties. For the most part, however, Travis kept to himself in the neighborhood.

No one remembered seeing or hearing anything odd on the last few days of Travis's life. However, several remembered Jodi.

Amanda and Chris Click lived directly across the street from Travis. About six months prior Chris remembered seeing a blonde around the residence driving a silver Infiniti, he told detectives. Travis was often seen arguing with Jodi outside the residence. Shortly after the funeral he saw the same female exiting Travis's backyard. Only now her hair had been dyed brown.

Dave Prusha, who had been to a Prepaid Legal conference, was the only neighbor of Travis's who had actually met Jodi. On the day of the memorial service he saw Jodi once again.

Initially Dave was surprised to see that the normally blond Jodi had darkened her hair. Jodi began talking about Travis's death. She mentioned how Travis always kept his doors unlocked.

"As she talked about Travis's death, I was surprised how disconnected and distant Jodi appeared," Dave Prusha told detectives. "She stared at me with a blank expression, showing no emotion as she spoke about Travis."

CHAPTER 27

The phone rang in Detective Esteban Flores's office on the afternoon of June 19, ten days after Travis's body was found. Glancing at the caller ID, he saw it was Detective Michael Melendez, the computer forensic investigator.

"You've got to come down here," Melendez said excitedly. "I have some photos you have to see."

A few minutes later, Flores stepped into Melendez's office. Melendez was sitting at his desk, his stare fixed on his computer screen. Animatedly, he spun around in his chair. "Check this out."

He told Flores he had retrieved images from the memory card found inside the washing machine. Although the pictures had been deleted, he had been able to restore the images—and they were unbelievable.

Melendez clicked his mouse and a photo of Travis Alexander appeared on the screen. He was standing in his master bathroom shower, his head tilted up, the water splashing his face. His arms were crossed, with his fists covering the center of his chest.

"The time stamp is June 4, 2008, at 5:22 P.M.," Melendez said.

Flores's eyes went wide. Someone had photographed

Travis on the last day of his life in the exact location where his body was discovered.

Melendez clicked again, slowly shuffling through a few more photos of Travis showering, posing awkwardly for the camera. Seconds after the first photo, Travis turned away from the lens. The next few were of Travis's backside. Six more were close-ups of Travis's face as he showered.

In one of the last haunting photos, Travis was staring directly into the camera's lens, the water dripping down his face. His expression was stern, his eyes slightly red. It was time-stamped 5:29 P.M.

At 5:30 P.M. Travis was sitting on the shower floor with his right side exposed to the camera. The lower right quadrant of his body was captured in the image.

"That's the last photo of him alive," Melendez said. "The next picture was taken forty-four seconds later."

A blurry, dark image appeared on the screen of the ceiling above the shower floor. It was out of focus as though the camera was moving at the time and the picture was taken by accident. It was time-stamped 5:31:14.

The next photo was taken at 5:32:16—just sixty-two seconds later. The image was also dark and unclear. The photo was shot while the camera was upside down, also possibly by mistake.

"I had to enhance it to make sense of it," Melendez said.

He clicked on the screen to display the enhanced photo. It took a moment for Flores to make sense of what he was seeing.

"My God," Flores muttered.

The photo was of the back of Travis's head. Blood was dripping down his arm—consistent with the neck wound. Someone was standing in front of the body.

Flores studied the image closely. All that was visible of the suspect was the person's right pant leg and a foot. The person was wearing a dark-colored sock or shoe with striped sweat pants that had a zipper on the back of the cuff. It was difficult to tell the color of the pants, but they appeared to be blue or black.

Flores would later compare the photo with crime scene pictures, matching together sections of the blood puddles with identifiers in the picture. The photo was taken at the northern end of the bathroom hallway, away from the shower, where the largest amount of blood was located at the scene.

"There's just one more," Melendez said.

The last picture was too dark and also had to be enhanced. It had also been taken when the camera was upside down. In the corrected image Flores recognized a close-up of the bathroom hallway and baseboards, which were smudged with blood. Next to the baseboard was a blurry image of a figure on the floor. It appeared as if the body was being lifted or dragged.

The pictures were unbelievable evidence. This meant that the killer had photographed the victim while committing murder. But Melendez pointed out that these weren't even the most salacious photographs he had discovered on the memory card.

"I retrieved several other photos from earlier that afternoon," he told Flores.

The second batch of photos had been taken four hours before Travis was murdered—starting at 1:42 P.M. on June 4.

Melendez clicked on the first photo. On his screen a slightly blurry image of a woman appeared. Flores immediately recognized Jodi Arias.

In the photo Jodi was nude, sprawled across Travis's bed. She was propped up on her elbows. Her hair was in two braided brown pigtails, her expression blank. In another she was on her back, her head turned to the side. The next two pictures were X-rated close-ups of Jodi's anus and vagina.

At 1:44 P.M. Travis was naked, lying on his back in the bed, next to a small bottle of K-Y Jelly, a sexual lubricant. His head rested on the pillow. Most of his face was blocked by his right arm.

At 1:47 P.M. Travis was glancing at the camera. His hand gestured with two fingers in the air—the sign for peace.

There were six photos total—four of Jodi and two of Travis.

Flores now had proof Jodi was lying about not seeing Travis since April. She had been there on the day of his murder.

On Saturday, June 21, Detective Flores received a call from Jodi. The call went to voice mail.

"Hi, Detective Flores. It's Jodi Arias calling in regards to Travis Alexander. It's Saturday, I'm not exactly sure what time. But maybe you're off; if so I hope you're enjoying your day off. If not, if you could give me a call back." Jodi left her phone number. "Thanks. Talk to you soon. Bye."

On Monday, Flores returned her call.

"What can I do for you?" Flores asked Jodi.

Jodi said she had called on Saturday because she was having a bad day. She had missed Travis's funeral in Southern California because she said she got a flat tire on the way to the airport.

"I was also calling to see if there are any updates on the case," Jodi said.

Flores said he was not at liberty to discuss updates on the case because it was an open investigation.

Jodi then mentioned what she had earlier said about not wanting to give an official statement before consulting an attorney. She said she now regretted it.

"I'm now willing to talk," she said. They scheduled a phone interview on June 25 at 10 A.M.

Before hanging up, Flores asked just one question.

"Did you send Travis an e-mail about coming down to visit him?" he asked.

Jodi admitted she had sent an e-mail about a week or so before he was found. When Travis hadn't responded Jodi said she assumed he was probably in California. She was planning on staying in his home while he was away in Cancún.

"Travis had an open door policy," Jodi said.

At the end of the conversation Jodi asked how she could retrieve belongings she left at Travis's house. She realized she left some clothing behind.

"It's nothing very valuable," Jodi said. "I don't want to bother anyone about it."

On June 25, Flores contacted Jodi for the scheduled interview. By then, Flores knew Jodi had been lying to him about her whereabouts on the day of the murder. The goal of the conversation was to get her story on tape. Throughout the conversation Flores led Jodi to believe they were still clueless about the murder.

"The reason I wanted to talk to you was to figure out what was going on the week we found Travis," Flores said. "We're still trying to figure out the day this happened."

At Flores's prompting, Jodi again reiterated the story of her whereabouts the week of June 2.

"He knew I was taking a road trip that week. And he was kind of guilting me because he knew I was going to Utah, not Arizona," Jodi said. "I didn't tell Travis this, but I was going there to meet somebody."

To avoid making him jealous, Jodi said she didn't admit to seeing Ryan Burns.

"I did talk to him on Tuesday night," she said. "It was brief. I was just calling to check in and say hey. I was calling people because I was bored on the road. He was nice and cordial, but he was acting like he had hurt feelings."

After getting lost Jodi said she slept in her car. By the time she reached Salt Lake City it was late in the morning on Thursday, June 5. She participated in the last day of the conference and spent time with Ryan Burns.

Once again Jodi explained her relationship with Travis and her move to Arizona. She also admitted to their ongoing sexual relationship.

"There was certainly a romantic side, or an intimate side," Jodi said. "But we weren't exactly on the path to marriage. And we both knew that."

Once again Flores asked her about the suspicions Travis's friends had.

"Some people have some unpleasant stuff to say about

you," Flores said. "I don't know why, you seem like a pleasant person."

"The only thing I can think of was I was at his house a lot," Jodi said.

Toward the end of the conversation, Flores asked Jodi about the camera.

"Did you discuss the purchase of the camera with Mr. Alexander?" he asked.

"Yeah, I remember that," Jodi said. "He called me for advice because I'm a photographer."

Jodi added that she knew he ended up purchasing a camera. "I don't remember what he got, but it sounds like it was a really nice camera."

"So you never got to see the camera or anything?" Flores asked.

"No," Jodi said.

"We found it and it's pretty much ruined and we have no idea why someone would destroy his camera," Flores said. "You never saw or touched the camera?"

"No," she repeated.

Flores knew she was lying—he had proof that she had used the camera on the last day of Travis's life.

When he got off the phone with Jodi, Flores calculated the trip using her route. The drive from Los Angeles to Salt Lake City took Jodi forty-eight hours to complete. Even allotting ten hours to rest, the trip should have only taken twenty-nine hours.

Next, Flores calculated the distance of a similar trip through Los Angeles, then to Mesa, and back to Salt Lake City. Allowing ten hours to rest, the entire trip would have taken thirty-seven hours to drive. It would have left ten to eleven hours to spend an afternoon photographing Travis and murdering him in the shower.

After speaking with Jodi, Flores called Ryan Burns to corroborate Jodi's story about meeting him in Salt Lake City. Ryan said Jodi had called him on the night of June 3 and planned to meet him the next day. About twenty-four hours later Jodi called him with the story about getting lost and driving in the wrong direction.

Ryan told Flores that many of his friends in Utah were pointing the finger at Jodi. At that point, he didn't believe it was possible.

As the days turned to weeks Jodi seemed absorbed by an impending sense of doom. While she tried to appear collected, fear and paranoia ate away at her.

She decided she needed to get away from Yreka. She told her parents she would soon be leaving town. Bill Arias was disturbed by his daughter's latest revelation, and asked her what was the reason for her sudden move.

"I can't tell you what's going on," Jodi told her father. "All I know is I have to leave."

"Why?" Bill said.

"I might get blamed for something," she said.

"What?" he pressed. "What could it be?"

"I can't tell you," Jodi said.

Jodi wouldn't say anything more. She began packing boxes and making arrangements to move away. She told several people she was relocating to Monterey, California—where she would be in close proximity to two ex-boyfriends: Darryl Brewer and Matt McCartney.

In late June she went to a nearby car rental agency and rented a 2007 Chevrolet Cobalt.

On July 1, she also bought a gun—a 9mm.

By late June, detectives received cell phone and financial records for Travis Alexander and Jodi Arias.

The phone records were valuable evidence. Using cell phone pinging technology to determine which cell towers the phone signal bounced off of, investigators would be able to approximate Travis's and Jodi's whereabouts during the week of the murder.

Sorting through Travis's records did not yield any surprises. During the last week of his life, he stayed in the East Valley—traveling between Mesa, Gilbert, and Apache Junction.

His last phone call was on the afternoon of June 4. Each subsequent call went to voice mail. By the time his phone had been confiscated, the voice mail box was full. There were twenty-three messages, four that had been reviewed and saved, and nineteen that had gone unchecked.

Jodi's phone records, however, were much more interesting.

The afternoon of June 2, cell records traced her six-hour drive from Yreka to Los Angeles. Late that night, calls began hitting off towers near San Francisco traveling south toward Monterey.

The next day, June 3, at around 8 P.M., calls were placed around Los Angeles, near Santa Fe Springs. At 8:16 P.M. she made her first call to Travis Alexander that night. The call was short, lasting about five minutes. At 8:34 P.M. she called Travis once again.

Shortly after, the calls stopped. For the next twenty-seven hours Jodi's movements were impossible to trace. Her phone was turned off, and all the calls went straight to voice mail.

The next call on her phone was made around 11:20 P.M. on June 4—the last day of Travis's life. The signal bounced off a tower along the Interstate 93, about forty-five miles north of Kingman, a small Arizona city about two hundred miles northwest of Mesa. When she was twenty-seven miles south of the Nevada border, Jodi phoned Ryan Burns.

Twenty-eight minutes later, at 11:48 P.M., she called Travis's phone, speaking for 168 seconds. At 11:53 P.M. she called Travis once again, the connection lasting sixteen minutes.

On June 5, starting at 12:37 P.M., the calls hit off towers near Las Vegas. By 11 A.M. the calls switch to a register off Salt Lake City, Utah. This was consistent with a path through Las Vegas en route to Salt Lake City, Utah. By June 6, Jodi's phone was back in California.

Jodi's bank and credit card records were also unusual. The activity documented her many stops as she drove through California, beginning on the morning of June 2.

At 10 A.M. she arrived in Monterey, where she made three

cash deposits. Five hours later, at 3:22 P.M., she made a purchase at a Walmart in Monterey.

The activity continued through Pasadena, where she made several purchases at a gas station around 8:30 P.M. All traceable purchases then ceased for more than twenty-four hours.

The next purchase began on June 6 at 10:38 A.M. in Reno, Nevada.

On June 26, Flores received a call from the Mesa Fingerprint Identification section.

"I was able to I.D. the bloody print on the bathroom wall," the senior print analyst said. It was matched to the left palm print of Jodi Arias, the analyst confirmed. Further DNA testing would need to be completed to determine whose blood was on the wall.

On July 3, the Mesa crime lab contacted Flores with results from the DNA typing. The bloody palm print was a mixture of DNA from two individuals. One was the victim, Travis Alexander; the other was Jodi Arias.

The match was decisive—matching Jodi on all sixteen genetic markers.

That same day, using DNA typing, the long hair found in the hallway, stuck to the wall with blood, was also identified as Jodi's. Flores now had a solid case against her.

On July 9, Jodi celebrated her twenty-eighth birthday—that same day a warrant was issued for her arrest.

CHAPTER 28

On the night of July 14, 2008, Jodi Arias was at her grandparents' house packing her belongings in boxes and stuffing her clothes in suitcases.

From his vantage point outside the residence, a detective from the Siskiyou County Sheriff's Department surreptitiously monitored her every move. He relayed the information to Mesa homicide detectives who were stationed at the local sheriff's office in Yreka.

"It looks like she may be attempting to flee," the officer told Detective Flores on his cell phone. "I can see her through a bedroom window. She's packing to go somewhere."

Earlier that day Flores, along with two other Mesa detectives, had flown to California to arrest Jodi Arias for the first-degree murder of Travis Alexander.

Accompanying Flores was Tom Denning, a stout twenty-year veteran of the Mesa Police Department who wore a wide mustache that took up most of the width of his face.

At 3 P.M. the Mesa investigators met with local detectives from the Siskiyou County Sheriff's Department to brief them on the case, obtain a search warrant, and formulate a plan to take Jodi into custody.

After locating Jodi at her grandparents', a local California officer was sent to survey the residence. Out front of the house at 352 Pine Street, parked in the driveway, was a 2007 Chevrolet Cobalt—Jodi's rental car. The officer watched as Jodi periodically stepped outside the house to load the luggage into the back of the car.

At 9:45 P.M. a car pulled into the driveway. Inside the vehicle was a woman the officer recognized from a driver's license photo he viewed earlier at the station—Sandra Arias, Jodi's mother. When Jodi saw the car from her bedroom window, she stepped outside and got into the passenger seat. Moments later Jodi got out of the car and went back inside the house as Sandra drove away.

The rest of the night the house was quiet. An officer continued to monitor the house until midnight with orders to arrest her if she attempted to leave. Meanwhile, with Jodi under surveillance, Mesa detectives convened at a nearby hotel to plan their next move.

Upon arrival in Yreka, Flores discovered intriguing new evidence. On May 28—six days before the murder—Jodi's grandparents had reported a burglary. Among the only items taken was a .25 automatic pistol—the same caliber weapon that had been used in Travis's homicide.

It was decided that the burglary would be used as an initial guise for the arrest. In order to alleviate the possibility of a potential stand-off, a Yreka police officer was recruited to contact Jodi under the pretense he was investigating the theft.

At 6:30 the following morning, the detectives from Mesa and Yreka met out front of the residence. An officer rang the doorbell; Jodi answered.

"Jodi Arias," he said. "Can I speak with you for a moment?"

When Jodi stepped onto the porch, she was placed under arrest. She calmly complied, placing her hands behind her back as the officer read her Miranda Rights.

"Do you understand your rights as they've been read to you?" the officer asked.

"Yes," Jodi said, seemingly unfazed. She paused. "Is there any way I can get my purse so I can get my makeup?"

The officers told her that would not be possible. Detective Flores placed Jodi in the back of a police cruiser and transferred her to the Siskiyou County Sheriff's Department.

Once Jodi had been taken into custody, two search warrants were executed on both her grandparents' and parents' residences. The detectives started at the grandparents' house.

In the room where Jodi had been staying, they found several boxes scattered across the floor. Sergeant Mark Hilsenberg, of the Siskiyou County Sheriff's Department, sifted through the boxes while a crime scene investigator photographed the premises. Lean and lanky, with sharp features and graying hair, Hilsenberg served in the army as a light infantryman before joining the police department in California, where he had worked for more than a decade.

Hilsenberg searched for guns, weapons, and anything else that could be related to the murder. Inside the boxes, he found clothes, books, and personal journals. Among the possessions were also two knives, which he seized to be tested.

In the storage room, locked inside a gun cabinet, the detective discovered a box of ammunition marked for a Winchester .25 caliber. The box, however, contained ammunition for a .22 caliber weapon. Someone had filled the box with the wrong caliber bullets.

Meanwhile, Detective Denning searched through miscellaneous paper documents for anything of evidentiary value. In one box, he located a receipt for a Hi-Point 9mm gun. By the July 1 date on the receipt, it appeared Jodi had purchased a weapon after the murder. She had taken possession of the gun on July 11, after a mandatory ten-day background check.

Another significant item was a confirmation receipt from Budget in Redding, California. Jodi had rented a car from June 2 through June 7—dates consistent with her trip to Utah and Travis's murder. There were also multiple receipts that documented her trip in California, Nevada, and Utah. The receipts would later be used to help fill in the gaps.

Later, Denning would review the information on Map-Quest. Jodi's grandparents' house in Yreka was more than a hundred miles away from Redding. Jodi would have had to drive 1 hour and 47 minutes to rent the vehicle. A simple search on the Internet showed there were numerous rental car facilities along the way, including one in Yreka itself.

Did she go to another town in a planned attempt to avoid detection? Denning wondered.

As Denning continued searching through the documents, Jodi's grandfather Carlton Allen approached him.

"You are wrong about Jodi," he said in a gruff voice.

Carlton insisted Jodi was working on the dates of the murder. He told detectives they needed to release Jodi immediately.

Unruffled, Denning insisted, "We have probable cause to arrest her, sir."

"Once I prove she wasn't even in Arizona, I demand you to release my granddaughter," Carlton said.

"Sir, we would not have traveled this far if we were not sure about our case," the detective said.

"Once I prove she was working in Yreka, you will let her go. We're going to sue the Mesa Police Department."

Eventually, Carlton asked if he could leave the house to obtain proof. Denning told him he was not being detained and was free to come and go as he pleased.

Jodi's grandfather left, and Denning continued his search. Around 1 P.M. he had concluded the search of the house, and had moved on to the Chevrolet Cobalt parked in the driveway.

While he was searching the vehicle, Carlton returned. He walked up to the detective and tried to hand him a sealed envelope.

"Here. I have proof." Carlton pushed it toward him. "After you look at this, you are going to let my granddaughter go."

Denning refused to take the envelope. "I applaud your efforts, sir. But I'm sure this would prove nothing."

Ripping open the envelope, Carlton unfolded three pages of photocopied records and displayed them in front of Denning's face. The detective scanned the documents—they were records of Jodi's payroll dates at the Purple Plum. Carlton flipped through the pages, which showed Jodi's last day was May 31.

Denning explained that it proved nothing for his cause. The victim had been murdered days later on June 4, he told Carlton.

Carlton dropped his head. "I apologize. I was just trying to help my granddaughter."

"I respect your efforts," Denning said. "I would probably do the same for a member of my family."

Meekly, Carlton stepped back inside the house. Denning continued his search of the car.

"Luggage and other personal effects had been placed inside the vehicle prior to Jodi's arrest," Denning later recalled. "It was apparent Jodi was preparing to leave based on what was inside the vehicle."

Zipping open one of the suitcases, the detective discovered mostly clothing and personal items. Tucked inside was also a box of 9mm ammunition—bullets that could be used for the gun Jodi had recently purchased. In the car, however, no weapon was found. Because a 9mm had not been used in the murder, the bullets were not considered evidence.

After completing the search of Jodi's grandparents' house, detectives transitioned to the residence where Jodi grew up, at 1021 South Oregon Street.

The premises were secured and photographed. It was quickly apparent that Jodi had not lived in the house for years. Few of her personal effects were discovered. In one room, however, detectives did seize a box of .25 caliber ammunition.

Also confiscated during the search of both houses were CDs and DVDs, two USB drives, three laptops, and a hard drive.

The searches were all concluded by 1:40 P.M.

Weeks later, detectives would receive a call from Jodi's mom, Sandra, inquiring about the 9 mm that Jodi had purchased. Sandra said she had reason to believe Jodi had hidden it somewhere inside the rented Chevrolet Cobalt. Somehow, detectives had missed it during the search of the car.

Eventually, detectives would track down the rental car in San Francisco, where a Hertz rental employee had located the weapon while servicing the vehicle.

Later, Detective Nathan Mendes would drive to Redding to speak with Raphael Colombo Jr., the owner of the Budget car rental office. Tall and brawny with thick black hair, Mendes was a seasoned detective for the Major Crime Unit for the Siskiyou County Sheriff's Department.

Mendes presented Colombo with a photo lineup of six petite young women with dark hair. Almost immediately Colombo pointed to the photo labeled number five—Jodi Arias.

"Except she had blond hair," Colombo told Mendes.

Jodi returned the car a day late—on June 7. Upon inspection Colombo noticed that the floor mats in both the back and front were missing. He also discovered some mysterious stains in the backseat, which he cleaned.

Mendes asked to see the vehicle and Colombo located it on the lot. He pointed out the faded stain in the middle of the backseat.

"I'm sure it wasn't there when she picked it up," Colombo said. "I know my cars. I'm meticulous about my cars. When she brought it back there was a stain."

The car was towed to the state crime lab for testing.

CHAPTER 29

Jodi Arias sat at the edge of her chair, her gazed fixed on Detective Esteban Flores as he repeated her Miranda Rights.

"You do have the right to remain silent," Flores said slowly. "Anything you say may be used against you in a court of law."

Jodi was wearing a dark blue short-sleeved T-shirt and tight white pants. As she listened, she rested her elbows on the table in front of her.

It was the evening of July 15, and Jodi was seated across from Flores in an interrogation room at the Siskiyou County Sheriff's Department. The small room was furnished with a round table, two small paintings, and a table lamp. Mounted on the wall, a digital video camera recorded the interrogation.

After Jodi waived her rights to an attorney, Flores, in his low, breathy voice, began by explaining some of the facts of the case. Many details of the investigation had not yet been released, he told her.

"I believe you know some of these details and that you can help," Flores said.

"I would love to help you in any way that I can," Jodi said politely.

For a third time, Jodi repeated the account of her whereabouts on June 4, using a manila folder to draw a map of her road trip through California and into Utah. Flores now confronted her with the gaps in her timeline.

"I have a problem with this trip," he said. "I've gone over and over it in my mind and on paper and there are still twenty-some odd hours unaccounted for."

"Did I tell you I got stranded?" Jodi interrupted, listing a litany of excuses for the holes in her story.

But Flores was done playing games. The road trip made no sense, he said. "Do I believe you came to visit Travis? Yes. I truly believe it."

Again, Jodi attempted to explain away the inconsistencies, but Flores told her he wasn't buying it.

"See the confusion that we're having?" he said, his tone more forceful. "Were you near Travis's house on Wednesday?"

"Absolutely not. I was nowhere near Mesa. I was nowhere near Phoenix," she said, leaning toward Flores.

"What if I could show you proof you were there?" He paused. "Would that change your mind?"

"I wasn't there." Jodi shook her head.

"Be honest with me, Jodi. You were at Travis's house. You guys had a sexual encounter—of which there's pictures," he said. "And I know you know there are pictures, because I have them."

In an earlier conversation, Flores had told Jodi the memory card located inside the digital camera had been destroyed. Now, he revealed the truth—that the deleted images had been recovered. "I have pictures of you in Travis's bedroom with Travis."

"Are you sure it's me?" Jodi asked inquisitively. "Cause I was not there."

Flores persisted. "Why did you go to see Travis that day? And what did you do?"

"I would never hurt Travis"—a phrase Jodi would repeat multiple times throughout the interrogation.

"I know you took pictures in the shower right before he died."

"I don't think he would allow that." Jodi shook her head.

Flores laid out the case for Jodi, writing down the evidence against her on the back of the file folder—the photos, Jodi's hair in the bathroom, DNA on wall, and the bloody palm print. "You left a palm print at the scene in blood."

Jodi sighed. "I can explain the blood and the hair. I used to bathe Napoleon all the time."

Flores interrupted. "This is over. This is absolutely over. You need to tell me the truth."

"The truth is I didn't hurt Travis," Jodi said.

Flores confronted her about the .25 caliber pistol, stolen from her grandparents' house one week before the murder. "You reported a gun stolen—a .25 auto. That just happens to be the same caliber as the weapon used to kill him."

"A .25 auto was used to kill Travis?"

"Yeah, along with multiple stab wounds," Flores said bluntly.

Jodi appeared to sob, burying her head in her hands.

Flores reclined in his chair, flipping through his file folder. "Have you ever shot that .25 auto?"

Jodi wiped her cheeks. "No. I've never seen it. My grandpa said it looks like a toy gun. I don't know what a .25 looks like."

"We're just playing games here. The gun was in your possession," he said. "When did you report it stolen?"

"I didn't even know that there were guns until my grandparents reported it stolen."

Changing the direction of the conversation, Flores discussed the crime scene and the condition of Travis's remains.

"If you want I can show you the pictures of him," Flores said. "Do you want to see the pictures of him?"

"Part of me does and part of me doesn't," Jodi said softly. "There's a morbid curiosity. I want to know how he died."

Repeatedly, Flores urged Jodi to explain her motive for killing Travis. Jodi admitted that she knew Travis's friends had been pointing to her as a suspect, casting her in a "bad light."

"This isn't about saving your reputation. It's about saving your life," Flores said.

"If I'm found guilty I don't have a life." Jodi threw up her hands. "I'm not guilty. I didn't hurt Travis. If I hurt Travis, if I killed Travis, I would beg for the death penalty."

The evidence didn't lie, Flores pressed. The photos proved Jodi was at the scene. "There are pictures of you in his bed with pigtails."

"Pigtails?" she asked with a tone of incredulity.

"It's you. It's obvious," Flores said. "Do you want to see the pictures? Would that change your mind?"

Jodi continued to claim she had no motive for the killing. "Let's say for a second I did it," she said. "I wouldn't even say I was jealous—if anyone, Travis was jealous."

"They know he was jealous. But they think that you were absolutely obsessed. Obsessed is the word that they used," Flores said, referring to comments from Travis's friends. "That's the word I've heard from everybody. *Fatal Attraction*—I don't know how many times I've heard that."

Flores asked her to come clean and reveal her motive. "I don't have answers of why it happened."

"There's nothing that could link me there," Jodi said.

For a minute Jodi was silent. Attempting a different tactic, Flores brought up Jodi's parents.

"I need you to think about what you're doing. I think your mom and your dad deserve the truth—because they're going to be asking," he said. "It's so important that you tell me why this occurred, what was going through your mind, what caused you to do this."

Flores stood up from his chair and left the room to retrieve a case file containing photos from the investigation. "I'll let you think about this."

As he walked away Jodi pleaded, "Detective, I'm not a murderer."

Alone, Jodi stared vacantly at the wall, not moving an inch. After nearly a minute she brought her hands to her face, wiped her eyes, and massaged her forehead. She leaned back, lifting her pelvis out of the chair and stretching into a backbend. She then flopped forward and rested her head on the table.

Minutes later, Flores reentered the room.

"What kind of gun is that?" Jodi nodded at the weapon holstered on Flores's hip. "Just curious."

"It's a Glock."

"I just bought a gun," Jodi said.

"We probably found it by now."

"Probably." She smirked. "I was taking it somewhere."

Flores flipped through a folder of photos, showing Jodi several images of Travis's house.

"If Travis were here today he would tell you that it wasn't me," Jodi insisted.

"My job is to speak for Travis right now." Flores looked her firmly in the eyes. "And everything Travis is telling me is that Jodi did this to me."

Thumbing through the folder, Flores stopped at a photo of Travis in the shower. "Remember him?"

"Yeah," Jodi said softly, gazing at the picture. Flores turned to the image of Travis sprawled on his bed naked.

"Travis would never go for that." Jodi shook her head.

Flores presented Jodi with a picture of herself naked on the bed, her hair braided in pigtails. Out of respect, he covered the photo from her face down with a piece of paper.

"That's you," Flores said. "All of you."

Jodi sat up out of her chair and lifted a corner of the paper, exposing her own naked body. "That looks like me."

"Let's just say I've seen all of you. And I've seen all of Travis," Flores said. "The one that sticks in my mind of Travis is on the autopsy table."

Flores turned to one of the last photos recovered from the camera.

"That's just one of the photos that were taken by accident." Flores pointed to the image of the back of Travis's head, with a socked foot in the foreground. "That's your foot, Jodi. Those are your pants. That's Travis."

"This is his bathroom," Jodi said. "That's not my foot."

Flores spoke about the crime scene and how Travis looked after decomposing for five days in the shower. "Couldn't even recognize him, he'd been there so long."

Flores turned to a picture of a bloody palm print on the

hallway wall. Jodi claimed she had no cuts that could have left blood. She pointed at scars on her arms, saying they were caused by her cat. Flores dismissed her claims as irrelevant.

"There's no doubt in my mind that you did this—none," Flores said. "So you can go until you're blue in the face and tell me you weren't there and you had nothing to do with it. I won't believe you. Because Travis is telling me you did this to him."

"There's no reason for it," Jodi said. "There's no reason why. There's no reason I would ever want to hurt him. . . . He never raped me."

Jodi dropped her head and began to cry.

"You have something to tell me. . . . I know you're afraid," Flores said. "Unfortunately, you're going to have to face the consequences."

"If I did that, I'd be fully ready to face the consequences," she said. "I'm all for the Ten Commandments—thou shall not kill."

Slowly and patiently, Flores continued to prod Jodi into admitting to a motive.

"There's no evidence to show that anybody else did this but you, you were the only one," he said. "Why won't you admit to it?"

"I just can't. I didn't kill Travis. I just didn't. I did not take his life," she said.

When Jodi last spoke to Travis, she said he urged her to come to Arizona, but she had refused. She said she felt guilty because she wasn't there when he was killed. "I don't think I had anything directly to do with it, but I feel responsible, somewhat, for it. I feel that if I would have gone there that I could have done something."

"But you were there, Jodi," Flores said, exasperated.

Again Jodi declared her innocence. The photos on the camera could have come from an old memory card, she said. Her blood and hair had likely been left in the house from when she had stayed there.

"Is that how you want to leave this?" Flores asked. "These farfetched excuses—about why your blood is there, why your hair is there, why your palm print is there, why those pictures were there?"

Jodi sat in silence as Flores reiterated the seriousness of the situation. "This is absolutely some of the best evidence I've ever had on a case. And I've convicted a few people on less than this."

"So I'm as good as done, right?" Jodi said. "With that evidence."

"Yeah," Flores nodded. "I'm begging you to at least come clean and tell me why. I don't want to leave here today not knowing, because it's going to follow me forever."

"I wish that I had answers. I'm sorry," she cried. "There's just no reason. There's just no reason."

"There's never a good reason why someone dies like this."

Jodi dropped her face in her hands, sobbing. "How many times was Travis stabbed?"

"More than I want to remember," Flores said. "Do you have anything else you want to tell me? I know this thing must be weighing on you pretty heavy. . . . I think you're feeling the reality in the moment now."

Jodi said she wasn't crying over guilt or remorse—she was lamenting all she would be losing if locked away in prison, and all that Travis had lost.

"I'm just feeling all the things I'm potentially going to miss out on with my family," she wept. "And I think of all the things Travis's family is going to miss out on with Travis. And it's not fair."

Flores made it clear—Jodi needed to face the gravity of the charges against her. "You are facing first-degree murder charges. And you are going to be booked in a jail. And eventually you will be brought back to Arizona and you will stand trial. That's the reality. And once you realize that, I think you'll be better for it."

But Jodi still seemed disconnected from the reality of the situation—expressing concern about the publicity her arrest would receive. "This is a really trivial question, and it's going to reveal how shallow I am, but before they book me can I clean myself up a little bit?"

Following the four-hour interrogation, Flores left the room. Quickly, Jodi composed herself, sat back in her chair, and ran her fingers through her hair. "Goodness," she whispered.

She turned her head, pulled her knees into her chest, and sighed. Glancing up at the ceiling, she chuckled. In the third person, she admonished herself for not doing her makeup.

"You should have at least done your makeup, Jodi. Gosh," she muttered.

As she waited for Flores to return, Jodi sang softly to herself, "Here with Me," by Dido.

"It might change my memory," she sang.

Then, she stepped over to the wall barefoot, flipped upside down, and did a handstand for nearly thirty seconds.

Minutes later an officer entered through the side door and directed Jodi to the corner of the room.

"Stop right there," the officer said. "Put your hands behind your back."

The handcuffs were slapped on Jodi, the clink of the metal resonating off the walls of the interrogation room.

That night Jodi was booked on charges of first-degree murder. She was fingerprinted, her clothes exchanged for a bright orange jumpsuit.

Even as she was being booked, Jodi seemed acutely aware that her arrest would make headlines. And it was important to her to look attractive in her mug shot. "I knew it would be all over the Internet," she said in a 2008 interview.

As she posed for the picture, Jodi tilted her head and grinned as if she were being photographed for the high school yearbook.

Once she was locked in her cell, Jodi had a chance to call her parents. While she whispered on the pay phone, another inmate overheard her side of the conversation.

"What comes up when you Google my name?" Jodi asked.

CHAPTER 30

Dressed in a baggy orange jumpsuit, Jodi pulled her knees to her chest, perched in her chair inside the interrogation room at the Siskiyou County Sheriff's Department. It was July 16, 2008—one day after her arrest—and Jodi had agreed once again to speak with Detective Flores.

A night in jail seemed to have an effect on her. She appeared anxious and uncomfortable, speaking in a stilted tone.

"I feel really powerless in here," she said, staring vacantly at the wall. "Do you know what my family is doing today?"

"I don't know. I know they're worried about you," Flores said. "Everyone's just in limbo right now."

Jodi hugged herself tighter. She told Flores she was ready to reveal the truth. "I can tell you everything that I know, that I remember."

"Okay, what do you remember?" Flores asked.

When she first set out on her road trip, Jodi said she had no plans to see Travis. Weeks prior, she and Travis had discussed getting together. But when Travis canceled their rendezvous, she made other plans.

A few hours after arriving in Los Angeles, Jodi called Travis and he urged her to come see him. At first, she declined.

Minutes later she called him back and told him, "I'm coming to Arizona."

"Really?" Travis asked. "What changed your mind?"

"Because I missed you," Jodi said.

Despite the fact that she was expected in Utah the next day, Jodi turned her car east and headed toward Mesa. It was a four-hundred-mile detour.

"So he knew you were coming?" Flores asked Jodi. "He expected you?"

Jodi nodded her head and whispered, "Yeah."

At around 4 A.M.—six and a half hours later—she arrived at Travis's Mesa home and quietly let herself inside. Travis was in his office, watching a YouTube video on his computer. Jodi asked about Travis's roommates and was told they were asleep upstairs.

In the interrogation room, Jodi explained to Flores that she never encountered Travis's roommates that day.

"You were pretty sneaky," Flores said. "You go up there and the roommates didn't even know you were there."

"I did that many, many, many nights."

Exhausted from her trip, Jodi went upstairs with Travis and fell asleep in his bed. Jodi was still sleeping when Travis woke at dawn and briefly encountered his roommates downstairs. Travis then crawled into bed next to Jodi, and fell back to sleep.

When they both woke again around 1 P.M., the roommates were gone. Travis and Jodi had sex in his bed. Afterward, Travis retrieved his new digital camera from his loft.

Jodi sprawled nude on his bed, posing for the camera, as Travis snapped a picture. Jodi spread her legs, and he snapped another. Jodi took the camera and turned it toward Travis, taking two pictures of him in bed.

"We also made a video," Jodi told Flores. "He deleted it. It was on the camera."

"Videos are hard to get once they're erased," Flores said. "Pictures are different."

That afternoon they went downstairs. Travis began

cleaning the house, moving the bar stools onto the couch. With her, Jodi had brought several CDs of photos from their many trips. In his office, Travis tried to download the pictures on his laptop, but due to a virus it wouldn't work.

"For some reason that was frustrating for both of us because he couldn't look at the pictures," Jodi said.

Instead, they had sex for a second time in his downstairs office. Around 5 P.M. Travis and Jodi went back upstairs. Jodi suggested another photo shoot, but Travis was reluctant.

"I asked if I could take pictures of him in the shower. He was like, 'No,'" Jodi told Flores. "He was very private about the shower."

"I'm surprised he allowed you to take pictures of him in the shower," Flores said.

Jodi convinced Travis it would look cool with the water droplets frozen in the images, like a Calvin Klein ad. Although he wasn't keen on the idea, Travis agreed.

At 5:22 P.M., he stepped into the shower. At first, he was uncomfortable.

"He's standing there and he's like, 'I feel gay.'" Jodi giggled, as if recalling the memory.

"The first few photos he didn't look like he was too comfortable. Obviously what you were saying to him made him more comfortable," Flores said. "What went wrong? Did he say something to you? Were you angry about something?"

In the interrogation room, Jodi paused, her face flush with emotion.

"What happened after that?" Flores prodded. "What went wrong?"

"I don't know what exactly happened after that." Jodi put her hand over her mouth and wept.

"What happened, Jodi? We've come this far," Flores said. "Did you plan on doing that the whole time?"

"No," she whispered.

Jodi laid her face in her palms.

"Jodi, please," Flores pleaded.

"I can't," she cried.

"Why not?" Flores asked. "Are you protecting someone else? Why would someone else do this?"

"I don't know," she said.

"He was sitting down, looking up at you. What did you do? . . . Did you plan on doing that the whole time?"

"No," Jodi said softly.

"You need to just let the answers come out," Flores pressed.

Slowly, Jodi began to discuss Travis's final moments. She directed Travis as he posed for the camera, showing off his physique. For the last two photos Travis was seated in the shower stall. Kneeling beside him, she browsed through the images.

Suddenly, a loud bang exploded in the bathroom, smacking against the walls. Before she could make sense of the blast, a violent jolt knocked her to the floor. She was lying next to the bathtub, across from the shower. The camera had slid across the tile. On the shower floor, Travis was bleeding.

"He was kneeling down in the shower and I don't really know what happened, but I think he was shot," Jodi said. "He was holding his head. . . . Travis was bleeding everywhere."

Shaken and bewildered, she said she tried to orient herself. She looked up and saw two tall strangers standing in the bathroom. They were wearing ski masks, gloves, and long-sleeve black shirts. One was wearing black pants, the other jeans. The man was holding a gun.

"I turn around and there are two people there. One was a guy, one was a girl," Jodi told Flores. "Travis was screaming the whole time. He wasn't screaming like a girl. He was screaming like he was in pain."

Terrified, Jodi got to her feet and ran.

"I ran into the closet and he stopped me. He held the gun to my head and said, 'Don't go anywhere,'" Jodi said.

For a moment she stayed frozen in the closet. Peering into the bathroom, she saw Travis on the floor, on all fours. Blood was dripping down his arms, pooling on the floor.

The woman was holding a knife. By the blood, Jodi said she "assumed" the woman had stabbed Travis. With adrenaline pumping through her veins, Jodi ran straight down the bathroom hallway, charging the woman and knocking her off her feet.

Leaping to Travis's side, Jodi pulled on his arm, trying to drag him to safety.

"Travis! Travis! Come on, come on, come on," Jodi yelled.

He looked at her, pain in his eyes. "I can't," he said. "I can't feel my legs."

Before Jodi could help Travis, the male attacker had re-appeared in the bathroom. Waving a gun at Jodi, the man screamed, arguing with the woman.

At some point during the encounter Jodi's fingers were cut, she said. In the interrogation room she showed Flores a scar on her left ring finger, which was crooked. She said her "CTR" ring no longer fit on her finger due to the injury.

In the bathroom, the woman approached Jodi.

"She came after me and he stopped her," Jodi said. "She wanted to kill me and he didn't. He said, 'That's not why we're here.'"

The man grabbed Jodi's purse and looked through her wallet. On her driver's license was a P.O. Box for an address in Yreka. "You must be that bitch from California," he said.

The man found Jodi's car registration, which had the address of her grandparents' home.

"If you ever say anything about this, we'll do your family the same way," he threatened, tossing her back her purse.

"He said, 'Leave now.' And part of me didn't want to leave," Jodi said. "Travis was still alive. He wasn't moving a lot, but I could see he was still alive."

With her purse and backpack, Jodi scrambled out of the bedroom. The last she saw of Travis he was on his hands and knees on the shower floor.

Clutching her keys, Jodi got behind the wheel of her car and sped away. She didn't run for help. She didn't call 911. She didn't rush to a neighbor's house. Jodi just left.

She said she told no one until this moment because the killers had threatened her family. Portraying herself as a martyr, Jodi said she was willing to face a lifetime in prison to protect her loved ones.

"There's a part of me inside that thinks they're going to come after my family," she said. "I'm just saying I think that as long I'm here, then there's less of a chance that my little brother is going to be hurt, or my mom, or my dad, or my sister."

"Are you trying to say that you're doing this to protect your family?" Flores asked. "Why would someone do this to you, or to him?"

"He said, 'If you ever say anything about this, we'll do your family the same way,'" she said. "I don't care much about myself at that point."

But Flores didn't believe a word of this new story.

"I don't believe you, Jodi," Flores said. "What was the motive of these two strangers? Why would anyone do this to him? He did nothing but help people. Everyone liked him."

Flores asked questions, attempting to debunk her story. Jodi maintained that it was the intruders that killed Travis.

"I came in here hoping you would tell me the truth and this is not the truth, Jodi. It does not make any sense," Flores said.

"It's all I know," Jodi murmured.

"Nothing changes for me."

"I didn't think it would," she said. "I feel responsible because I should have done more."

"You feel responsible because you did this," he said.

"I did not," Jodi insisted.

"You did this and nothing you can say is going to make me believe you," Flores said. "This is an elaborate story that does not make any sense."

Flores pointed out the scars on her hands were common in knife attacks. Blood can be slippery—when she was killing Travis she accidentally cut hands, he said.

"I was hoping you were going to be completely truthful with me today. Obviously that's not the case," Flores said. "I've been doing this a long time and this is the most far-fetched story I've heard in a long time. Is that how you want to leave this?"

"I know it was obvious I was there."

"No," Flores said, his tone more forceful. "It is obvious that you committed a crime, that you hurt Travis."

"What is my motive?"

"Jealousy, anger, fear, fear of being alone, angry at him for not keeping you in his life. I don't know? That's what I'm trying to figure out. There are so many motives with you—too many."

Jodi sat quietly, her gaze cast downward at the table. "I wasn't jealous of anything. I was a little envious that he was going to Cancún, but that was not the reason."

"So you're going to continue to tell me you didn't do this to him," Flores said.

"If I planned to hurt him in any way, I'm not the brightest person, but I don't think I could stab him. I'd have to shoot him continuously until he was dead," Jodi said. "I would never stab him. If, if I had it in me anywhere to kill him, the least I could do is make it as humane as possible, or quick, or something."

Jodi continued to prattle on about the two intruders, until Flores interrupted her.

"If you're going to continue with this, I don't think I want to go any further." Flores stood up to leave the room. "I gave you an opportunity. This was the only opportunity."

For the next week, Jodi remained locked up in California as she fought extradition to Arizona. On July 24, she lost her dispute and was transferred to Maricopa County's Estrella Jail in Phoenix.

In later interviews, Detective Flores questioned Bill and Sandra Arias in the case against Jodi.

Both parents told Flores about their ongoing issues with their daughter and her history of suspected mental issues. They also each spoke about the suspicions they had following the murder.

During her interview with Flores, Sandra was overwhelmed by emotion.

"How are you doing?" Flores asked. "You okay?"

"Not good. No," Sandra said, her voice trembling.

"As good as can be expected, I guess, huh?" Flores said sympathetically.

"I feel like I'm going to puke," she cried.

"Did you have any suspicion at all that she had anything to do with his death?" Flores asked.

Sandra admitted she had asked Jodi if she had been in Arizona, but said her daughter denied it—and claimed she had proof. After returning from her trip to Utah Jodi had acted completely normal. Dismayed, Sandra wondered out loud how anyone could commit a murder and act as if nothing was wrong.

"Why would she do something like that? She just snap or what? I don't know . . . And how could she come back here and be normal?" Sandra wept. "And then when her friends called her and told her he died she totally freaked out like she knew nothing about it."

CHAPTER 31

News of the arrest spread quickly among Travis's family and friends. From the beginning many had been convinced Jodi was the killer.

Still, when it was confirmed that she was arrested, many were shaken. It was unbelievable that such monstrous evil lurked underneath a benign-looking facade.

Jodi had attended the funeral, wrote loving things in the guest book, even hugged Travis's loved ones as they were grieving. Through it all she was harboring the abhorrent secret that she had taken Travis's life.

Many felt angry and wanted justice to be swift. For others, it was a relief that the case would not go unsolved.

For weeks after Jodi's arrest, police declined to reveal any details on the case to the public. All anyone knew was that the investigation uncovered some sort of evidence that led to the arrest.

On September 7, for the first time, Mesa police released details of the evidence against Jodi. This included the sexually provocative photographs discovered on the digital camera. The next day the local papers ran articles, focusing primarily on the photographs of Travis as he was dying.

"The last few moments of Travis Alexander's life—before he was shot in the head and stabbed to death—were captured on the memory card of his own digital camera," read an article in the *East Valley Tribune* on September 8, 2008. "There were pictures of his ex-girlfriend, Jodi Arias, lying nude on Alexander's bed. Then there were naked pictures of him posing in the shower. Finally, there were two pictures of a person on the floor of the bathroom, bleeding heavily."

Across the Valley many of Travis's friends opened up their newspapers and logged onto the Internet to read the disturbing details for the very first time. For many, the news was baffling. The Travis they knew was a devout Mormon and a virgin. Now it seemed as if he was living a second life.

Some took to his memorial Facebook page to express their shock, anger, and disbelief.

"I just wanted to say that I feel completely sick to my stomach after reading the news article," wrote a friend. "This changes the whole picture to me of what I thought the relationship between Jodi and Travis was, and of his worthiness to the gospel."

Others doubted the validity of the stories. They questioned the media's interpretation of the evidence and whether Travis was actually "posing" for the pictures.

"The article makes me feel sick to my stomach as well. But, just don't let that change your opinion of who Travis was," commented another. "For all we know, he was probably unaware she was even in the house."

As the days passed, however, the facts became difficult to ignore. More news outlets reported details of the evidence. Travis's family and many of his close friends were informed by the police directly about the photos.

The photos didn't lie. Travis had broken his promises to God. But despite his indiscretions, no one believed he deserved to be brutally murdered. Judging him in death would cause nothing but further pain. As the anger and disbelief subsided, most came to the conclusion they would not let this information influence their opinion of the man they knew.

"Regardless of any of the information that has been brought to light, the fact still remains that Travis changed lives—and was a friend to many, many people," wrote a loved one. "God is taking care of him, and things beyond our knowledge are being sorted out."

While the sexual photographs were difficult for his loved ones to comprehend, Lisa Andrews found them impossible to grasp. The idea that Travis had been sleeping with Jodi ran so contrary to the man she knew. For a while, she refused to believe it was possible.

"The media tells us what they want us to believe. But their facts are not always accurate and their stories are often biased or skewed. It's hard to know if they can ever really be trusted," Lisa wrote on her blog in the summer of 2008. "I know one thing is for sure: Heavenly Father knows all things. And He spares us from the pain and grief that we cannot handle."

Later, the facts would be impossible for Lisa to ignore.

Jodi Arias's case was assigned to one of Arizona's top prosecutors, Deputy Maricopa County Attorney Juan Martinez.

Short in stature, Martinez was in his mid-fifties with a dark complexion, graying hair, and round-framed glasses. His dogged demeanor and confident swagger were belied by the quiet gray suits and muted ties he typically wore in court.

The seventh of eight children born to illiterate Mexican farmers, Martinez and his family migrated to California when he was six. As a child, he resolved to learn English, which he primarily taught himself.

After earning an undergraduate degree, he managed a drug store. In 1984, he graduated from Arizona State University with a degree in law. For a few years he did some defense work, before joining the Maricopa County Attorney's Office in 1988. For the previous seventeen years of his career, he had focused solely on prosecuting murder cases.

With an aggressive courtroom demeanor, Martinez was meticulous in preparation and presentation. He was legendary for his no-nonsense tactics and his combative, sometimes theatrical style.

Widely despised by defense attorneys, Martinez rarely entered into plea bargains. And while other prosecutors in his office worked in teams, Martinez always went solo—handling his trials alone. During his career, he had prosecuted more than three hundred cases, and had an extremely high conviction rate.

His office inside the Maricopa County Courthouse was adorned with framed news clippings from his many wins—including against one of Arizona's only female death row inmates, Wendi Andriano.

In the early-morning hours of October 8, 2000, Wendi had bludgeoned her terminally ill husband to death inside their apartment in the Phoenix suburb of Ahwatukee. Police found thirty-three-year-old Joe Andriano, who had been diagnosed with cancer, beaten with a barstool and stabbed in the neck.

The subsequent autopsy revealed that he had sustained twenty-three blows to the skull and had traces of poison in his system. Despite his weakened state, Wendi told the police her husband was physically and psychologically abusive and that she killed him to save her own life.

In 2004, Martinez prosecuted Wendi, who pleaded self-defense. At the trial, she testified in her own defense for nine days on the stand, where she claimed to be a battered wife.

Martinez not only secured a first-degree conviction, but also a death sentence. Since her conviction, Wendi had been awaiting execution alongside just two other female death row inmates: Debra Jean Milke, who was convicted of murdering her five-year-old son, and Shawna Forde, ringleader of a group that killed a man and his nine-year-old daughter during a home-invasion robbery.

In an atypical twist, during Jodi Arias's trial, Debra Milke's death penalty and conviction would be overturned on appeal, leaving just two women on Arizona's death row in 2013.

As her case crept through Arizona's justice system, Jodi would rotate through numerous public defenders. But her ultimate lead trial attorney, and Juan Martinez's courtroom foe, would be Laurence Kirk Nurmi, who went by Kirk.

Nurmi was tall and rotund, with a head of gray buzzed hair, a neatly trimmed salt-and-pepper beard and mustache, and square-framed glasses. He carried himself with a touch of brassy arrogance, accessorizing his ill-fitting suits with brightly colored ties and matching socks.

A graduate of University of Wyoming, Nurmi began practicing law in Arizona in 2001. Originally working as a public defender, Nurmi would eventually open a private practice where he would earn a reputation for defending some of the state's sleaziest accused criminals. Specializing in sex crimes, he primarily defended those accused of sexual assault and child molestation. His Web site boasted his high record of not-guilty verdicts in these cases.

"At the Law Office of L. Kirk Nurmi we understand that you do not have to commit a sexual offense to be accused of being a sex offender," his Web site reads. "We understand that innocent people can be accused of sex crimes such as sexual assault, sex conduct with a minor or sexual exploitation of a minor, or any sex offense with very little evidence. We also understand that being accused of committing such a crime is devastating and daunting. . . . Our results speak for themselves."

Also assigned to assist in Jodi's representation was Victoria Washington, a heavyset African American woman in her forties, with short black hair and glasses.

A graduate of Arizona State University, Washington began practicing in Arizona in 1997. She worked for the Maricopa County Office of the Public Defender as a death penalty–qualified attorney.

On September 11, 2008, Jodi stood with a public defender by her side as she was arraigned on charges of first-degree murder. She wore black-and-white horizontal stripes with her booking number stenciled across the back. Her hands were in front of her, restrained with pink cuffs.

"How do you plead?" the judge asked.

"Not guilty," Jodi said softly.

Because of the heinous nature of the crime, the judge set her bail at $2 million, an amount her family could not afford. Until the trial, Jodi would remain behind bars.

In secure lockdown at the Estrella Jail, Jodi Arias was housed with another inmate in an eight-by-twelve square-foot cell twenty-three hours a day. There, she was fed twice a day. There was no organized recreation. She could mail letters, but would be unable to receive any in return. Jailhouse correspondence was only permitted by postcard. Visitors would only be able to speak to her through a steel cage.

In the days following her arrest, Jodi was in a deep depression. She would later testify that she was suicidal and had plans to end her life. She began her plan by slowly stocking up on Advil from the jail store—which she believed would prevent her blood from clotting. One night she asked for extra laundry, packing it around her body so she would not bleed on the bunk mate below her. Digging the small blade out of a shaving razor, she prepared to slit her wrists. As she considered her final moments of life, Jodi accidentally nicked her finger.

"It just stung so bad. I just sat there and I couldn't bring myself to do it," Jodi said.

As the weeks passed, Jodi's mood would periodically alternate from despondent to upbeat and defiant.

Meanwhile, her reputation still seemed her most immediate concern. The idea that people would think of her as a murderer was inconceivable.

After her arrest, Jodi wrote an eighteen-page letter addressed to Travis's grandmother. In it, she explained in detail the story of the two mysterious intruders who she claimed killed Travis. At the end of the letter, Jodi wrote that she did something she was not proud of.

"I kept my eye on the front door as I backed out. Awful I know. I didn't look as I backed out. I probably never should have been driving in that state. It wasn't heightened awareness, it was blind confusion. The front door never opened."

When Travis's family received the letter, they were disgusted. By then they had learned of the evidence against her and were convinced the right person would stand trial for the murder.

Slowly, Jodi began to adjust to life behind bars.

When she was first transferred to Estrella Jail in Phoenix, Jodi was locked up with another inmate named Donavan Bering. With a ruddy complexion, Donavan was an obese, middle-aged woman with short graying hair and glasses.

Donavan was being held on charges of accessory to arson. In May 2008, she helped her friend burn down a dental office in Sun City West in order to collect the insurance money. They had doused the office with gasoline and set it ablaze using matches. Investigators immediately suspected arson, and four months later Donavan and her friend were arrested.

In jail, Donavan took Jodi under her wing and provided her protection. They passed their days reading books and playing cards.

Meanwhile, as the facts of the case were uncovered, the media gravitated to the scandalous "fatal attraction" murder. And Jodi Arias suddenly became a very popular inmate.

CHAPTER 32

Jodi Arias gently patted her nose with cosmetic powder and dabbed a bit of gloss on her lips.

"Sorry," she said. "Don't roll the tape yet."

Jodi was surrounded by television cameras inside an interview room at the Estrella Jail. She was dressed in the shapeless black-and-white striped prison garb, with a pink ID tag around her wrist. She sat poised, her legs crossed at her ankles, as she checked her makeup.

Behind bars, just days after being extradited to Phoenix, Jodi was holding a press conference. Television crews from every local station, and several print reporters, gathered to speak to her about the heinous charges. As she primped for her debut, Jodi appeared to relish the attention.

"There have been a lot of people that have been speaking out and saying things, you know, on their side. This isn't a two-sided story. This is a multifaceted story," Jodi said, her tone flat. "There are many sides to this story. And I just don't feel like mine has been represented."

As she spoke about her relationship with Travis, Jodi softly smiled. "He was the first person to share the gospel with me and give me a copy of *The Book of Mormon*. And he challenged me to read it and I did."

Jodi described her adoration of Travis. "I cared very much for him."

"Were you in love with Travis?" a reporter asked.

"I think that being in love and loving someone are two different things," Jodi said. "And there was a point in time where we were in love but it was short lived."

"Why did you guys break up?" another reporter asked.

"Umm." Jodi glanced at the floor. "There was sort of a breach of trust in our relationship."

"On your part or his part?" asked a reporter.

"Both."

"And you guys couldn't move past it?"

"Um, no," Jodi said with a wry grin. "We really couldn't move past it."

Jodi openly spoke about her sexual relationship with Travis and how it continued after they broke up. "We both kind of knew that what we were doing wasn't for the best. We needed to correct our behavior for spiritual reasons."

Jodi said she knew their sexual relationship was considered a sin. Throughout their relationship it was a closely guarded secret. "As much as Travis and I told ourselves and everyone that we were just friends at the time, I think that our behavior was not as innocent as we tried to make it."

A reporter asked about allegations that Jodi snooped through Travis's phone. "But were you obsessed with texts? Those are the allegations."

"No. No, not at all," Jodi said.

Travis was the one who was obsessive when it came to text messages, according to Jodi. He had a strong, persuasive personality and she said she went to his house when summoned. "He wouldn't allow me to not answer a text message. If I didn't respond, he would keep calling and calling until I did. And so to me that was an obsessive behavior on his part. It was just—I took it as a compliment. He wanted to talk to me."

Reporters also asked about allegations that Jodi was obsessed with Travis.

"He admitted a lot—he got a lot of grief from his friends about the amount of time that we spent together," Jodi said.

"Did they not like it?"

"I don't know that it was so much that. I think they were more concerned with his future prospects for marriage."

Most important, Jodi addressed the charges against her.

"I have to ask you this. Did you kill Travis Alexander?" asked a reporter.

"Absolutely not." She shook her head. "No. I had no part in it."

"So you had nothing to do with Travis Alexander's death?" another asked.

"Nothing to do with it," Jodi said adamantly. "I didn't commit a murder. I didn't hurt Travis. I would never hurt Travis. I would never harm physically. I may have hurt him emotionally and I'll always regret that."

When she left his Mesa home, Travis was alive, according to Jodi. She declined to address the state of his well-being. Concerning the forensics Jodi said, "There's a good reason for all of that, but it will be saved for the courtroom."

She did, however, admit the evidence was overwhelming. "I need to be honest. There's a lot of evidence and it's very compelling. None of it proves that I committed a murder, none of it."

Jodi said that at times, sitting in jail, she had felt helpless, but her faith in the Lord left her with a deep sense of peace.

"I would be shaking in my boots right now if I had to answer to God for such a heinous crime," she said, her tone flat. "But I'm very grateful that this is one thing I will never have to answer to. This is not one of those things that will be brought up. I've done many things that are shameful, but this is not one of them."

Over the subsequent weeks, Jodi granted numerous interview requests. In most murder cases, the accused rarely speaks to the media because their statements could later be used against them in court. Against the recommendation of her public defenders, however, Jodi spoke to any reporter who visited her.

At first, she never mentioned the story she told Flores about the two intruders. Instead, she seemed more interested in exposing Travis as a sinner. Many of her statements focused on their sexual relationship.

Then in September, Jodi was visited by a producer from the tabloid news program *Inside Edition*. She granted the request and sat down in front of the camera. With national exposure, Jodi now publicly revealed her story of the two intruders.

"What really happened in there?" the reporter asked.

"Two people took Travis's life—two monsters," she said.

Jodi claimed she didn't know who they were and said she couldn't pick them out of a police lineup.

"You did not stab him twenty-seven times," the reporter asked, "or slit his throat from ear to ear?"

"That's heinous." She shook her head in disgust. "I can't imagine slitting someone's throat."

The interview ended with Jodi addressing the charges and her unwavering confidence she would be vindicated.

"No jury is going to convict me," she said. "Because I'm innocent. And you can mark my words on that one. No jury will convict me."

In her most high-profile interview, in the fall of 2008, Jodi spoke with reporters from the CBS crime show *48 Hours Mystery*. By then she had been locked away for more than a month, which seemed to have an effect on her.

"I've been sitting a lot in my cell thinking, what a waste. You know, I did have my whole future ahead of me," Jodi said. "I had everything to lose and nothing to gain if I were to kill Travis."

On the episode, Jodi went into further detail about the mysterious intruders, embellishing the story she told Flores. In this version, the male intruder put the gun to her head and squeezed the trigger, but nothing happened. The gun had jammed or misfired. Jodi grabbed her purse and ran out the front door.

"It was the scariest experience of my life. It just was so unreal; it was like a movie unfolding—a horrible movie. I could think only, if there was a way that I could get to Travis and get us both out of there, but it just seemed impossible," Jodi said. "I ran down the stairs, and out of there. And I left him there. I ran out the front door and I got in my car. I drove forever and ever until I was in the middle of the desert. The rest of it is a blur."

CHAPTER 33

On Halloween 2008, the Maricopa County Attorney's Office filed a notice of intent to seek the death penalty against Jodi Arias.

In seeking to execute Jodi, prosecutors concluded the first-degree murder was committed in an "especially cruel, heinous or depraved manner." It wasn't just the brutal manner in which Travis was killed. Her behavior following the slaying had been so cold, had shown such lack of empathy, that she was classified in a rare group reserved for only the most inhumane of murderers.

Even for a veteran prosecutor like Juan Martinez, it would likely be a challenge to convince a jury to sentence a pretty young woman to death. But considering the vast amount of evidence against her, Martinez felt the punishment was warranted.

Jodi's case was assigned to Maricopa County Superior Court Judge Sherry K. Stephens, a shrewd former prosecutor. The trial was originally scheduled for February 2010. Over the next five years, however, it would be delayed numerous times.

A potential death sentence somewhat divided Travis's friends. While some objected to it on principle, others believed Jodi Arias deserved no less than death for her crime.

As for Travis's family, his siblings believed Jodi was pure evil. They wanted her to die for murdering their beloved brother in cold blood.

"I hope to get to watch her die someday after she's on death row," said Travis's sister Tanisha Sorenson in a television interview. "Even if it's in twenty years from now, the death penalty is what she deserves."

In jail, Jodi seemed undisturbed by a possible death sentence. In interviews she actually said she would prefer execution.

"If a conviction happens, I know I won't be the first person to be wrongly convicted and possibly wrongly sentenced to either life in prison or the death penalty," Jodi said during her interview with *48 Hours Mystery*. "Personally, if I had my choice I would take the death penalty, because I don't want to spend the rest of my life in prison."

Later, Jodi's own words would come back to haunt her.

As the seasons passed, broken hearts slowly began to heal.

For nine months, the house on East Queensborough Avenue sat vacant. The lights were off, the shutters closed tight.

Travis's family considered selling it. But by then property values had plummeted. Travis owed $359,373 on the house, but it was worth less than $290,000. They let the house slip into foreclosure. In February 2009, it was sold at auction and the new owners moved in.

Travis's beloved dog, Napoleon, was willed to Travis's best friend, Deanna Reid. In California, she gave the dog the kind of life that Travis would have if he had lived.

Meanwhile, Mesa homicide detectives continued to build a case against Jodi, focusing primarily on information recovered from the electronics seized during the searches. Travis's and Jodi's phones and computers contained hundreds of photographs, text messages, and e-mails that needed to be examined.

During the year and a half they had known each other, Travis and Jodi had exchanged over 82,000 e-mails and text messages. By combing through the files, detectives attempted to piece together the complicated nature of their relationship. While in the very beginning, Travis had been loving toward Jodi, by the end his words were filled with hurt and anger.

By the time of his murder, something had divided Travis and Jodi.

A deep resentment, born of jealousy and pain, seemed to consume Jodi. Love turned to hate. Her obsession grew deadly.

By 2009 Jodi's press tour came to an end. At the insistence of her attorneys, she stopped granting media interviews and eventually the news coverage became less frequent.

Over the next few months, Jodi made use of her time in jail—getting her GED and learning Sign Language. She passed her days drawing, mainly with colored pencils she purchased from the jail commissary and cardboard from the back of a yellow legal pad of paper.

Behind bars, she was regularly visited by Mormon missionaries and even a bishop. While maintaining her innocence for the murder, Jodi sought redemption for her sexual encounters with Travis.

Periodically, a few of Travis's friends came for jailhouse visits, primarily in desperate attempts to make sense of the unexplainable. Jodi also maintained regular correspondence with many of the people she had met through Travis—penning dozens of letters.

In September 2008, she had written one of the executives from Prepaid Legal concerning her case.

"I am writing this letter in regards to Travis Alexander, whose life was taken last June. He was a good friend of mine. I am also, at present, in custody as I am being charged with his murder," Jodi wrote. "I am not writing this solely to plead my own innocence. That goes without saying—as Travis meant the world to me and I would never harm him."

Jodi explained she was aware of the upcoming Prepaid Legal conference in Las Vegas where Travis's memory would be honored. She insisted that it be made clear at the event that she was innocent until proven guilty. In closing, she made a plea.

"It is with a spirit of humility that I would ask that if I am in any way referenced during Travis's memorial at the team breakout, that my implied innocence is taken into account."

Months later, in March 2009, Jodi wrote a four-page letter to her former love interest Ryan Burns.

"I know you probably think I am a total psychopath and frankly, that is among the lighter things I've been labeled in the preceding months," she wrote.

Jodi explained that, while in jail, she had come to accept that "which seems beyond comprehension," and had come to "grips with what seems so impossible to accept."

"Yet, accept it I have mostly," she wrote. "I still indulge in a little resistance on occasion, a bit of grinding my heels into the ground."

In mentioning Travis, she maintained she was innocent of the murder.

"Ryan, you were never in danger with me. I hope you truly know that somewhere within, although what others think has gradually become less and less important to me," she wrote. "The only danger Travis was ever in because of me was 'spiritual danger' and of that we were both guilty of endangering each other."

She finished by thanking him for the ways he had enriched her life.

"It is no longer important to me that you believe me," she wrote. "You will know for yourself one day."

In 2009, Donavan Bering pled guilty and was released from jail, after being sentenced to five years of probation. But her friendship with Jodi continued, as they spoke periodically by phone and met for regular jailhouse visits.

Through it all Jodi's family would stand by her. But because they were out of state, Donavan asked her friend, Ann Campbell, to visit Jodi in jail as well.

Among Jodi's most ardent supporters was her ex-boyfriend Matt McCartney. In their relationship, Matt had always been chivalrous. Visiting her in jail, he vowed to do anything possible to save her.

As often is the case with high-profile murders—especially involving a beautiful female—Jodi attracted a lot of attention. Intrigued by Jodi's many media appearances, dozens of people reached out to her—sending postcards and making regular visits.

Many offered their support and claimed to believe in Jodi's innocence. She wrote each of her followers, forming several pen pal relationships.

One of her regular visitors was a man named Bryan Carr. Husky, with a shaved head, Bryan reached out to Jodi after discovering they had mutual friends on Facebook. He visited her regularly and they became friends.

Eventually, she would attract a loyal network of defenders who—although they never met her—were somehow captivated by Jodi Arias.

CHAPTER 34

Even in the dead of night, the jail was never silent. The omnipresent moans and cries of other inmates continuously echoed off the cement walls.

Jodi, who was once a sound sleeper, became easily stirred awake. She spent many sleepless nights lying in her bunk, staring into the darkness.

Memories of Travis haunted her. During the day she would be reading a book or eating a meal when suddenly Travis consumed her thoughts. As much as she tried, she couldn't erase him from her mind.

In 2009, Jodi began relating stories of these "intrusive thoughts" to a forensic psychologist who was hired by her defense to evaluate her.

Heavyset and bald, with a ring of thinning gray hair, Dr. Richard Samuels had worked for over thirty years as a psychologist, before specializing in forensic evaluations, examining criminals—primarily sexually violent perpetrators.

Over the next few years, Samuels would meet with Jodi more than a dozen times. In the beginning, Jodi was despondent and appeared to be suicidal. At various times throughout her incarceration, she would be medicated with tranquilizers and antidepressants. Because he was concerned about her mental health, Samuels later sent her a self-help book on self-esteem and depression.

During their first few visits, when Samuels inquired about the murder, Jodi stuck to the story of the two intruders. While the doctor was skeptical, he didn't question her claims. Instead, to conduct his evaluation, he administered tests to determine if she was suffering from any mental illnesses, including post-traumatic stress disorder.

Months passed and Jodi remained steadfast—she had done nothing to harm Travis. Then in the spring of 2010, she had an abrupt reversal.

During one of their visits, Dr. Samuels and Kirk Nurmi confronted Jodi and encouraged her to reveal the truth. And for the first time in two years, Jodi admitted her involvement in the crime.

"I lied," she said through tears.

Over the next few visits, Jodi began presenting a new version of her relationship with Travis, claiming Travis was physically and sexually abusive. On the day of the murder, he attacked her, throwing her to the ground. Jodi picked up a gun and shot Travis in self-defense, she said. After that, she said her memories were a blank.

Jodi claimed she had kept it all secret because she still loved Travis and wanted to protect his reputation.

With this new story, Nurmi and Washington began building a new case based on her claims of self-defense. But the attorneys also faced a problem. In Jodi's multiple media interviews she had claimed an entirely different account of the crime. These statements would most certainly be used to discredit her in court.

If Jodi was to be believed, her attorneys needed proof. Fortunately for her defense, evidence was about to be delivered.

In the summer of 2010, Kirk Nurmi received an anonymous e-mail. Attached were electronic copies of handwritten letters, dated between November 27, 2006, and May 27, 2008.

The letters were a series of dark confessions, revealing

disturbing acts of pedophilia and sexual deviance. They were signed Travis Alexander.

Seemingly authored by Travis, the letters were correspondence he had with Jodi throughout their relationship. In one, Travis asked Jodi to wear "boy's briefs," that he could "rip off," and requested her to perform oral sex on him while he wore one of his shirts with engraved cuff links so he could see his initials.

In another, dated March 2, 2008, Travis admitted to hitting Jodi, "in the face," and claimed that marrying her would help erase his "deviant" thoughts.

These mysterious letters were peculiar. Throughout Jodi's life, it seemed anonymous strangers were constantly coming to her rescue. If her boyfriend was cheating, someone always delivered a warning. When Travis wouldn't commit, a stalker's e-mail convinced him otherwise. Now, with her life hanging in the balance, evidence appeared out of nowhere to help prove her case.

At first, Jodi's attorneys were excited by the letters, believing they backed up Jodi's claims of abuse. In 2010, Nurmi submitted the letters to the court to be reviewed by experts, who would determine if they could be used as evidence during Jodi's trial.

Meanwhile, Jodi's attorneys urged her to cut a deal. If she would admit to second-degree murder, she could get out in a few years. Perhaps she would still be young enough to marry and start a family.

Jodi agreed to negotiate a plea, and on October 26, 2010, Nurmi and Washington submitted a plea proposal for second-degree murder.

When Juan Martinez saw the documents, he balked. His case for premeditated, first-degree murder was overwhelmingly strong.

Martinez didn't even bother to respond.

CHAPTER 35

Jodi gripped the microphone stand with both hands and closed her eyes. Her long brown hair was parted down the middle, and she wore a pink thermal under her baggy prison stripes.

"O Holy Night! The stars are brightly shining," she sang in an almost angelic voice. "It is the night of the dear Savior's birth."

It was December 2010, and while families everywhere were celebrating the holidays, Jodi was performing this Christmas carol behind bars. Arizona Sheriff Joe Arpaio, a man notorious for media stunts, had organized a unique holiday celebration—a jail-wide prison caroling contest.

Contestants—held on charges ranging from burglary and DUI to rape and murder—participated in the singing contest. Along with Arpaio, detention officers dressed as Santa Claus judged the inmates.

Competing against fifty other inmates, Jodi won the top prize. That Christmas, she was awarded with a special turkey dinner and a stocking full of presents.

In July 2011, Jodi's attorneys made another plea offer for second-degree murder. This time her attorneys pressed for a plea, citing the "collateral damage" that would impact Travis's friends and family if the true nature of his relationship with Jodi was revealed.

A trial would reveal that Travis exhibited "extremely demeaning, degrading, and abusive behavior," the plea read. Evidence including Travis's texts, e-mails, and voice mails would "paint a tawdry picture not of a choir boy steadfastly practicing his faith, but of a playboy expert manipulator and sexual deviant."

"Mr. Alexander carried on numerous relationships that while in and of themselves are really not a big deal," Nurmi wrote in the plea. "However, when you consider them in the context of all parties' relationship and affiliation with the Church of Jesus Christ of Latter-day Saints, they become a very big deal."

If the case went to trial, and details of Travis's secret life were revealed, it would cause further pain.

"Personal friendships would be affected, and most of all very poignant and cherished memories of Mr. Alexander would be tarnished," Nurmi wrote. "The relationship was chaotic and unhealthy to say the least."

By this point, Jodi was unconcerned about the death penalty. If the jury knew the details of her relationship with Travis, she felt there was little chance she would be executed. If she lost at trial, the most severe sanction she would likely receive was life without parole. Due to this Jodi had no incentive to plead to anything but second-degree murder, Nurmi insisted.

"Ms. Arias is willing to resolve this case," Nurmi wrote, "because she has grave regrets for the falsehoods she told the media after Mr. Alexander's death and how such falsehoods might have caused the family even more pain."

Martinez consulted with Travis's family, but his siblings wanted no part of it. Again, Martinez rejected the offer.

By the summer of 2011, Jodi and her attorneys were at an impasse. The trial date was fast approaching, but there was a problem.

The "pedophile letters" had been analyzed by handwriting

experts who concluded they were forgeries. Someone had used Travis's writing to create the messages. It appeared as if samples of his writing, possibly taken from his journals, were later cut up and used to create the letters.

In addition, these letters were copies. The originals could not be produced, Jodi claimed, because they had been destroyed.

But Jodi said she had someone who could back up her claims. During her relationship with Travis, Jodi said she had shown them to her ex-boyfriend Matt McCartney.

A few days later, Jodi's attorneys interviewed Matt McCartney about the letters, and he claimed he could verify the originals.

In August 2011, Juan Martinez was visiting the Estrella Jail for a deposition when he noticed Jodi in the visitors' area meeting with a large middle-aged woman.

As Juan waited for a prisoner he planned to interview to be brought out from lockdown, Jodi handed something to one of the guards to be passed to the woman. It was two magazines—a *Digital Photo Pro* and an issue of *Star,* which featured a cover story about Casey Anthony, who had been arrested for the murder of her two-year-old daughter, Caylee. Ironically, throughout Jodi's trial, she would often be compared to the Florida woman, who seemed to exhibit similarly erratic behavior after her daughter's death.

The guard flipped through the magazines and, seeing nothing out of order, was about to hand them to Donavan Bering's friend, Ann Campbell.

But something about the magazines raised Martinez's suspicions.

What could be the possible point of providing magazines to someone on the outside? he thought. *Jodi is up to something.*

Martinez intercepted the magazines, asking the guards to hold them. He called his legal assistant and asked him to get a warrant.

When Ann realized the magazines were being confiscated,

she left the visitors' area. An hour later, Martinez had seized the magazines. Flipping through the pages, at first he didn't notice anything peculiar.

Then, on one of the pages he noticed the faintest of writing. Printed neatly in pencil near the binding on page 20 of the photography magazine were the words, "You testify so."

Martinez flipped through the pages carefully examining every inch of the page, while writing down what he found.

On page 37 were the words "We can fix this"; on 40, "Directly contradicts what I've been saying for over a year."

The messages made no sense. They were written in some sort of code.

Back at his office, Martinez and his legal assistant pored over the magazines trying to decipher the code.

That's when Martinez noticed a series of numbers. In the *Star,* at the bottom of one page was the following set of numbers: 43, 40, 56, 20, 37, 54. Each number corresponded to a page from the photography magazine that contained part of the message.

Once deciphered and strung together, the entire message read, "You fucked up. What you told my attorney the next day directly contradicts what I've been saying for over a year. Get down here A.S.A.P. See me before you talk to them again and before you testify so we can fix this. Interview was excellent! Must talk A.S.A.P.!"

This was incredibly damning for Jodi's case. From jail it appeared she was soliciting false testimony.

It didn't take much detective work for Martinez to figure out the intended recipient. Just days earlier Matt McCartney had spoken with Jodi's attorneys about verifying the letters mysteriously submitted to the defense.

From the messages, it seemed Matt had failed in backing up Jodi's claims.

Matt never acted on Jodi's suggestion that he see her before talking with her attorneys, and in fact never testified in court. Shortly after the incident, and based on expert testimony, the judge ruled the letters would be inadmissible in court. When

Jodi's attorneys informed her that experts had ruled the letters forgeries, Jodi was incredulous. The letters were her only "proof" of Travis's true character, and were necessary to her defense.

On August 8, 2011, on the eve of her trial for first-degree murder, Jodi sat at the wooden defense table. Beside her at the table were her public defenders Victoria Washington and Kirk Nurmi. With her hands neatly folded in her lap, Jodi stared straight ahead.

When the time had come, Jodi stood to address the judge.

"Your honor," she said. "I'd like to represent myself."

The judge gave her an inquiring look.

"Ms. Arias, do you have any experience?" Judge Stephens asked.

"No," Jodi said meekly.

"Do you have a law license?"

"No."

"Have you even read the statute you're accused of?" the judge asked.

"No," Jodi replied.

The judge explained the complexities of the legal system and informed Jodi that she would face a severe disadvantage in choosing to represent herself. Jodi acknowledged these difficulties but told the judge she wanted to proceed.

Stephens granted the request, but did not allow her to fire her attorneys completely. Nurmi and Washington were to remain as advisory counsel and be ready to step back in as her attorneys if needed.

Jodi, the high school dropout, would go up against Juan Martinez, a prosecutor with a reputation for going straight for the jugular. It would be a battle for her life.

Although the trial was scheduled to begin August 9, 2011, Jodi's legal maneuver caused another lengthy delay.

Jodi seemed determined to get the letters admitted into evidence. With the assistance of her attorneys, Jodi filed several motions. The prosecutor immediately countered with motions of his own to preclude the letters as evidence, pointing out Jodi's documented history of lying.

"Defendant had previously attributed the crime to intruders. She now argues that all of the letters must be admitted to support her domestic violence defense," Martinez wrote in a motion.

The judge ruled against Jodi, barring the letters from being admitted during her trial. Less than a week later, on August 15, Jodi was back in court.

Only now, she wanted to reverse her previous request. She told the judge she realized she was not qualified to represent herself.

"I'm over my head," she admitted.

Stephens reinstated her defense counsel.

Following Jodi's brash courtroom move her relationship with Nurmi and Washington became acrimonious. On many of their legal decisions Jodi openly expressed her dissension. Her defense came to believe Jodi was a difficult client.

On December 16, 2011, Victoria Washington filed a motion to withdraw from the case, which was granted six days later.

Nurmi also attempted to withdraw from the case multiple times, citing in several motions that he had opened a private practice. However, it was too close to the trial date to completely replace Jodi's entire defense team and his motions were all denied.

Washington was replaced—postponing the trial once again. In January 2012, a new attorney was assigned to assist in representing Jodi.

In her early forties, Jennifer Willmott was pretty, with shoulder-length brown hair and a round face framed with heavy bangs and thick-framed glasses. In court she wore designer suits and high heels, which added an extra few inches to her petite frame.

Willmott received her undergraduate degree from the University of Arizona in 1992. Three years later she graduated from the Arizona State University's Sandra Day O'Connor College of Law. After finishing law school, she joined the Maricopa County Office of the Public Defender. As a trial attorney, she defended thousands of cases ranging from misdemeanor DUI charges to homicides.

Willmott was a smart, capable attorney—a necessary complement to Nurmi's somewhat relaxed style.

With her new attorney came a new twist to Jodi's defense. Once it became clear that the letters would not be submitted in court, Jodi's attorneys began submitting motions claiming Travis "became angry when she dropped his camera" and she was forced to kill him in self-defense, according to court records.

By the summer of 2012, it had been four years since the murder of Travis Alexander. For those who loved him, the pain of his loss was still overwhelming. His friends and family spoke of him constantly. Many also kept memories alive on a Facebook page dedicated to him, which by then had amassed more than a thousand friends.

"Travis, you will be missed as a leader, a mentor, a teacher and one who led and inspired many," wrote a friend. "We will keep your memory alive in hearts, minds and by our actions. May you now enjoy the blessings promised by our Savior. Until we meet again."

"You have truly touched more lives than one could ever count," wrote another. "You have a more important work to do now and will be missed."

Travis's family found some comfort in knowing how much he was truly loved and how many people were touched by his story.

On December 14, 2012, the Alexander family suffered another tragic loss. Shortly before the trial was scheduled to begin, Travis's beloved grandmother Norma Sarvey passed away at the age of eighty. Norma was laid to rest alongside the murdered grandson she had raised at the Olivewood Memorial Park in Riverside.

As they grieved for both their grandmother and brother, Travis's siblings prepared for their chance at long-awaited justice.

By the end of 2012, when it appeared the trial date was near, they rented a house in Phoenix. Travis's sisters, Samantha Turbeville and Tanisha Sorenson, and their brother Steven Alexander vowed to come to court every day, partially to show the jury that their brother's loss was felt deeply.

Jodi's family also wanted to show support for their daughter. In late 2012, Sandra Arias quit her job as a dental assistant to be able to attend the trial. By then Jodi's father was in poor health and on dialysis, and could not regularly make it to court.

Meanwhile, media outlets from across the country were booking tickets to Phoenix, for what they deemed would be the trial of 2013.

CHAPTER 36

Four and a half years after the murder of Travis Alexander, the trial of the *State of Arizona vs. Jodi Ann Arias* was called to order on January 2, 2013.

The trial—one of the most high-profile in Arizona history—would take place inside a cavernous, wood-paneled courtroom on the fifth floor of the Maricopa County Superior courthouse.

Perched at the center of the room sat Judge Sherry Stephens, a slight woman with shoulder-length, honey blond hair. From behind her oval-framed glasses she peered down on the court.

To the judge's right, Juan Martinez scribbled notes on a yellow legal pad. At his side was Detective Esteban Flores, who was assigned to assist with the prosecution.

Across the aisle, on the opposite side of the room, defense attorney Kirk Nurmi lounged in his chair. Seated next to him at the heavy wood table, Jennifer Willmott periodically whispered to Jodi.

More than four years in jail had a dramatic effect on Jodi—transforming her from a sexy seductress to a dowdy schoolmarm. She appeared frail, having shed about twenty pounds from her already thin frame. Her dark-brown hair was cut bluntly below her shoulders with a thin wisp of bangs and she wore mousy, horn-rimmed glasses. On the first day of trial, Jodi was dressed in gray slacks and a baggy black blouse concealing the bulge of an electronic stun belt worn by accused murderers.

Throughout the testimony, Jodi often dabbed her eyes with a tissue and wiped tears away from her cheeks. When graphic crime scene photos were shown to the court, she hid her face behind her hand or hair.

In the front row behind the defense, Sandra Arias sat quietly with her twin sister and the occasional family friend.

Huddled together behind the prosecution was a revolving group of Travis's loved ones. Fixtures each day were Travis's sisters Samantha and Tanisha, and their brother Steven Alexander.

The back three rows were comprised of an array of TV reporters from network news and court commentary shows. A television camera stationed in the last row broadcasted the testimony, while a satellite link provided a live Web stream on dozens of sites. Millions tuned in to watch the trial; the most dedicated crime followers packed the courtroom's visitors' gallery, at times waiting for a seat for hours.

The trial would be like none other—a rare concoction of sex, religion, and death. Testimony would be filled with salacious phone sex and graphic text messages, juxtaposed with gruesome crime scene photos capturing the viciousness of the murder.

At 11 A.M. on January 2, Juan Martinez began his opening statement.

"This is not a case of whodunit," he said, standing before the jury. "The person who done it, the person who committed this killing, sits in court today. It's the defendant Jodi Ann Arias."

Martinez spoke in a measured tone as he painted a portrait of the victim—a good man and devout Mormon who had the misfortune of meeting Jodi.

"She slit his throat as a reward for being a good man," he said. "She knocked the blessings out of him by putting a bullet in his head."

At the defense table Jodi sobbed, although no tears appeared to run down her cheeks.

Martinez walked the jury through Travis and Jodi's relationship, beginning with their meeting in Las Vegas in September 2006. Five months later, after she converted to Mormonism, the two became a couple.

"They both did what can be expected by young people," he said. "They engaged in sexual relations."

After their breakup, Jodi moved to Mesa, where their sexual relationship continued. Ten months later, Jodi returned to Yreka.

Then, on June 9, after not hearing from Travis for five days, his friends discovered his decomposing body. Using a poster board with a diagram of Travis's bedroom, Martinez pointed out the layout of the crime scene.

"Whoever had done this killing had taken the time to wash the body," Martinez said. "Someone had taken the time to stage that kind of scene."

The murderer also tried to dispose of evidence by throwing the camera in the washing machine, he said. During the subsequent investigation, the camera and memory card were discovered in the washer. "The camera was destroyed. It was messed up. It could never take pictures again."

Ultimately, the deleted images were recovered, however. For the jury, Martinez described the explicit pictures from earlier that afternoon: Jodi, sprawled on the bed; Travis lying beside a bottle of K-Y Jelly. "These are salacious photos. What they are doing is what people do behind closed doors."

A second batch of photos showed Travis showering, with the last image taken at 5:31 P.M. Just forty-four seconds later, a photo was accidentally taken of the shower ceiling as Travis was being attacked.

Then, for the first time, Martinez publicly announced his theory of the crime.

As Travis showered, he was first stabbed in the heart. The

wound had not been fatal. As Travis staggered to the bathroom sink, he was repeatedly knifed.

"He was more likely than not dead at that point," Martinez said.

Throughout the attack, Travis had attempted to defend himself, as evident from the wounds to his hands.

"Mr. Alexander did not die calmly," Martinez said. "He fought. He was conscious at the time of the crime."

While he lay dying, Jodi shot him in the face, likely after he was already dead, Martinez said. "She wasn't through with him. She took a shot and stuck it in the temple."

The scenario was a calculated move on Martinez's part. If he could show that Jodi fired a bullet into Travis's dead body, it would prove the murder was cold and calculated—not a sudden passion that could lead to a second-degree murder conviction.

Martinez then explained Jodi's actions following the murder, including her trip to Utah to see Ryan Burns.

The day of her arrest, on July 15, 2008, Jodi repeatedly denied she had been inside the house, even when presented with the evidence. The next day, she told Detective Flores the twisted tale about the mysterious intruders. Now, in court, she was claiming self-defense.

At the conclusion of his opening statement, Martinez played a clip from Jodi's 2008 appearance on *Inside Edition*. In the video, Jodi told the reporter that she was innocent.

"No jury is going to convict me," Jodi said on *Inside Edition*, "because I am innocent, and you can mark my words on that. No jury is going to convict me."

Martinez paused. Then, he implored the jury to "mark her words."

"Remember that while you're marking a premeditated murder verdict."

"Jodi Arias killed Travis Alexander—there's no question about it," defense attorney Jennifer Willmott said in her opening statement. "The million-dollar question is what forced her to do it."

As Willmott spoke, Jodi seemed momentarily agitated, but quickly seemed to compose herself. Willmott began by explaining Jodi's background, including her relationship with her ex-boyfriends. During her presentation, photos of Jodi flashed on the TV monitors around the courtroom.

"Throughout the trial you will learn much more about Jodi Arias," Willmott said. "Jodi was a talented photographer, artist. She was a bright, articulate young woman."

In March 2006, Jodi signed up for Prepaid Legal. Six months later she met Travis. During their first weekend together in Las Vegas, Travis spoke about his Mormon values.

"Jodi was captivated," Willmott said. "He was someone to be admired by Jodi. He was a good Mormon man."

Four days later, Jodi broke up with Darryl. After converting to Mormonism, Jodi's relationship with Travis blossomed, especially during their frequent out-of-town trips.

"Certainly on the outside it appears they were involved in a healthy relationship." Willmott paused. "Nothing could be further from the truth. In reality Jodi was Travis's dirty little secret."

From their first meeting, Willmott claimed, Travis was using Jodi to fulfill his sexual desires. In the beginning their encounters never reached the point of vaginal intercourse.

"As Travis would explain to Jodi, 'Oral sex wasn't as much of a sin as vaginal sex,' so he convinced her to have oral sex," Willmott told the jury. "And later in their relationship, Travis would tell her that 'Anal sex wasn't as much of a sin as vaginal sex,' as a way to convince her to engage in that as well."

As Willmott described, Travis and Jodi's relationship was wrought with psychological and sexual abuse. Travis was a sexual deviant, living a secret second life, she said.

"Being an executive, outward appearances would have been very important to Travis," she said. "On the outside he could pursue the appropriate Mormon woman."

Blinded by her love for Travis, Jodi was naive. Travis would often tell her to date other men, but if she did, he became irate.

"Jodi was easily manipulated and controlled," she said.

"Anytime she started talking to another man he would degrade and humiliate her. She became humble, compliant, and agreeable."

Following the breakup, Jodi didn't move to Mesa because of an obsession with Travis, she did so because he was sending mixed signals. But while he was sleeping with Jodi, Travis told many friends she was stalking him, Willmott said. "You'll hear how Travis degraded Jodi to his friends, how he referred to her as a 'stalker' or 'crazy,' called her a 'slut' or 'whore.'"

On the monitors an image of Jodi appeared, wearing a gray T-shirt with the lettering TRAVIS ALEXANDER'S. "That T-shirt is the perfect example of how Travis treated her."

By April 2008, Jodi had had enough and returned to Yreka. But Travis's hold on her didn't diminish.

"Even though she moved, he wouldn't let her go. He continued e-mailing, texting, and calling," Willmott said. "The more Travis distanced himself the more he could control her."

The sexual manipulation escalated until the last day of Travis's life. "On June 4, it reached a point of no return. On that day he told her he was going to kill her."

After being persuaded by Travis to come see him in Mesa, Jodi arrived at his house at around 4 A.M. on June 4. That afternoon, they had sex. In preparation of their tryst, Travis had purchased rope to fulfill his fantasy of tying Jodi up during sex, Willmott said.

"He used softer rope, like the kind to hold curtains with," she said. "He used a knife to cut the rope when at the appropriate length."

After sex that afternoon it was Travis who asked to take pictures of Jodi. "The kind of pictures that Travis wanted to take of Jodi would make most people cringe with embarrassment."

On the monitors a nude photo of Jodi appeared, her hair braided in pigtails. The next two close-up pictures were of Jodi's anus and vagina.

Following the photo session, Travis and Jodi went to his downstairs den and he tried to download photos from a CD on his computer. Because of a computer virus, the software wouldn't download. In anger, Travis threw the CD. Jodi tried to calm him down.

"She knew that the one thing that calms his temper the quickest is sex. So as she's telling him, 'It's ok, I'll fix it, don't worry,' Travis grabbed her and spun her around," Willmott said. "Afraid that he was going to hurt her, Jodi was actually relieved when all he did was bend her over the desk."

They had sex in the den, after which Jodi washed herself in the downstairs bathroom. Hours later, it was Travis who urged Jodi to photograph him in the shower, according to Willmott.

On the monitors one of the last images taken of Travis alive appeared. The next photo was the blurry image of the ceiling above the shower—time-stamped 5:31 P.M. At that moment, Willmott said, Jodi dropped the camera.

"He lunged at Jodi in anger," she said. "Jodi's life was in danger. He knocked her to the ground in the bathroom, where there was a struggle."

Jodi was forced to defend herself. The next picture showed the back of Travis's head lying on the shower floor, with Jodi's foot in the foreground.

"In under two minutes she had to make a choice. She was going to live or she was going to die," Willmott said. "Had Jodi not been forced to defend herself, none of us would be here. In that one minute, had Jodi not chosen to defend herself she would not be here."

Over the next nine days of the trial, Martinez would present his case to the jury as it unfolded through the investigation—beginning with the discovery of the body.

Following opening arguments, Martinez called his first witness: Mimi Hall. For court Mimi, then thirty-three, wore her hair curly and wore thick-framed glasses and a loose-fitting gray sweater.

On the stand, she explained her relationship with Travis, their planned trip to Cancún, and the discovery of his body on June 9, 2008. With the help of Travis's roommate they had unlocked the master bedroom door.

"I looked through the crack in the door," she said. "When they said they saw blood, I stopped looking."

On cross examination, Kirk Nurmi attempted to paint Travis as a sinner. He questioned Mimi about what constitutes sin in the Mormon religion. Murder and denying the Holy Ghost were at the top of the list, Mimi said. Ranked below that was sexual immorality.

"It's a very serious sin and something you could lose your good standing in the church or even be excommunicated over," Mimi explained.

On redirect, Martinez asked Mimi about the process of repentance in the church. Through his questioning, Martinez tried to show that while Travis had sinned, he was also in the process of making amends.

"Was he or was he not temple worthy?" Martinez asked.

"I actually remember him telling me a story that he was no longer able to go to temple," Mimi said. "I don't think he was temple worthy."

Over the next few days Martinez called officers and detectives who worked the investigation to the stand. In court, he frequently used photos of Travis's corpse to shock the jury.

During the testimony of one of the patrol officers who had responded to the 911 call, Martinez entered into evidence one of the more gruesome photos: a close-up of Travis's decomposing face.

"This was the body that was found in the shower?" Martinez asked.

"Yes," the officer said. "His face was very dark purple, almost black. The rest was very pale."

As the images were shown, Travis's sisters averted their eyes, silently sobbing in agony.

Later, two latent print examiners from the Mesa crime lab testified about taking fingerprints, palm prints, and buccal swab samples from Jodi, which matched the palm print and DNA found in the house.

A Mesa fingerprint examiner also led the jury through a photographic tour of Travis's house. Displayed for the jury were images of the inside of the washing machine showing the digital camera lying on top of a bleach-stained towel and clothes. During the testimony, evidence was presented, including a section of bloodstained carpet, Travis's laundry, sheets, the camera, and the camera's memory card.

Forensic scientist Lisa Perry also detailed bloodstains and spatter found at the scene, as well as the .25 caliber bullet casing, which was discovered lying in a pool of congealed blood. It was shown as proof Travis was stabbed and sliced prior to being shot.

"In relation to the blood—when was that casing placed there in relation to the blood?" Martinez asked.

"After the blood was deposited there," Perry said.

"So the blood source was already bleeding?" Martinez asked.

"Yes," Perry said.

Later, a firearms examiner testified that the bullet casing on the shower floor would have been automatically ejected from a .25 caliber pistol.

On the third day of trial, the medical examiner, Dr. Kevin Horn, inventoried Travis's twenty-seven stab wounds, using autopsy photos. As images of Travis's bruised and bloated body flashed on the monitors, Jodi readjusted her seat to shield her gaze. In the front row, Tanisha and Samantha sat doubled over to hide their faces from the horror. About twenty minutes into the explicit testimony, Travis's family members stood up and bolted from the courtroom.

The most contentious part of Horn's testimony came when discussing the bullet wound to the skull. Because of the location of the wound, Horn determined the brain had been perforated.

"He would be incapacitated . . . rapidly," he said.

Both the neck wound and the gunshot would have caused

unconsciousness within a few seconds. The stab to the chest "would definitely cause death without medical attention."

"How did Mr. Alexander die?" Martinez asked.

"Primarily from rapid blood loss," said Horn.

In heated cross-examination, Willmott questioned Horn's perception of the sequence of the murder. In pretrial hearings, Detective Flores had testified that he believed the gunshot wound had come first. Yet Horn maintained this was not possible.

"For the most part if you have a bullet pass through the brain you won't be standing," Horn said. "You won't be functional."

Repeatedly, Willmott tried to raise doubt that the bullet had actually passed through the brain. Horn, however, remained resolute in his assessment.

"It had to have passed through the brain," he said. "The skull is perforated where the brain is. It would have passed through the right hemisphere."

"Are you sure of that?" Willmott asked.

"Yes," Horn said.

Throughout the prosecution's case, the defense tried to dispute the prosecution's theory on the sequencing of the murder.

On January 10, Nurmi grilled Detective Flores about testimony he gave in 2009 during a probable cause hearing, in which he said he believed Travis had been shot first.

"That was my understanding at the time," Flores said. "I'm not a doctor."

In interviews and sworn statements, Flores had repeated this theory of the crime. Over vigorous objections from Martinez, Nurmi pushed Flores about the discrepancy.

"It was not inaccurate, it was mistaken," Flores said.

"That's a pretty big misunderstanding, isn't it?" Nurmi asked.

"No, I don't think so," Flores replied.

After the jury was dismissed for the day, Nurmi requested a mistrial, claiming Flores had committed perjury in his testimony. The motion was denied.

Throughout the month of January, Detective Esteban Flores took the stand multiple times, testifying primarily about interactions he had with Jodi throughout the investigation.

Each recorded phone call, voice message, and both interrogation videos were played for the jury. On cross-examination, Kirk Nurmi asked about instant message conversations discovered on computers seized from the house, in which Travis referred to Jodi in crude sexual terms.

"Do you recall her saying he had said several mean things to her?" Nurmi asked.

"Yes," Flores answered.

Nurmi asked if Travis had ever referred to her as a "three-hole wonder."

"Yes," the detective said.

"As a slut?" Nurmi asked.

"Yes."

"As a whore?"

"Yes."

On redirect Martinez clarified why Travis had been using degrading terms toward Jodi in his e-mails to her.

"You read that e-mail, didn't you?" Martinez asked. "What did that e-mail say? Why was he upset?"

Flores explained that during the conversation Travis was actually accusing Jodi of using him sexually. "I think I was little more than a dildo with a heartbeat for you," Travis had written.

On the fifth day of the trial, Ryan Burns testified about his relationship with Jodi and her trip to Salt Lake City, seventeen hours after the murder.

Nearly five years after meeting Jodi, Ryan was now married and a father. He had put on some weight and looked different from how he had in 2008. In court, he wore a black suit and a green tie.

For the jury, Ryan described how during her stay, he and Jodi became intimate.

"When we woke up we were kissing and she eventually

kind of grabbed me and adjusted me a little bit," Ryan said. "And that's when she got on top of me and we were kissing."

Ryan said he was surprised by Jodi's physical strength.

"I complimented her on being very feisty and was kind of referring to her being a lot stronger than she looks," he said.

On cross-examination, Nurmi questioned Ryan about his expectations of Jodi's visit to Utah.

"You were hoping for a romantic interaction?" Nurmi asked. "Were you interested in pursuing a romantic relationship with her?"

"Yes," Ryan said.

Throughout the trial each day, Sandra Arias sat quietly in the front row behind the defense. She smiled softly as Jodi was led in and out of the courtroom. She walked briskly by reporters, ignoring all requests for interviews. And when explicit photos of her daughter were shown, she dabbed tears from her eyes.

Through it all, Sandra supported her daughter and was willing to do anything she could to save Jodi's life. Midway through the prosecution's case, her allegiance was put to the test.

In early January, at Jodi's request, Sandra met with the *National Enquirer* in a twisted scheme to help combat the growing negative public sentiment against her daughter. With her, Sandra had electronic copies of letters, supposedly written in Travis's handwriting, describing his "deviant" sexual thoughts and discussing desires for Jodi to wear "boy's briefs."

"Jodi wanted me to get these letters out to the public. I am only doing this because she asked me to," Sandra tearfully told an *Enquirer* reporter. "Jodi has several other letters in her possession, but she's holding off on releasing them."

When asked, Sandra said that the electronic copies were the only copies in existence. "Jodi told me that the originals were destroyed," she said.

The scheme, however, backfired. Instead of publishing the letters as an exposé on Travis Alexander, the *Enquirer* wrote

about Jodi's desperate, last-ditch plan to walk free from jail
by selling the letters, quoting anonymous sources condemn-
ing Jodi for the scheme.

"These letters are quite literally the only card Jodi has left
to play," said a source. "Getting them out to the public is her
strategy to be acquitted of murder and escape the death penalty. That's how desperate and evil she is. She's manipulating her own mother from behind bars."

In an attempt to further profit from the publicity of the
case, in January, a family friend began selling Jodi's art on
eBay, including fifteen colored-pencil drawings she created
in jail.

One series consisted of celebrities from the 1950s, including Grace Kelly, Frank Sinatra, and Lucille Ball. Others were
pictures of beautiful women named after the zodiac signs. A
third set included photo-realistic drawings of hands, one holding a baby's feet.

They were initially listed from between $150 and $450 dollars. They all sold, raising thousands.

According to the auction listings all profits went toward
"Jodi's family traveling expenses to the trial, other fees, and
of course money for Jodi so she can eat better food than what
they serve in jail."

At the bottom of the listing was a note from Jodi.

"Jodi thanks everyone that has helped during these tough
times. Please continue to pray for her family and for Travis's
family."

Meanwhile, in court, prosecutor Juan Martinez continued to
build his case.

A detective from the Siskiyou County Sheriff's Department testified about receipts found during the search that
traced Jodi's journey across California the week Travis was
killed. A Yreka police detective also spoke about the unusual
burglary at Jodi's grandparents' house. Photos of Jodi's grandparents' house were shown, including one of the gun cabinet, on top of which were stacks of quarters.

"Anything unusual about this robbery?" Martinez asked.

"Yes," the officer said. "I believed it was unusual that small items worth money were not taken, for instance the money."

On cross-examination, the officer admitted there had been a rash of burglaries in the Yreka area.

Following the Yreka investigator, Mesa detective Michael Melendez detailed how the digital camera was found broken inside the washing machine.

"Just because an item is deleted does it mean that it's gone?" Martinez asked.

"No, it does not," Melendez said.

Martinez presented the time-stamped photo taken forty-four seconds after the last shot of Travis alive in the shower. In opening arguments the defense said the attack began forty-five seconds after the camera was dropped.

While questioning Melendez, Martinez dropped the camera for dramatic effect.

"Is that forty-five seconds?" he shouted.

On the third week of the trial, Martinez called an employee from Verizon Wireless and a Mesa detective who testified about the calls Jodi made to Travis late on the night of June 4, after she knew he was dead. Additionally, a Sprint employee discussed calls Jodi made to Travis in the days before and after his death.

A Utah police officer also took the stand relating the traffic stop and Jodi's upside-down license plate. And Raphael Colombo Jr., the owner of the Budget in Redding, spoke about the encounter with Jodi on June 2.

"Do you remember her hair color back then?" Martinez asked.

"It was blond," Colombo said.

The prosecution's final witness was Leslie Udy, Jodi's former friend.

As Leslie spoke about their friendship, Jodi, wearing a green button-down blouse, stared at her almost apoplectically, occasionally wiping away tears.

The day after the murder, when Jodi met Leslie in Utah, she had discussed her relationship with Travis.

"She said they weren't together anymore, which I kind of already knew," Leslie said. "But that they'd always be friends and they had joked and laughed about the fact that at some point, further on, they would see each other at Prepaid Legal events, and their children would play together and be friends."

On cross-examination, Leslie said the fact that Jodi killed Travis ran contradictory to the person she knew. "Jodi was a soft-spoken person. She was a gentle person. I couldn't imagine she would do something like this."

On redirect Martinez attacked Leslie's assessment of Jodi.

Grabbing the explicit photos of Jodi nude on Travis's bed, he said, "Ma'am, I don't mean to be indelicate with you, but you said you knew her."

"Yes." Leslie nodded.

"Did you know anything about that?" he said, as he laid a naked photo on the courtroom's overhead projector. He then presented a shot of Alexander bleeding on his bathroom floor.

"You said you knew her well, but she never confided to you that she killed him, did she?" the prosecutor asked.

"No," Leslie answered.

Minutes later Martinez stood at his desk. "The state rests."

CHAPTER 37

Throughout the defense's case, Jodi and her attorneys attempted to destroy the only thing left of Travis Alexander—his reputation.

They began by attempting to airbrush over the image created by the prosecution of Jodi as a manipulative murderer. Their first witness: Darryl Brewer. At the sight of her ex, Jodi raised her hands and touched her cheeks, as if she were blushing. Darryl, now fifty-two, walked briskly through the courtroom, wearing a dark gray suit and wire-rimmed glasses. He took his seat at the witness stand and folded his hands in front of him.

Because he didn't want his son to be somehow associated with this case, he asked for, and was granted, permission to have his face not shown on video.

On the stand, Darryl was stoic, occasionally glancing at Jodi, but staying primarily focused on the attorney questioning him. He spoke about the details of their four-year relationship and how it abruptly shifted after she met Travis.

"Jodi became more actively religious," Darryl said. "We stopped being intimate. Jodi told me she was saving herself for her husband."

At the time, however, Darryl never knew about Travis.

"In the fall of 2007, were you aware of her being in a relationship with Travis Alexander?" Nurmi asked.

"No," Darryl said.

On cross-examination, Martinez asked Darryl about his
encounter with Jodi on June 3, 2008—the day before Travis's
murder.

"She was asking for gas cans so she could make the trip
to Mesa, Arizona, wasn't she?" Martinez asked.

"She said she needed them and was taking a long trip,"
Darryl said.

It was a crucial point for Martinez. The fact that Jodi had
borrowed two red gas cans a day before the murder was further evidence of premeditation. It appeared as if she had
brought enough gas to avoid stopping anywhere in Arizona
and to avoid leaving a paper trail.

Over the next few days, the defense called several of Travis's
friends who had witnessed arguments between him and Jodi.

A former Prepaid Legal mentor spoke about seeing Jodi
cry and shake after a phone call with Travis. Dan and Desiree Freeman each discussed the fights they had witnessed
on their trips with the couple in the summer of 2007.

On January 30, Travis's former girlfriend took the stand.
In four years life had changed dramatically for Lisa Andrews,
who by then had the last name Daidone. She was now twenty-
five and married with a newborn baby.

Under questioning by Jennifer Willmott, Lisa explained
her on-again, off-again eight-month relationship with Travis.

"When you were together, did you know he had cheated?"
Willmott asked.

"I did not know that," Lisa said. "I had my suspicions but
I didn't know the details of their relationship."

At the mention of Travis's infidelity, Jodi smiled weakly.

Throughout their relationship Lisa said she never had
intercourse with Travis.

"Did he always profess to be a virgin?" Willmott asked.

"Yes," said Lisa.

On cross-examination, Lisa told Martinez that Travis was

never inappropriate, never forced himself upon her. Theirs was a "normal" relationship, she said.

Halfway through his questioning, and without warning, Martinez picked up a photograph from his desk.

"Is this what a normal relationship looks like to you?" he asked, throwing an image on the projector of Travis's throat slit on the autopsy table.

A croaked gasp was heard from Travis's sisters in the front row. Lisa covered her mouth with her hand. At the defense table, Jodi buried her face and sobbed.

On the thirteenth day of the trial, the defense shocked the courtroom. Kirk Nurmi's next witness was none other than Jodi Arias.

CHAPTER 38

Jodi Arias locked eyes with each juror as the eleven men and six women filed into the courtroom.

She was dressed in beige pants and a short-sleeve black top, a strand of hair pulled to the side in a partial ponytail. Taking a deep breath, she folded her hands and took her seat on the witness stand.

It was Monday, February 2, 2013, and Jodi Arias was testifying in her own defense. At the center of the room, in a gentle tone, Kirk Nurmi began by addressing the defining issue of this case.

"Did you kill Travis Alexander on June 4, 2008?" he asked.

"Yes, I did," Jodi said, glancing at the jury.

"Why?"

"The simple answer is that he attacked me. And I defended myself."

Nurmi then asked about the interview Jodi gave with *Inside Edition*.

"In that tape you said that no jury would convict you," he said. "Do you remember saying that?"

"I did say that," she said softly.

"Why?" he asked.

"I made that statement in September 2008," she said. "At the time I had plans to commit suicide. So I was extremely confident that no jury would convict me because I didn't expect any of you to be here. I didn't expect to be here."

Because she was in jail monitored by an armed guard, however, she couldn't admit to being suicidal, Jodi told the jury.

"I was very confident that no jury would convict me because I planned to be dead." Her gaze fell to her lap. "Those are probably the most bitter words I'll ever eat."

Over the next eight days of direct examination, Jodi told her life story in painstaking detail. She was composed and unemotional, answering questions in a flat tone. For the majority of her testimony, she looked directly at the jury. When it turned sexually graphic, she cast her gaze downward.

While Jodi's mother looked on from the front row, Jodi described her early childhood and the physical abuse she claimed drove her out of the house as a teenager. She explained how she bounced from relationship to relationship, while moving up and down the California coast and supporting herself as a waitress.

Most important, she spoke about the intimate details of her relationship with Travis Alexander. She described the relationship as dysfunctional and wrought with sexual abuse. She claimed Travis used his religious influence to exert control over her and demean her sexually.

During her first encounter at the Hughes house, she said she felt "obliged" to perform oral sex on him.

"I felt apprehensive, but I was going with it. I didn't want to tell him no. I didn't want him to feel rejected or get his feelings hurt, or spoil the mood by saying stop," she claimed. "Even though it was uncomfortable, I kept going with it. He wasn't aggressive but definitely doing the initiating at that point."

Discussing the explicit details, including encounters where she both performed and received oral sex, Jodi paused for words, fidgeted with her fingers, and touched her face. At one point she paused and said, "This is embarrassing."

Jodi claimed her second sexual encounter with Travis was about ten days after leaving Vegas, when he joined her at a Starbucks and gave her a copy of *The Book of Mormon*.

"He wanted oral sex . . . he wanted to receive it," she said. "I was attracted to him and I wanted to do what he wanted to do. I liked him."

"How did you feel after that encounter?" Nurmi asked.

"I don't recall feeling really bad. Maybe just a little deflated," she said. "He refused to kiss me afterwards because he said it was gross."

The next time they met up was in a motel room in Ehrenberg, Arizona, where they spent the weekend having sex. After Travis left he didn't call her for a few days.

"I hate to put it this way, but I felt a little bit used," she said. "We get a hotel room, we have sex. We check out and he takes off. I kind of felt like a prostitute, sort of."

Over the next few weeks, their sexual behavior continued long distance, through explicit text messages and phone sex, she testified. At one point she said he sent her a photo of his erection, which was admitted into evidence and displayed on the monitors for the jury.

Perhaps most perverse, Jodi discussed a sexual encounter that occurred the day of her baptism on November 26. Following the ceremony, Travis returned to her house where they once again became intimate.

"The kissing got more passionate, more intense. Then he spun me around. He bent me over the bed. He was on top of me," she said. "I thought he was just going to keep kissing me."

She had her head down, face turned to the side.

"His hands were wandering and he lifted up my skirt, and he pulled down my underwear, and he was pressing against me—his whole body," she said. "He began to have anal sex with me."

As Jodi explained, the interaction was painful. Through clenched teeth she told him to stop, which he did.

"After this encounter, on this spiritual day, how did you feel about yourself?" Nurmi asked.

"I didn't feel very good," she said. "I felt like a used piece of toilet paper."

Meanwhile, Travis was also educating her about the Mormon religion. Although she said she was taught a little about the Law of Chastity, she believed that it only applied to intercourse.

While in private, Travis and Jodi were sexual, in Mesa their interactions were the opposite—Jodi claimed he wouldn't even hold her hand.

When she pressed him on the disparity of affection, Travis encouraged her to date other people. In December Jodi went on two dates. But when Travis discovered the men were not Mormon, he grew angry, according to Jodi.

"I was sort of reprimanded for that because they weren't church members," she said. "He explained to me the importance of dating in the church, so I agreed with him."

Despite their issues, in February 2007 the couple became exclusive and began traveling, crossing off destinations on the list from *1,000 Places to See Before You Die*.

In court, Nurmi entered into evidence several photos of Travis and Jodi posing together during their trips.

On the monitor he presented an image of Travis and Jodi standing in the Sacred Grove in Palmyra, New York.

"Were you in love with him at the time this photo was taken?" he asked.

"Yes." She looked down and sniffled.

A second photo was displayed, showing Travis and Jodi at the New Mexico balloon festival.

"Is this picture hard for you to look at?" Nurmi asked.

"It is very sentimental. It was happier times," she said softly. "When you look back, you just don't think it would end up the way it did."

On her fourth day on the stand, Jodi began establishing the foundation for claims that Travis was a sexual deviant.

For Valentine's Day 2007, she said she received a package with a letter, melted candy, and a gray shirt and pink shorts printed with the words TRAVIS ALEXANDER'S. Nurmi tried to present the clothing as a part of Travis's possessive attitude toward Jodi, although she seemed to dismiss the significance.

"It was a joke that came up occasionally," Jodi said. "I didn't think he would actually make me a shirt like that."

More disturbing were Jodi's claims that the package included boy's underwear emblazoned with the image of Spider-Man. According to Jodi, Travis wanted her to wear the underwear during sex, which she did, although she had to cut the leg holes to make them fit.

By this time, Jodi was deeply in love and willing to submit to his devious desires in an effort to please him, she said. In the spring of 2007, Jodi claimed she and Travis had vaginal sex for the first time. It began while Jodi was sleeping, without her consent, just days after they had prayed together to be more chaste, she said.

Then in June 2007, Jodi read texts on Travis's cell and discovered he was cheating. After their trip to New York and Huntington Beach, she broke up with him by phone on June 29. But the next day they resumed speaking.

"I still loved him and I thought he was serious about changing, so I continued to be intimate with him," she said.

Once Jodi had moved to Mesa, their sexual relationship grew increasingly kinky. Performing each of Travis's sexual fantasies, they had sex on the hood of a car, in a bathtub, and while he was dressed in his designer suits.

"He had a list of fantasies he wanted to fulfill," she said. "I enjoyed making him happy, so I was willing to do the things he liked to do. And while he was doing these things, he was paying attention to me. So I got something out of them too in that regard."

She dressed up as a schoolgirl, wore lingerie while he took pictures, and used sex toys in their lovemaking. According to Jodi, they also incorporated candy in their oral sex play—using Tootsie Pops and Pop Rocks.

On one occasion, she acted out a fantasy where he came to her house and she gave him oral sex on her porch, without uttering a word. At the end of the encounter, he threw her a Toblerone chocolate bar.

After she moved to Mesa, Travis paid Jodi to clean his house. In court, Nurmi presented an e-mail with a photo of a woman dressed as a sexy French maid, wearing a short black skirt, a tiny apron, stockings, and stilettos. According to Nurmi, it was another way Travis demeaned Jodi sexually.

Throughout her testimony, Nurmi submitted several pornographic text messages from Travis to Jodi, lending a glimpse into the X-rated nature of their relationship.

"When it's done, the intensity will make your body feel like you've been raped, but you will enjoy every moment of it."

"You'll rejoice in being a whore that's sole purpose in life is to be mine to have animalistic sex with and to please me in any way I desire."

Nurmi addressed Jodi's feelings about these messages.

"Were you willing at this point in your life to have animalistic sex with him?" Nurmi asked.

"Probably." Jodi glanced at the floor.

By then, Jodi knew Travis was dating other women, but could not stay away.

"Why not break up with this guy?" Nurmi said.

"Right now we're focusing on the negative things. There are things he did that made me feel like a million dollars," Jodi said. "He would say little things that were sentimental that had meaning between us. He would still allude to the fact that he wanted to marry me, even though I don't think he was very serious."

On her fourth day on the stand, Jodi made a disturbing claim—portraying Travis not only as a sexual deviant, but as a pedophile.

On January 21, 2008, Jodi said she unexpectedly entered Travis's bedroom to retrieve a porcelain angel he had given her.

"I walked in and Travis was on the bed masturbating, and I got really embarrassed," Jodi said. "He started grabbing at something on the bed."

A picture went sailing off his bed and landed faceup near her feet. It was a photo of a young boy wearing nothing but briefs, according to Jodi.

"I was frozen for a minute," she said. "I didn't know how to react. It seemed like one of those dreams where something is really off."

Nauseated, Jodi said she ran out of the house, drove home, and vomited. To collect her thoughts, she went to the visitors' center of a Mormon temple. Eventually, she said she spoke to Travis about the incident.

"Did you come away with the understanding that Mr. Alexander had a sexual interest in children?" Nurmi asked.

"Yes," she said. "He preferred sex with women. It made him feel more normal."

Even though she said she now believed Travis to be a pedophile, she continued to have sex with him.

"He seemed very ashamed with himself. He didn't want to be that way," she said. "When he had sex with women he felt like a normal heterosexual man, and that's what he wanted to be."

Contradictory to her claims, however, no pornography of any kind was discovered on Travis's computers.

On Jodi's fifth day of testimony, a recording of a sexual conversation between Travis and Jodi, which she had recorded just weeks before the murder, was played for the jury.

The recording was extremely graphic as they reminisced about their sexual history. Travis began talking about sex acts he wanted to perform on Jodi in the future.

"I am going to tie you to a tree and put it in your ass all the way," he said.

"Oh my gosh!" Jodi gasped. "That is so debasing! I like it."

They discussed a previous encounter where she braided her hair and they had sex in a bathtub. Jodi complimented his sexual stamina and called their encounters "surreal."

"You were amazing," she said. "Seriously, you made me feel like a goddess."

They both began to moan and breathe heavily. Travis said he was touching himself.

"I wish those were my hands giving you a hand job," she whispered.

Travis spoke of a future fantasy to video record him and Jodi having sex.

"It could be like legitimate porn in every sense," he said.

"You make me so horny," she said.

In court Jodi buried her head as she seemed to climax on the tape.

"The way you moan, it sounds like you're a twelve-year-old girl having her first orgasm. It's so hot," Travis said.

"You're bad," she squealed. "You make me feel so dirty."

After the recording was concluded, Jodi told the jury that she taped the sex talk at Travis's request. She also claimed she was only pretending to climax because "when I masturbate it requires both hands."

"I was faking then," she said. "I wanted him to be turned on. I wanted him to like it."

Over the course of their relationship, Travis and Jodi argued constantly. On the stand, for the first time, Jodi claimed that on several occasions Travis grew violent.

"Whenever he got mad it was like being in an earthquake. You don't know how long it is going to last or how bad it was going to be until it stops," she said. "I was afraid, not for my physical safety, but just intimidated by him."

Over time, Jodi became fearful of Travis. When he grew angry, she admitted to shaking, not in fury, but in fear.

"When he got mad at me I would visibly shake," she said. "I would feel some sort of trepidation or apprehension or unsettled."

She said Travis pushed her down twice. During an argument, he once backhanded her; during another he grabbed her wrist. In April 2008, he choked her, nearly leaving her unconscious.

"Did you fear for your life that day?" Nurmi asked about the day she was choked.

"It happened so fast," she said.

Her most serious injury occurred on January 21, 2008, when during an argument, he picked her up and body slammed her. Calling her a "bitch," Travis kicked her and broke her left ring finger, Jodi told the jury.

"I screamed really loud," she said. "He stormed out of the room and left."

After calming down, he helped make a splint for her finger, using Popsicle sticks. On the stand, Jodi lifted her hand, revealing a crooked left ring finger she claimed was a result of the incident. It was the same finger, and injury, she had once told Detective Flores occurred on the day of Travis's murder.

Over the months she lived in Mesa, the back-and-forth relationship with Travis left Jodi despondent. At one point she considered suicide, she testified.

"Throughout the fall I had been feeling suicidal, and I thought that was the point I wanted to go through with it," she said.

She asked to borrow a gun and eventually called a suicide hotline.

On the stand Nurmi asked why she continued to talk to Travis.

"He pawned his car off on me, so I still had that connection," she said.

On other occasions, however, Jodi had said he helped her out by giving her the vehicle, providing her the "easiest terms possible."

Nurmi pressed. "Why were you so craving, or so desirous of positive attention from Mr. Alexander?"

Jodi said she was still in love. She knew she was making a mistake but at that point in her life Jodi was admittedly making bad decisions.

In April, Jodi moved back to Yreka, where she said the "fog lifted."

But while she seemed to be moving forward, she continued to talk to Travis. Long distance, however, he became increasingly cruel.

Angry text messages and e-mails were presented in court.

Through April and May Travis called her a "pure whore,"

"sociopath," "liar," and referred to all the "crazy shit" she had done.

"You are a liar to the core of who you are, it seems," he wrote.

The broken BMW also appeared to have become contentious.

"You are a real piece of work. By the way, thanks for keeping your end of the contract by paying for the car you destroyed," he wrote. "You are more and more like your mom every day."

In other messages he wrote: "Bitter feelings are brewing in me towards you"; "I'm asking for you to stop doing it." He also called her "the sociopath I know so well."

On the stand, Jodi claimed Travis's anger was due to her insistence he get mental help for his sexual deviancy and jealousy because she was talking to other men. Days later, however, Travis's tone took an abrupt turn.

"You're one of the prettiest girls on the planet," he sent her in a text.

In her testimony, Jodi said the constant swinging pendulum of emotions left her despondent.

"I felt bullied," she said. "It was just miserable."

After seven days of testimony—detailing every aspect of her life—Jodi finally began describing the events leading up to the murder.

When it came to her hair color, Jodi maintained that she changed it in April or May, weeks before the crime. Photos were admitted into evidence showing time-stamped photos of her hair colored brown before June.

On May 28, when the gun was stolen from her grandparents' house, Jodi said she was at a Buddhist monastery on the Oregon border without cell phone reception.

"Did you break into your grandparents' home to steal this gun?" Nurmi asked.

"No," Jodi said.

"Did you orchestrate or tell anyone else to steal this gun?" he asked.

"No," she maintained.

On June 2, she said she did not rent a car a distance from her home to conceal her movements, but because the rental agency only offered cars in certain towns. She chose one where her brother lived.

As for the car color, Jodi did ask for a replacement because red is too flashy. "I've always been told not to drive red cars. They get pulled over more often."

During her road trip, Jodi admitted to stopping by Darryl Brewer's house to borrow gas cans, but it was only because gas was cheaper in Utah and she was on a budget. She confessed to buying a third gas can at Walmart but said she returned it that very same day, receiving cash.

Jodi also stuck to her story about a group of kids outside of Starbucks flipping her back license plate upside down. "I noticed some skaters hanging around there, and they were all laughing as I was walking up to my car."

She maintained she had not originally intended to go to Mesa to see Travis. Rather, she said, he persuaded her over the course of several phone calls to make a detour.

"He said he would wait up," she said.

After speaking with Travis the last time, Jodi turned off her cell phone, but not because she didn't want her phone traced in Arizona. She did so because she couldn't find her car charger. "My battery was getting low, I didn't want to be without cell phone service or gas driving across the desert."

Jodi arrived at Travis's house in Mesa around 4 A.M. and parked in the center of the driveway. She walked around to the side of her house, carrying with her a suitcase, backpack, purse, and laptop.

"Did you have a gun with you?" Nurmi asked.

"No," she said.

"Did you have a knife?"

"No."

Inside the house she found Travis on his computer in his home office, his dog by his side. For a minute, Jodi stood watching him. Napoleon barked, alerting Travis to her presence. Travis approached her.

"He greeted me. He had a big smile on his face, and he kissed me on the lips," she said. "He had his hands around my waist at the top of my butt, and he was pulling me towards his body."

Although Travis wanted to have sex, Jodi was tired, and they just went to bed. Jodi said she was the one to awake first. When Travis woke up at 1 P.M., they had sex.

For the encounter, Travis tied her up—something they had done before, Jodi said. Only this time they used soft decorative rope, which Travis cut using a knife.

He put the length of rope behind his sleigh bed and tied two nooses at the ends for her wrists. But when Nurmi asked where Travis placed the knife, she said she couldn't remember—an early indication of where her testimony was headed.

"There are a lot of things I don't remember about that day," she said.

As Jodi described how Travis performed oral sex on her with her wrists tied to the bed, she stared downward, speaking quietly.

"Are these sexual subjects difficult for you to talk about?" Nurmi asked.

"Yes," she said, "this one in particular because of how the day ended."

Quickly Travis and Jodi both grew bored with the rope. She slipped her wrists out of the nooses and tossed it on the floor.

They began photographing each other in sexual poses. She said they also made a sex video by setting the camera on the night stand. It was never recovered by forensics.

"We reviewed it, then deleted it," she said.

After sex, they went downstairs and into his home office. Jodi gave Travis a CD of photos from their vacations together. Jodi lay on the floor beside Napoleon as Travis inserted the disk into his computer.

But because the disk was scratched and Travis's computer had a virus, he was unable to view the pictures. In frustration and anger, he threw the disk against the wall.

"It ricocheted against the wall and landed on my head and hit the carpet," she testified.

As Travis's temper flared, Jodi stood up. He grabbed her, spun her around, and bent her over the desk. Grabbing both her arms, he twisted her right arm behind her back.

"Were you thinking he was going to hit you?" Nurmi asked.

"I wasn't thinking that." She shook her head. "He had only done that once at that time."

She claimed Travis pulled down her pants, had rough intercourse with her, and ejaculated on her back. In the downstairs bathroom, she cleaned herself off.

Travis and Jodi then proceeded upstairs for the last photo shoot of Travis's life.

Jodi said Travis wanted the photos because he had gotten to his top physical peak in preparation for his trip to Cancún.

"Why was the shower selected?" Nurmi asked.

"It was selected for the water. We were going for a certain effect with the pictures and the water."

Travis posed in the shower as she snapped photos, reviewing them and deleting the ones she didn't like.

After snapping the last image of him seated on the shower floor, the camera slipped out of her hands, skidding across the tile floor and landing on the bath mat.

At that moment Travis "flipped out," she said.

"He stood up, and he stepped out of the shower," she said. "He picked me up and body slammed me on the tile."

Travis was screaming at her, calling her a "stupid idiot."

While he stood seething and spitting, Jodi rolled on her side and sprung up. With Travis in pursuit, she ran down the long bathroom hallway into a walk-in closet that met the bedroom. Suddenly, she remembered something she had found in his closet during a cleaning project—a .25 caliber gun he stored there.

With the sound of Travis's footsteps behind her, she jumped up, grabbed his gun, and ran out the other end of the closet, back inside the bathroom.

While she pointed the weapon at him, Travis charged at her, like a "linebacker."

"I turned around and pointed it at him so he would stop chasing me," she said. "I didn't mean to shoot him or anything. I didn't even think I was pulling the trigger. I didn't know that I shot him. He lunged at me and I fell."

Travis landed on top of her, screaming, "I'll fucking kill you, bitch."

After that, Jodi said her memory became foggy.

"There's a lot of that day I don't remember," she said. "There are a lot of gaps."

"What do you remember?" Nurmi asked.

"Almost nothing for a long time. There are some things that have come back over the years," she said. "There is like a huge gap. I don't know if I blacked out or what."

On the stand Jodi claimed she had no memory of stabbing him, slicing his throat, dragging him across the bathroom floor, or putting him in the shower stall. "I just remember trying to get away from him."

The next thing she remembered was dropping the knife. It hit the tile floor with a clank. Jodi looked down at the body next to her and started screaming.

"I just remember dropping the knife and being very freaked out and screaming," she said.

Few details emerged beyond a vague memory of putting the knife back in the dishwasher.

"What else do you remember?" Nurmi asked.

"Not much," she said. "I remember more the feeling at that time, not pictures, and things that I can bring back. It was like mortal terror. I'd pissed him off the worst I've ever seen him pissed off. He was angry at me and he wasn't going to stop."

The next thing she knew she was driving west, barefoot and bloody, the sun in her eyes.

"I don't remember bringing the gun with me, but I remember throwing it in the desert," she said.

"What about the rope, did you take that with you?" Nurmi asked.

"Yes," she said. "Eventually it went into the Dumpster. It was behind a gas station."

Looking at her hands on the steering wheel, she saw they were stained with Travis's blood. She pulled over in the middle of the desert and washed off with bottled water from the trunk of her rental car. At that moment, she was unsure if Travis was even dead.

"I don't think I fully realized, but I knew that it was really bad and that my life was probably done now," she said. "I thought he was not alive at that point."

"Was there a part of you that hoped he was alive?" he asked.

"Yes. Of course," she said. "I wished that it was just a nightmare that I could wake up from."

"Did you still love him?" Nurmi asked.

"Yeah, I did," she said quietly.

"Do you still love him now?" he asked.

"Yeah," she said. "It's a different love, but yeah I do."

Eventually, Jodi said she found her phone charger. She got back in her car and continued driving. Passing a sign that said she was a hundred miles from Las Vegas, she came upon a checkpoint for the Hoover Dam.

"At this point I realized I was in really deep trouble. I started thinking of what I could do to delay the inevitable," she said. "I was scared what would happen to me. I was thinking of all sorts of things—my family, myself, what would happen."

Her following actions and lies were all an attempt to cover up her crime.

"I knew my life was pretty much over. I didn't want anyone to know that that had happened or that I did it," she said. "I started taking steps to try and cover up that I was there. So I did a whole bunch of things to try and make it seem like I wasn't there."

On her way to Utah, she called Ryan and told him she had gotten lost and slept in her car. Then, she also called Travis and left the voice mail. Because she was crying, she kept replaying and rerecording the message so she sounded cheery, explaining the sixteen-minute phone call on the cellular records.

When Jodi arrived in Utah, she did her best to act like nothing was wrong. She told everyone the story of getting lost and explained the bandages on her fingers were due to cutting her hand on a broken glass at work.

On the stand, Jodi said the cuts were unrelated to the killings and she had actually broken a glass at Travis's house, a wound that reopened during the attack.

That night in Utah, Jodi admitted to being intimate with Ryan, partially because she was trying to please him and give him what he expected.

"I just wanted to seem like normal, like I was okay, like I didn't just do what I did," she said.

Creating an illusion of normalcy, she returned to Yreka, went back to work, and waited for the phone call that Travis's body had been found. As "the clock ticked down" to her inevitable arrest, she tried to convince herself and everyone else that nothing had happened.

Just after midnight on June 10, she got the call from Dan Freeman.

"I saw his name on the caller ID, and I thought that would probably be the phone call I was dreading," she said.

Dan told her the police were at Travis's house. Phoning Travis's bishop, Jodi confirmed the discovery. At that moment, reality sunk in for Jodi.

"I doubled over and started sobbing really hard and I couldn't stand up," she said. "I was hoping the whole thing wasn't real, that it was just a nightmare and none of it had ever happened."

The next afternoon she called Detective Flores, offering her assistance in the investigation in an effort to disassociate herself with the killing.

"I thought that if I didn't call him it would look more suspicious than if I did call him," she said. "I was kind of also calling him to see what information I could garner from him. . . . I wanted to try and determine how much time I had."

In court, Nurmi asked Jodi why she didn't confess.

"I couldn't imagine admitting to something like that; I couldn't imagine doing something like that," she said. "I began that facade right away."

A few days later Jodi attended Travis's memorial service. "I thought that if I didn't show up it would look suspicious because Travis and I were close."

Knowing the arrest was imminent, she threw out items related to the sexual encounters with Travis—including the Spider-Man underwear. At the time of the arrest she admitted she was preparing to flee Yreka, but claimed she was moving to Monterey, so she would be away from her family at the time of her arrest. On July 1, she purchased the 9 mm handgun for her own protection.

"I didn't feel safe at all after June 4," she said. "I wanted to someday see myself being a responsible gun owner."

After taking possession of the gun, she started to contemplate suicide.

"The idea to kill myself didn't occur to me until I had possession of the gun, and I realized how easy that could be," she said.

Jodi was arrested the morning of July 15, as she was packing her car and preparing to leave Yreka. She now admitted to lying to Detective Flores in the interrogation room.

"The main reason was because I was very ashamed of what happened," she said. "It was just shameful. I didn't want anyone to know I had anything to do with that."

After being confronted with the evidence, however, the gravity of the situation set in. She concocted the story of the two intruders.

"I began to tell him things that would connect with their forensics and create a way for me to not have been responsible for it," she said.

She said she didn't admit to the physical and sexual abuse, because she wanted to preserve Travis's memory. "I was very concerned about both of our reputations. I didn't feel like I had a future anyway. There's no benefit to me, there's no benefit to anyone else to say those things."

Over the next few months she repeated the story of the intruders to various news outlets because she said she cared about how she would be perceived.

"I didn't want to be known or remembered as someone capable of what happened. I wanted to portray a different picture of myself," she said. "I made up this big stupid story for Flores, and I felt I should stick with it. I stuck with it for a long time."

All the while she said she wanted to die. Yet in jail, she made only one suicide attempt, stocking up on Advil and trying to slit her wrists with a razor.

Finally, in the spring of 2010, she said she confessed to "the truth." It was after much soul searching and the realization that her family would love her regardless.

On the stand, she repeatedly stated she wished she could take it all back, but said she found solace in the knowledge that Travis was in heaven.

"I have a million regrets. I was scared of him and I reacted, but I will always regret everything about that," Jodi said. "It helped me to know he was okay and he was in a better place. And maybe he wasn't mad anymore."

For eight days Juan Martinez sat at the prosecution table, scribbling notes and making occasional objections. On February 21, Martinez sauntered to the front of the room and began his grueling, five-day cross-examination of Jodi Arias.

His questioning was often bogged down in lengthy sidebars and detours through the evidence. At times, his antagonism lapsed into vitriol as he bantered with Jodi.

Through most of it, Jodi seemed defiant. She called Martinez "angry," corrected his grammar, and dodged questions. She appeared haughty, smirking at the prosecutor and, at one point, giggling.

By the end Jodi would crumble.

In meticulous detail, Martinez examined Jodi's long litany of lies.

"You have problems with the truth," he said, his voice rising. "You lie, don't you?"

Martinez pried into details of her sex life and excoriated her for her frequent memory lapses.

"Give me the factors," he said. "I want to know about a specific circumstance. What factors influence when you're having a memory problem?"

Jodi shot back, "Usually when men like you are screaming at me or grilling me or someone like Travis is doing the same."

Martinez raised his voice and acted out scenarios in dramatic fashion. As she dodged questions, he cut her off midsentence. Jodi held her own, appearing to smugly toy with Martinez as she grinned and repeatedly answered yes-or-no questions with "sure" and "I guess."

The exchanges rattled the seasoned prosecutor as the case at times devolved into a showdown of wit and will. The judge had to admonish both to stop speaking over each other.

"You are making my brain scramble," Jodi said, blaming the circular questions for her not being able to give responses. "I think I'm more focused on your posture and your tone and your anger, so it's hard to process the questions."

"Are you having trouble understanding?" Martinez asked.

"Sometimes," she said, "because you go in circles."

The back-and-forth sniping went on as the focus turned to Jodi's claims that she tried to kill herself while in the county jail—with Advil and a razor—but couldn't go through with the act because it "stung" when she nicked herself.

"You said it stung and that's why you stopped," he blasted. "Can you imagine how much it hurt him when you stuck that knife right into his chest?"

Martinez also confronted Jodi with the two magazines that contained the secret coded messages. On the large monitor at the center of the room, Martinez showed each message printed in the margins of the magazine.

Once strung together, he had Jodi read the message for the court. "You fucked up. What you told my attorney the next day directly contradicts what I've been saying for over a year," the message began.

Martinez pointed out the magazines were intercepted just

days after the prosecution interviewed Matt McCartney and just four days before a pretrial hearing.

"You tried to get someone to lie at that hearing, didn't you?" Martinez asked.

"No," she replied.

For hours Martinez grilled her about her make-out session with Ryan Burns, while Travis's body lay rotting in the shower.

"Did you know he was dead when you and Mr. Burns were kissing?" Martinez asked.

"I guess I knew, I wasn't accepting it," Jodi said.

"So if you didn't think he was dead, it was okay with you to roll around with Mr. Burns?" Martinez pressed.

Under the ruthless questioning, Jodi had difficulty explaining the state of her mind as to how easily she could end up in the arms of another man.

"I wasn't 'there' in my head," she replied through her tears.

But Martinez tore into her once again, charging that she was "there" enough to call Ryan, and to leave a voice mail on Travis's cell phone in an attempt to cover up her grisly attack.

"Are you ashamed that you killed him?" asked Martinez.

"Most definitely," she replied.

Throughout his cross-examination, Martinez frequently showed video clips from interviews that Jodi did with police. He juxtaposed her text messages, e-mails, and journals with her testimony about being assaulted by Travis, challenging whether the abuse really happened.

Martinez forced Jodi to admit that during these assaults she never called the police or told anyone who could back up the claims. In fact, on the dates in question Jodi actually wrote loving things about Travis in her diary.

Martinez displayed one journal entry from the date Jodi claimed Travis had backhanded her in his car.

"It doesn't say anything there that he backhanded you, does it?" Martinez shouted.

"No, of course not," Jodi said.

"Please take a look at it," Martinez said, pointing to the screen. "It doesn't say 'I love the backhand,' it says 'I love his lips.'"

Martinez also challenged her assertion that she once caught Travis pleasuring himself to a photograph of a young boy.

"You caught Mr. Alexander masturbating to some images of boys, correct?" Martinez said. "And it's so noteworthy to you that you waited until after you killed Mr. Alexander to tell anybody about it, right?"

"I waited years," she said.

"You chose to keep that allegation until about two years ago?" he countered.

Martinez then presented text messages from the date of the alleged encounter that showed Travis and Jodi exchanged text messages throughout the day, making no reference to any unsettling incident.

Martinez noted the duplicity of her portrayal of Travis and painted Jodi as a stalker and the aggressor in the couple's sex life, although she denied his allegations.

The graphic and often antagonistic testimony continued throughout the week, with Martinez arguing that Jodi was hypocritical in her attitude to sex—switching between actively instigating it and then claiming she felt used.

"Your participation was equal to him?" asked Martinez.

"I would say it was mutual," she claimed. "I didn't feel like a prostitute during, it was just afterwards that I did."

Martinez recounted Jodi's admitted lies to authorities, friends, and family in the days after she killed Travis. He pointed out that even her lies were changing as she spoke to various media organizations.

"I couldn't keep my stories straight," Jodi confessed. "It's all the same thing, just different versions—I couldn't keep my lies straight."

Martinez also played the cheery voice mail that Jodi left for Travis.

"Did you send it so he could reach you from the grave?" he asked.

For most of Martinez's onslaught of questioning, Jodi maintained a tough and confident demeanor on the stand. But on the final day of cross-examination, Martinez seemed to break her.

Flustered and floundering, she gave teary admissions about the slaying.

Her arrogance fell away to emotion, as Martinez guided her through the last minutes of Travis's life. Presented with the photo of Travis's body slumped in the shower, Jodi began to sob.

"Were you crying while you were shooting him?" Martinez asked.

"I don't remember," she blubbered.

"Were you crying when you were stabbing him?"

"I don't remember."

"How about when you cut his throat, were you crying then?"

"I don't know," she cried repeatedly.

She acknowledged that she attacked him with a knife.

"Would you agree that you're the person who actually slit Mr. Alexander's throat from ear to ear?"

"Yes." She took off her glasses and dropped her head in her hands.

"You're the one who did this, right? And you're the same individual that lied about all of this, right?" he pressed.

Martinez concluded his cross-examination, returning to Jodi's previous statement where she said no jury would convict her because she planned on committing suicide. He pointed out that in the interview Jodi said she would not be convicted because she was innocent.

Finally, he questioned her cover-up of the crime scene, including taking the gun and the rope.

"You were trying to alter the crime scene, right?" he shouted.

"It would appear that way," she said.

At the end of the fifth day, Martinez turned to the judge and said simply, "I don't have anything else."

Unassumingly, he returned to his chair at the prosecutor's table.

* * *

Nurmi spent two days during redirect on reviewing the evidence. Diary entries were reread, the phone sex tape was replayed.

He questioned Jodi about the gaps in her memory and whether she actually remembered stabbing Travis. Jodi said she had attempted to piece together the events of the day based on what she had learned after the fact.

"The events of June 4, 2008, do you want to remember those events?" Nurmi asked.

"I have made attempts to piece things back together," she said, her voice cracking. "There's a part of me that doesn't ever want to remember it. It feels like I'm the person who deserves to sit with those memories that I don't have right now. Those were my actions and it's my responsibility."

Jodi was asked to repeat the exact events of June 4. This time she made a key change in detail, describing the gun as being in a holster.

Finally, Jodi spoke in loving detail about the man she killed and expressed profound regret.

"I wish I could turn back the clock and make some different decisions. If I could go back in time I would choose differently as far as Travis of course. But it goes back further than that," she said. "If I had never gone to the MGM Grand, if I had never signed up for Prepaid Legal, if I had never watched the DVD and just left it sitting collecting dust—at any point in time I could have made a different decision and we'd all be in different places today."

After fifteen days and more than sixty hours of Jodi's testimony, the jury had a chance to ask her direct questions.

Arizona is one of three states that allow jurors to pose questions to witnesses after the lawyers have finished their questioning. The more than two hundred juror questions largely focused on the details of the killing and gaps in Jodi's story.

"Why did you take the rope and gun with you?" "Why did

you put the camera in the washing machine?" "Why didn't you call 911 after the shooting?"

Most of Jodi's answers were "I don't remember" or "I don't recall."

The jurors asked about Jodi's memory problems and why she took so long to come forward with this latest version of events.

"Did you ever see a doctor for your memory issues?" "Have you ever taken medication for your memory issue?" "How is it you remember so many of your sexual encounters, including your ex-boyfriends, but you do not remember stabbing Travis and dragging his body?"

The questions seemed to show skepticism from the jury.

"Were you mad at Travis while you were stabbing him?" one question read.

"I don't remember being angry that day," she said calmly.

"Why were you afraid of the consequences if you killed in self-defense?"

"I believed that it is not okay, in any circumstance, to take someone's life, even if you are defending your own life," Jodi said. "I felt like I had done something wrong and I was afraid of what the consequences would be."

"After all the lies you told, why should we believe you now?" The question brought groans from the spectators' gallery.

"Lying is not something I typically do," Jodi said. "The lies I told in this case can be tied to protecting Travis's reputation or my involvement."

Jodi would spend one more day going over final questioning from both Nurmi and Martinez. In total she would spend an unprecedented eighteen days on the witness stand.

When she was finally dismissed, she calmly returned to her seat at the defense table.

CHAPTER 39

By the time Jodi Arias stepped down from the witness stand, the public's fascination with her high-profile murder trial had grown fanatical.

Trial watchers flew in from as far away as Canada, lining up outside the courthouse before dawn for a chance to score one of the coveted seats open to the public.

While in line for a spot in the gallery, friendships formed, fights broke out, and one woman even sold her place in line for $200. Because the transaction was witnessed by court staff, the woman was forced to return the money.

In the waiting area the banter was often loud and raucous as the trial watchers debated the facts of the case. As the chatter grew louder, security guards occasionally ordered the gaggle to be quiet.

While a small segment of the trial watchers backed Jodi—believing she was a victim of domestic violence—the vast majority supported the Alexander family and prosecutor Juan Martinez. Frenzied followers vilified Jodi and demonized her defense, turning Martinez into a celebrity. After court, prosecution groupies hounded Martinez for pictures or to get his autograph—spurring the defense at one point to ask for a mistrial for prosecutorial misconduct, a motion that was denied.

Behind bars, Jodi seemed to relish the attention. Through

her friend and former cellmate, Donavan Bering, she established a Twitter profile where she promoted the sale of her artwork and posted derogatory comments about the prosecutor. Through periodic phone calls Jodi relayed messages to Donavan, who posted them on the social networking service. Jodi also penned a manifesto and autographed several copies of the book.

In her life outside of jail, Jodi had always sought control in her relationships, spying on her boyfriends' private correspondence. And in court, Jodi attempted to direct the trial.

On multiple occasions court was canceled when Jodi claimed she had a migraine headache. When spectators began wearing navy blue ribbons in support of the Alexander family, she complained to the court, prompting the judge to disallow anyone other than the Alexander family to wear them. At one point, Jodi even filed an order of protection against three of the journalists covering her trial.

Meanwhile, Jodi remained optimistic and told several of her supporters she believed her testimony had swayed the jury. She thought she may be found guilty of manslaughter, or possibly second-degree murder, but expected her trial would likely result in a hung jury.

As the chaos surrounding the trial trickled into the courtroom, the defense continued to present their case, calling two expert witnesses to back Jodi's claims that she was abused and experienced a blackout during the slaying.

Psychologist Dr. Richard Samuels testified that following his evaluation he had concluded Jodi suffered from post-traumatic stress disorder that had caused amnesia. Samuels claimed a large percentage of people subjected to a traumatic event have "cloudy and foggy" recollections. "There are many people that never remember the actual events," he said.

On cross-examination, however, Juan Martinez claimed Samuels's diagnosis of PTSD was flawed because when he examined Jodi, three years prior, she was still telling the story of the phantom intruders.

"You confirmed the presence of PTSD, even though you've

just now told us that this is based on a lie," Martinez said with a tone of incredulity.

"Perhaps I should have readministered that test," Samuels reluctantly admitted.

In making his diagnosis, one of the qualifying symptoms Samuels had observed were Jodi's bouts of irritability and anger. But under questioning, Martinez forced Samuels to admit that Jodi had anger issues throughout her life.

"When she was a teenager, isn't it true that the defendant had such anger toward her mother, Sandy, that she treated her like crap?" Martinez asked.

"Yes," Samuels replied.

"Isn't it true that they argued all the time?" asked Martinez. "And isn't it true that during that time, the defendant hit Sandy for no reason?"

"Yes."

"And this was all before this June 4, 2008, incident?"

"But it's irrelevant for the diagnosis," Samuels contended.

Finally, Martinez attacked Samuels's integrity, asserting that by sending her a self-help book in jail, the doctor's relationship with Jodi had become inappropriate.

"You have feelings for the defendant, right?" Martinez asked.

"I beg your pardon, sir!" retorted Samuels.

Following Samuels, domestic violence expert Alyce LaViolette recounted incidents of physical and emotional abuse Jodi claimed she endured.

"Do you believe in your expert opinion that Jodi was a battered woman?" Jennifer Willmott asked.

"Yes, I do," LaViolette said.

"How would you characterize their relationship?"

"I would call it a domestically abusive relationship," said LaViolette.

On cross-examination, however, Martinez pointed out that the only evidence of abuse were Jodi's statements.

To undermine her credibility, Martinez ridiculed LaViolette for a presentation she gave in 2012 where she made the case that Snow White was a battered woman, illustrating that she could find abuse even in a fairy tale.

"What this shows us is that even if it's a myth—all made up—you can come up with the opinion that the person is a victim of domestic violence," Martinez said.

As the questioning grew increasingly aggressive, LaViolette shot back at Martinez, "If you were in my group I'd ask you to take a time-out, Mr. Martinez."

Martinez went on to question LaViolette about her evaluation of Jodi.

"So when you're interviewing then you're not talking, right?" Martinez asked.

"Mr. Martinez," said LaViolette, before being interrupted.

"Yes or no? My question is: are you talking—yes or no?" Martinez snapped.

"Mr. Martinez, are you angry at me?" LaViolette suddenly asked, prompting laughter from the gallery.

"Is that relevant to you?" Martinez barked back. "Does that make any difference to your evaluation, whether or not the prosecutor is angry?"

Meanwhile, outside the courtroom, trial watchers, angered by LaViolette's testimony, attacked her online, posting more than a thousand negative book reviews on Amazon, calling her a fraud and a disgrace. Hundreds also called organizations that had booked LaViolette for speaking engagements in an attempt to persuade them to cancel her appearances.

The barrage of harassment was the subject of lengthy closed-door meetings in the judge's chambers and later sent LaViolette to the emergency room for anxiety attacks and heart palpitations.

In concluding their case, the defense asked the jury to look deep into Travis's eyes in his last seconds of life.

The defense called a forensic audio and video expert who had examined one of the final photographs Jodi had taken of Travis while he was still alive.

In a hearing held outside the presence of the jury, the expert enlarged the photo to show a reflection in the cornea of

Travis's left eye. In one shot, he had sketched a white outline around the shape of a head and elbows that he identified as arms holding a camera. The image was intended to support Jodi's claims that she had no weapon when she was photographing Travis and had to run to get the gun and knife.

Initially, Juan Martinez scoffed at the blurry reflection and demanded tests to prove the expert's opinion. "I don't see a camera, I don't see a knife. I don't see anything but a blotch," Martinez said.

After a two-hour meeting in the judge's chambers, however, Martinez grudgingly admitted that the figure in the image was holding a camera.

Following the closed-door meeting the jury was brought into the courtroom, where the enlarged photograph of Travis's eye was displayed on the screen. Judge Stephens explained to the jury that the lawyers had stipulated that Jodi was not holding a gun or knife when the picture was taken.

On April 16, after thirty-eight days of graphic and emotional testimony, the defense rested its case.

Over the next few weeks Juan Martinez presented his rebuttal case, refuting many of the defense's claims. A psychologist, Dr. Janeen DeMarte, was called to dispute abuse allegations, noting that even those claims varied wildly during Jodi's many evaluations.

"This reporting of domestic violence has changed over time, frequently," she said. "My opinion is that there did not appear to be significant abuse."

DeMarte also dismissed claims that Jodi had suffered memory loss from post-traumatic stress disorder. She explained that PTSD could not result from a fabricated event, such as the intruder story. Further, she said Jodi's memory lapse wasn't consistent with PTSD, which usually involves short bursts of blackouts.

"She does not have post-traumatic stress disorder," DeMarte maintained.

According to tests she had administered, DeMarte concluded that Jodi suffered from borderline personality disorder.

Her diagnosis was based on Jodi's history of unstable personal relationships, inappropriate anger, feelings of emptiness, suicidal thoughts, and paranoia she was being persecuted. DeMarte compared a person suffering from borderline personality disorder to an immature teenager with identity issues.

The disorder caused Jodi to have an irrational fear of abandonment, according to DeMarte.

"You could see it in her journal entries that went from happy to sad very quickly," she said. "There is some indication that she has some anger problems, that she has strong feelings of anger, internally."

As Martinez continued to poke holes in the defense's case, Jodi seemed defiant, disregarding the witnesses while silently sketching on a notepad.

As part of Martinez's rebuttal, a friend and former co-worker of Travis's testified he observed Travis and Jodi being affectionate in public and even shot photos and video that captured romantic public exchanges.

A Tesoro employee spoke about three gas purchases made at a Tesoro gas station in Salt Lake City, two days after Jodi killed Travis.

Returning to the stand, Michael Melendez testified that he did not find any pornographic images of any kind on Travis's computers. Detective Flores also told the jury that Travis was not a registered gun owner and no evidence of a gun was found in his house—no bullets, no holster.

Martinez also disputed Jodi's claims regarding a gas can she had purchased from Walmart the day before the murder. Jodi said she returned the gas on June 3, 2008. However, a Walmart employee, who had reviewed records from the Salinas store, said no one had returned a five-gallon gas can that day. According to the store's records, Jodi returned the gas can one week after the purchase.

Finally, Travis's best friend, Deanna Reid, spoke about her relationship with Travis.

"Would he ever call you names?" Martinez asked.

"No, he did not," Deanna said.

"Did he ever strike you or physically advance on you or inflict any physical violence on you?"

"No, never."

On cross-examination, Nurmi questioned Deanna about the intimate details of her relationship with Travis, forcing her to admit she had sex with him several times while keeping it secret.

"That was our private business," Deanna said.

CHAPTER 40

After four months of testimony, and over six hundred pieces of evidence, closing arguments began on May 2, 2013.

Dressed in a navy blue suit with a striped tie, Juan Martinez spoke directly to the jury. "This individual, Jodi Ann Arias, the defendant, killed Travis Alexander."

Repeatedly raising his voice, Martinez reminded jurors that it was Jodi who manipulated and abused Travis, not the other way around.

"Even after stabbing him over and over again, even after taking a gun and shooting him in the face, she will not let him rest in peace," he said. "Now instead of a gun, instead of a knife, she uses lies. She uses these lies in court when she testified to stage the scene for you like she did for the police."

Throughout his arguments, Jodi doodled, ignoring Martinez. When Martinez described Jodi faking an orgasm during the phone sex call, Jodi flashed a smirk. Later, she slowly shook her head.

Martinez described Jodi as a manipulative liar, who craved the limelight and sought out the media attention. She lied from the beginning and continued to lie on the stand, he said. "This is an individual who will stop at nothing, and who will continue to be manipulative and will lie at every turn."

Presenting some of the text message exchanges between Travis and Jodi, Martinez spoke of the heated argument the former couple had on May 26, 2008. During their fight Travis had written: "You are the worst thing that ever happened to me."

"No one can dispute that those are the truest words that are spoken in this case, and they are spoken by Mr. Alexander—even though he is not here—through his writing," said Martinez. "Any doubt that that's the truth? Do we need to look at the pictures of his gashed throat?"

During the fight Travis had called Jodi a "sociopath," "liar," and a "scammer."

"Whatever reason, he believed that she had done something to him," Martinez said.

Two days after the fight Jodi stole the gun from her grandparents. She then borrowed gas cans, rented a car, and turned off her cell phone to avoid leaving a trace of her presence in Arizona. On June 4, Jodi came to Mesa intending to slaughter Travis. "This is a meticulous approach to premeditation. This is a meticulous approach to killing."

Once again Martinez presented the images of Travis's decomposing body covered in stab wounds. As a close-up image of Travis's throat wound was displayed on the screen, gasps could be heard from the spectators. "This was a strike to kill, right at the neck."

Finally, Martinez reviewed the charges, explaining that Jodi committed murder in the first degree under both theories of premeditated and felony murder—a murder that takes place during the commission of a felony. If Jodi brought the gun to Travis's house, then the murder was premeditated; if after killing Travis she took his gun with her, it was considered robbery and therefore felony murder.

Martinez concluded by imploring the jury not to be manipulated by Jodi's lies, making an analogy about the gas cans she brought on her road trip.

"She wants you to carry those gas cans. She wants you to help fill them with gas," Martinez said. "Don't leave this courtroom with the stench of gasoline on your hands."

"Sex, lies, and dirty little secrets," Kirk Nurmi began his closing statements. "These aspects of the human condition may not be universal, but each one of these aspects of the human condition played a prominent role in the relationship Jodi Arias shared with Travis Alexander."

In stark contrast to her distracted disposition during Martinez's closing, Jodi watched Nurmi intently as he laid out his case.

On the screen, Nurmi displayed one of the last photos taken of Travis alive and then the blurry picture of his body on the bathroom floor—time-stamped three minutes later.

"What happened in those three minutes is ultimately what you have to decide," he said. "Was this three minutes in time the culmination of a plot that Jodi hatched in June 2008? Or was it an act of self-defense forced on Ms. Arias by the actions of Mr. Alexander?"

Aware that his client came across as unlikable, Nurmi pleaded with the jury to take an impartial look at Jodi.

"It's not about whether or not you like Jodi Arias. Nine days out of ten, I don't like Jodi Arias," Nurmi said. "But that doesn't matter." Jodi smiled briefly at the statement before returning to an unemotional gaze.

Repeatedly, Nurmi argued the prosecution's theory of a planned attack "didn't make any sense" and disputed the evidence that seemed to point to premeditation. It was never a "covert mission," he said, dismissing his client's behavior after the crime as insignificant.

"Why, if someone is there to commit a murder, do you hang out and let the intended victim take pictures of you in what's soon to become a crime scene?" he said. "That doesn't make any sense, does it?"

Nurmi described the saga of Travis and Jodi as a "sad ending to a toxic relationship."

"This relationship was one of chaos," he said. "The sex, the love, the fear, the lies, and the dirty little secrets all culminate on June 4."

Toward the end of his closing, Nurmi speculated that Jodi simply "snapped."

"What this evidence shows is that either what happened is that Jodi Arias defended herself and didn't know when to stop, or she gave in to a sudden heat of passion," Nurmi said. "Ultimately, if Miss Arias is guilty of any crime at all, it is the crime of manslaughter and nothing more."

The jury deliberated for less than three days, a total of fifteen hours, before reaching a verdict on May 8, 2013.

As the word spread through e-mail, Twitter, and Facebook, hundreds mobbed the courthouse, some carrying homemade signs in support of the prosecution.

Inside the courtroom, Jodi remained stoic as the bailiff handed the verdict to the judge, who silently read it and handed it to the clerk.

Unfolding the paper, the clerk spoke. "The state of Arizona versus Jodi Ann Arias, verdict count one." She paused. "We the jury duly impaneled and sworn in the above entitled action upon our oaths do find the defendant as to count one—first-degree murder—guilty."

Jodi blinked hard; her lips parted as she sucked in a deep breath.

Travis's friends and family cried and consoled each other. Outside, as word spread to the public and the crowd, they cheered loudly.

Jodi's eyes welled with tears; her face reddened. She glanced back at her mom, who was softly sobbing. Beside her, Willmott rubbed Jodi's arm in a comforting gesture.

The clerk polled each juror, asking if they agreed to a guilty verdict—five jurors had found her guilty of only premeditated murder; seven had decided she was guilty of both premeditated and felony murder.

As each of the jurors spoke the word "guilty," Jodi's face contorted with emotion, while fighting back tears.

* * *

Twenty minutes after the verdict was read, Jodi granted an interview with a local Phoenix television reporter. Calm and collected, she expressed shock at the decision of first-degree murder.

"It was unexpected for me, yes, because there was no pre-meditation on my part," she said. "I can see how things look that way."

When asked about her sentence, Jodi said she actually hoped to get the death penalty. "Longevity" had run in her family, she said, and the worst possible outcome for her would be a life sentence without parole.

"I said years ago that I'd rather get death than life, and that still is true today," she said. "I believe death is the ultimate freedom, so I'd rather just have my freedom as soon as I can get it."

Jodi's comments prompted authorities to temporarily place her on suicide watch.

Following the guilty verdict, Jodi's relationship with her attorneys grew increasingly hostile. Jodi blamed her lawyers for her conviction, saying in multiple television interviews that they hadn't done enough to prove her innocence.

Following the verdict, both Nurmi and Willmott attempted to withdraw from the case several more times, but the judge denied their motions.

A week after the verdict the jury decided the murder was exceptionally cruel, making Jodi eligible for the death penalty.

On May 16, during the penalty phase, two of Travis's siblings gave tearful statements about how their lives had been torn apart since their brother's murder.

"I thought my brother couldn't be knocked down or cut down," Steven Alexander said, standing in front of the jury. "He was unbreakable."

Choking back tears, he spoke of the nightmares that had plagued him since learning of Travis's death.

"Why him?" Steven asked. "Unfortunately I won't ever get

the answers to most of my questions. Questions like, how much did he suffer?"

Sobbing through her statement, Samantha Turbeville described the torment her family had endured throughout the trial, learning the heinous details of Travis's death.

"He was full of life," she said. "To have Travis taken so barbarically is beyond any words we can find to describe our horrific loss."

Finally, Samantha told the jury what Travis had meant to their family.

"Travis was our strength, our constant beacon of hope, our motivation. His presence has been ripped from our lives," she said. "Our lives will never be the same. We're never getting him back."

Two weeks after telling the world she'd prefer to be sentenced to death, Jodi Arias had an abrupt reversal.

During the penalty phase, standing calmly in front of the jury, she said she "lacked perspective" when she claimed she wanted to die. She begged the jury to spare her life, if only for the sake of her family.

"I couldn't imagine standing in front of you asking you to give me life. To me life in prison was the most unappealing outcome. I can't in good conscience ask you for death because of them." She pointed to her family. "I'm asking you to please, please don't do that to them. I've already hurt them so badly, along with so many other people."

In a bizarre, nineteen-minute statement she spoke of all the "positive contributions" she could make in prison. Locked behind bars for life, she planned to start a recycling program, create a book club, and donate her hair to be made into wigs for cancer victims.

"I didn't know then that if I got life there were many things I could do to affect positive change and contribute in a meaningful way," she said. "In prison there are programs I can start and people I can help."

While she said killing Travis was "the worst mistake of my life," she maintained she was a victim of domestic violence. At one point she held up a shirt printed with the word SURVIVOR, saying she was selling the T-shirts to raise money for victims of domestic abuse.

"To this day I can hardly believe I was capable of such violence, but I know that I was. And for that I'm going to be sorry for the rest of my life, probably even longer," Jodi said. "I want everyone's healing to begin and I want everyone's pain to stop."

As the jurors deliberated Jodi's fate, she conducted a series of media interviews, expressing little remorse.

Two days passed and late on the afternoon of May 23, everyone filed back into the courtroom for what should have been the sentencing verdict.

Judge Stephens addressed the jury. "I understand you have reached a verdict." Glancing at the verdict form, Stephens's voice cracked as she said, "The clerk will now read and record the verdict."

The clerk spoke, "No unanimous agreement." The jury was deadlocked, unable to decide on a sentence. Eight favored the death penalty, while four voted for life.

Jodi put her hand to her cheek and smiled slightly.

In the front few rows, Travis's loved ones wept in anguish. Tears running down her cheeks, Samantha dropped her head in her hands. Dazed, Steven stared vacantly at the jury. Travis's friends sobbed, wiping away tears.

In Arizona, a mistrial in the penalty phase meant that the guilty verdict remained, and the state had the option of accepting a life sentence or convening a new jury to retry the penalty phase.

The lack of courtroom closure was devastating—Travis's family so yearned to end this horrifying chapter of their lives.

They found peace in the knowledge that regardless of the ultimate punishment, Jodi Arias had been held accountable for the murder of Travis Alexander.

Over the last five agonizing years, in times of great despair, Travis's siblings had sought strength in remembering their brother's remarkable spirit.

In life, one of Travis's sayings had been: "The difference between a stumbling block and a stepping stone is the character of the individual walking the path."

In this case, the road to justice was long and paved with many stumbling blocks. Walking that path many others would have faltered, but those who loved Travis refused to fall.

AFTERWORD

May 8, 2013

Today the house on East Queensborough Avenue bears little resemblance to the crime scene it was on the day Travis Alexander's decomposing remains were discovered upstairs in the master bathroom shower.

Absent are the red and blue revolving lights reflecting off the glossy yellow crime scene tape. Police officers no longer swarm the property among the weeping, distraught witnesses standing by the curb.

Sold and occupied since 2009, the interior of the house has been remodeled—the carpet replaced, the walls repainted, the hole in the bathroom hallway covered with fresh drywall.

Still, every once in a while one of Travis's friends will drive by the house and see the windows glowing brightly from outside on the street, sparking memories of how it appeared when Travis was still alive.

I first passed by the house in 2009, around the time I began covering the case as a writer for a Phoenix-based magazine. I was curious to get a glimpse of the property that had served as Travis's mausoleum for five long days in June 2008.

When I first heard about the case, I was immediately intrigued by the tale of the attractive aspiring photographer who was apprehended because she had accidentally photographed her victim.

As I began researching the background of both Travis and Jodi, however, I quickly learned the story ran much deeper. Searching online, I discovered their blogs and respective MySpace pages, and was amazed by how much of this case played out through social media.

Online, Travis's and Jodi's lives seem frozen in June 2008. Travis's childhood—written in his own words—remains posted on his blog. Photos from their many trips are displayed on their respective MySpace accounts. And most haunting is Jodi's final MySpace status update, which remains in cyberspace: "Jodi Arias misses Travis Alexander."

In a twist unique to the Internet age, the story has continued to develop online. During the trial, hundreds of Web sites, blogs, and Facebook groups were established where people dissected each detail with rapt attention—some describing it as an obsession.

Today, even after the verdict, Travis's memory continues to live on through social media. The memorial group established for Travis has attracted thousands of members—most of them strangers who felt somehow connected to his story.

As the trial progressed, however, I believe the story became detached from its foundations. Instead of a tale of obsession and murder, it devolved into a debate over domestic violence and sexual deviancy. Many people lost sight of the story's real victim.

Travis wasn't a saint, but he also wasn't a deviant. Throughout his life he tried to be a good person and I don't think he ever fully realized the effect he had on Jodi. To maintain the closeness in their relationship, Jodi tried to seem so at ease with their nonmonogamous sexual relationship. She feigned tolerance of the fact he was dating other women, all the while desperately in love and seething with jealousy.

The intense chemistry that brought them together festered inside Jodi to the extent she could no longer imagine a life without Travis—an admission she made in her own diary.

Sometime in the spring of 2008, I believe that Jodi decided Travis had to die. And so she began planning her crime.

Meanwhile, Travis had begun to see Jodi for what she truly

was—a liar and a sociopath. It is possible Travis's blog also contributed to Jodi's breakdown. In his last entry he had written about how after he turned thirty he decided to date with "marriage in mind." For Jodi, it must have been like a knife to the heart to realize she was never marriage material—that she was just someone to keep his bed warm until a nice Mormon girl came along.

By late May, Jodi had begun plotting the murder—taking special care to rent a plain colored vehicle, outside of Yreka, to avoid detection. Then, she began establishing an alibi, stopping to see her ex-boyfriend and borrowing gas cans to prevent being captured on surveillance videos making any purchases.

When she arrived at Travis's home in Mesa at 4 A.M., she didn't kill him right away, likely because his roommates were home. It was possible she wanted one last night with the man she loved, one more chance to say good-bye.

The next evening she lured him into the shower with a photo shoot, possibly as a ploy to get him naked and vulnerable. While snapping photos, she may have even held the knife and gun behind her back, in the waistband of her pants.

Jodi directed him to the shower floor and snapped one more picture before plunging the knife into Travis's body. As he was being attacked, if even for a split second, I imagine it finally dawned on Travis—for maybe the first time—how truly dangerous Jodi had become.

By the time he was shot and his throat was slit, Travis was already a dead man. Somehow he made it all the way to the edge of the bathroom hallway, where he collapsed and died.

After the murder, Jodi dragged Travis to the shower, cleaned up the crime scene, and deleted the photos from the camera. She thought she was smart enough to get away with the crime. Instead, every measure she took to ensure she wouldn't be caught left a trail of evidence that proved premeditation.

At some point after years in jail, I believe Jodi started to transfer blame onto Travis, continuing the assault on his character in an attempt to paint herself as the victim.

Through it all, Jodi maintained an almost peculiar interest in her reputation. She said as much in court—admitting she lied to the police and the media because she cared about how she was being perceived.

In my personal encounters with Jodi, I experienced this firsthand. Before the trial, I had sent postcards to Jodi in jail, informing her I was writing a book. Before granting an interview, she requested a copy of my first book, which I sent to the Estrella Jail.

Weeks later, during a preliminary hearing, I was in court when Jodi gave me a double take, apparently recognizing me from my photo on the back inside cover of my book. Soon after, she delivered a message to me: "If you ever want an interview, you are sitting on the wrong side of the courtroom."

At the time I was sitting where the media was permitted, which I explained to Jodi in a subsequent postcard. But the encounter made me realize something surprising about Jodi. Even as an accused murderer, and a documented liar, she still cared deeply about how she was perceived. It bothered her that someone writing a book on her case would be "against her," on the other side of the courtroom.

While I once considered interviewing Jodi for this book, after she took the witness stand I realized it would have been futile—I would have never learned the truth. Speaking for hours in television interviews and in court, Jodi publicly said all I needed to know to fairly convey her perspective.

For me, only one question remains unanswered. If I spoke to Jodi I would want to know, during the last five years, how many days have gone by where Travis hasn't consumed her thoughts? Back in 2008, Jodi was so fixated on Travis that she couldn't imagine a future without him. After years in jail, have the daily comings and goings of a life in confinement erased the deep imprint Travis left on her heart?

Anyone who has ever experienced unrequited love can understand the pain of heartbreak, although most people walk away. As difficult as it is to believe at the time, eventually the pain and attachment subside.

If only Jodi had moved on when she moved away; if only

Travis realized how crazed she had become—both their lives would have turned out much differently. Instead, Jodi decided to slaughter Travis in one of the most monstrous ways imaginable. And in doing so, she tossed away her own life.

Locked away in prison until the day she dies, time will stand still for Jodi. While she will certainly make new memories, experiences, and interactions with other inmates, as the years pass, she won't move forward in life. Her life will never exist outside those looming prison walls. She'll never be a wife or mother—goals she once cherished.

If in life we are defined by our actions, then Travis and Jodi will leave behind very different legacies.

Jodi will be forever haunted by her most unpardonable actions, permanently linked in history to the man she killed.

To the thousands of lives he touched, however, I don't believe Travis will be defined by the way he died, but by how he lived.

In the end Travis's memory will extend far beyond that of a murder victim. But Jodi Arias will never be more than a cruel, calculating killer.

UPDATE TO THE PAPERBACK EDITION

Life or death—Jodi's fate dangled, undecided for more than a year.

Following the jury deadlock in the penalty phase, both the prosecution and defense rallied and reassessed the case.

Nurmi and Willmott pushed for a settlement of a life sentence. But Martinez was relentless—anything less than death was unacceptable.

That meant there would be a second jury convened, another trial just to decide Jodi's sentence.

A trial date was set but soon vacated. There were scheduling conflicts and a medical leave by the prosecutor.

Months passed and the case remained in limbo as the trial was postponed time and time again. Sixteen months after the guilty verdict, a September 2014 date would be scheduled.

Meanwhile, as the attorneys prepared for the retrial, dozens of hearings were held. The judge heard arguments concerning sequestering the new jury, moving the retrial out of Phoenix, and Jodi's increasingly strong desire to fire her attorneys.

But all that courtroom drama unfolded under a shroud of secrecy.

Due to the chaotic nature of the first trial, Judge Stephens shut the media and public out of each and every hearing.

In December 2013, the judge also banned electronic devices, including TV cameras from the courtroom. There would be no tweeting of the testimony, no live coverage of the retrial on television or the Internet.

After allowing every moment of the murder trial to be broadcast, it was a complete about-face for Judge Stephens.

The trial went from total transparency to a bewildering blackout.

Stephens' controversial ruling drew complaints from constitutional lawyers that it violated the public's right to attend proceedings.

Suddenly, Jodi vanished from the public view. As time passed, interest in the convicted murderer flagged.

In the 16 months between her trial dates, new sensational murders consumed people's attention. Wars were fought, planes crashed, countless lives lost and somehow, inexplicably, the bizarre case of the attractive femme fatale no longer seemed all that important.

The fame and attention Jodi had grown to adore faded. Fan mail from fawning supporters dwindled; donations for a potential appeal became infrequent.

It should have been the beginning of the end.

Perhaps Jodi couldn't stand losing the spotlight. In any event, she played the very last card she had left.

Four weeks before the trial was set to begin, Jodi apparently decided she would no longer share what little time she had left in the limelight with her attorney. She would take her life in her own hands and represent herself.

The judge reluctantly and wearily approved the request.

"I do not believe it is in your best interest," the judge told Jodi. "I strongly urge you to reconsider."

Before granting the motion Stephens asked Jodi whether she was taking prescription drugs. Jodi admitted she was but denied that it was affecting her judgment.

Jodi would now go head-to-head with the hard-nosed prosecutor in the fight for her life.

It was grotesque.

Another attempt to further antagonize Travis's siblings and prolong their grief.

Weeks later, however, Jodi changed her mind, relinquished her right to serve as her own attorney and Nurmi resumed his role as lead counsel.

Because of the media ban, by the time of the retrial no one will care as much about what happened to Jodi Arias. Life or death—it was almost irrelevant. Either way she would almost certainly die behind prison walls.

Between the trial and court hearings, Jodi will still return to the confines of her stark and lonely cell. Convicted murderer, prisoner No. 438434, locked in a 7-by-11-foot cell in solitary confinement. Always alone—left to her own wretched existence.

In that cell, there was no fame, no cameras, not even a television or radio for Jodi to watch her own final act.

There, Jodi Arias was simply just another prisoner.

ACKNOWLEDGMENTS

When I first started this project in 2010—years before Jodi Arias became a household name—I had no idea where this story would take me or the level of exposure the trial would garner.

Throughout 2013, as the publicity grew, I often gave commentary on TV about the case. During many of these interviews I was asked to give my opinion—one which I tried to leave out of the pages of this book until the final chapter. For the story I tried to show just the facts and let the readers decide for themselves.

I would like to thank those who helped me give Travis a voice, including his many friends who interviewed with me for this project. First and foremost I would like to express my gratitude to Taylor Searle, for trusting me exclusively with personal audio recordings, text messages, and instant message conversations he had with Travis. Because of these, Travis was able to tell much of his own life story in the pages of this book.

I would also like to thank Chris and Sky Hughes, who worked closely with me over two years to help form an accurate portrayal of the relationship between Travis and Jodi.

In addition, I'd like to express my appreciation to Juan Martinez, Esteban Flores, and the dozens of other police officers and detectives who were involved in Jodi's arrest and conviction.

Thanks to Travis's siblings who supported this project. I

have tremendous sympathy for your loss and my condolences are with you and your loved ones.

I owe special gratitude to my literary agent, Sharlene Martin, for her continual support of my career. Additionally, my gratitude goes out to my superb editors at St. Martin's Press: April Osborn and Charles Spicer.

On a personal note, thank you to Kimberly Hundley for your editing advice. To my beloved Mimi, Carol Hogan, for being my first reader—I send my love. To my entire family, namely my parents, Dann and Debbie Hogan, as well as my mother-in-law, Joann LaRussa—I truly love and appreciate you.

Most important, I would like to thank the one person who has made my career possible and my life remarkable, my husband, Matt LaRussa.